D1188048

1905
ORIGINALS

1905
ORIGINALS

The remarkable story of the team that went away as
the COLONIALS and came back as the ALL BLACKS

BOB HOWITT
DIANNE HAWORTH

National Library of New Zealand
Cataloguing-in-Publication Data

Howitt, Bob, 1941-
1905 Originals : the remarkable story of the team that went
away as the Colonials and came back as the All Blacks /
Bob Howitt, Dianne Haworth.
Includes bibliographical references.
ISBN 1-86950-553-0
1. All Blacks (Rugby team)—History.
2. Rugby Union football— New Zealand—History.
3. Rugby Union football—Great Britain—
History. I. Haworth, Dianne. II. Title.
796.33365—dc 22

HarperSports
An imprint of HarperCollins*Publishers*

First published 2005
HarperCollins*Publishers* (New Zealand) Limited
P.O. Box 1, Auckland

Copyright © Bob Howitt and Dianne Haworth 2005

Bob Howitt and Dianne Haworth assert the moral
right to be identified as the authors of this work.

All rights reserved. No part of this publication may be
reproduced, stored in a retrieval system or transmitted in
any form or by any means, electronic, mechanical,
photocopying, recording or otherwise, without the
prior written permission of the publishers.

ISBN 1 86950 553 0

Designed by Darren Holt, HarperCollins Design Studio, Sydney
Cover image by Nolan Howitt
Typeset by Pages LP
Printed in China by Phoenix Offset on 128 gsm Matt Art

COVER IMAGE: An artist's impression of Wallace (carrying ball), Stead and Smith in full cry on tour.

CONTENTS

PHOTO CREDITS

t = top; b= bottom; l = left; r = right

Auckland War Memorial Museum
20, 36t, 138, 139

Hocken Library
50r, 51, 53, 137r, 155, 157

Malcolm Dick collection
24–29, 50l, 54r, 59b, 61, 67, 71, 73, 83, 86, 91,
95t, 99, 103b, 107, 111, 115t, 118, 125b, 129, 133t,
137l, 142t, 147t, 152, 166, 171b, 175b, 178b

New Zealand Rugby Museum
2, 36b, 37l, 37r, 39, 46, 47, 49, 50t, 55, 57, 58, 59t, 62,
65, 66, 74, 77, 79t, 82, 87, 90, 94, 98, 102, 103t, 106, 109,
115b, 119, 124r, 125t, 142b, 143r, 143b, 144, 145, 158, 159,
163, 165, 170, 171t, 174, 175t, 178t, 181, 193b, 195, 197, 202

W.G. Garrard scrapbooks
(property of Canterbury Rugby Museum)
17, 19, 38, 40, 45, 54l, 63, 69, 79b, 93, 95b, 114,
121, 122, 124l, 132, 133l, 135, 141, 143l, 147b, 153t,
153r, 160l, 160r, 161, 162t, 162b, 169, 173, 179l,
179r, 183, 185, 186, 187, 188, 193t, 194, 200

ACKNOWLEDGEMENTS

Putting together a book on the 1905 Originals has led the authors on a fascinating voyage of discovery through superbly detailed scrapbooks, the musty archives of the New Zealand Rugby Union in Wellington and the New Zealand Rugby Football Museum in Palmerston North, to museums where unexpected rugby treasures exist and to private homes where century-old memorabilia has been, in many instances, fondly preserved.

The authors are indebted to the late W.G. 'Gun' Garrard, secretary of the Canterbury Rugby Union in the early 1900s (and a New Zealand selector) whose meticulously compiled scrapbooks on the '05 tour, now the property of the Canterbury Rugby Union, inspired this project.

How he managed to secure newspaper clippings from so many diverse and intriguing sources throughout the UK while the tour was unfolding remains a mystery, but whatever his secret, the authors remain eternally grateful.

A debt of appreciation must also go to Bob Luxford, the dedicated and eternally cheery curator, and John Sinclair of the Rugby Museum, to Lee Golding, the protector of Garrard's scrapbooks at the Canterbury Rugby Union, to Joslyn Titus of the New Zealand Rugby Union, to the Auckland War Memorial Museum, to the Hocken Library of Otago University, to former All Black and NZRU councillor Malcolm Dick (who just happened to be in possession of Charlie Seeling's original 1905 jersey), to Geoffrey Vincent, who willingly shared his thesis on early All Black rugby with us, and to the Rugby Football Union at Twickenham.

Bob Howitt and Dianne Haworth
February 2005

PROLOGUE

We authors have a confession to make. Our 1905 Originals project has turned out quite differently to the way we planned it.

It was our original intention to present a centenary book in which we expounded on the triumphant exploits of manager George Dixon's heroic team. But about three months into our research we completely re-assessed the project because of the incredible wealth of material we were uncovering.

Instead of simply narrating their story, we decided we would re-create the tour.

This would not have been possible without the two magnificent scrapbooks painstakingly pieced together by Christchurch's 'Gun' Garrard, himself a New Zealand selector in 1904. His diligence in compiling these two 100-page volumes with newspaper clippings, predominantly from British newspapers supplemented with items from New Zealand's leading dailies of the time, the *New Zealand Herald*, the *Christchurch Press*, the *Otago Daily Times* and the *New Zealand Times*, a national morning newspaper, provides a vivid insight into the tour.

If we felt privileged to be in possession of these priceless works of love, imagine our delight when, by chance, we became aware of the presence in the Auckland War Memorial Museum library of manager Dixon's personal diaries, cash books and tour memorabilia. Ten boxes of them.

Patently a workaholic, Dixon, besides almost single-handedly managing 27 players throughout their seven-month tour and maintaining the team's financial accounts (no minor responsibility, given that the team received 70 per cent of the net gate from every match and the players received three shillings a day out-of-pocket expenses), still found time to write a book about the tour and keep a detailed diary.

That book, *The Triumphant Tour of the NZ Footballers, 1905*, has become a collector's item and faithfully records the team's exploits. But the diaries go further and give a more intimate account of happenings along the way.

Given Dixon's conservative nature, it is surprising to find him fingering the opponent who pulled Bob Deans back from the goalline in the Welsh test, a controversial incident that led to the Originals' only defeat and is, incredibly, still a hot issue 100 years on.

While the astute Dixon provides a fascinating window into the events of 1905 from a manager's viewpoint, it was obvious that the book would be incomplete without some more earthy observations.

Come in Billy Wallace. We were in raptures at discovering in the bowels of the New Zealand Rugby Museum in Palmerston North boxes containing countless copies of the *New Zealand Sportsman* published in the mid-1930s in which were featured Wallace's personal memoirs. We have quoted extensively from Wallace's memoirs, which are so deliciously revealing they virtually merit a book on their own.

Wallace, wonderfully eloquent and obviously a gifted storyteller, recaptures events in Britain, France and America with great clarity. Thanks to Billy, not everything that happened on the bus stayed on the bus. Actually, it was trains and brakes back in 1905.

Wallace recounts how through their onfield exploits and rave reviews the players became a target for the local ladies. A favourite approach from a fair maiden would be to inquire which player was, say, No. 12, that day's hero. Billy says if the woman in question was good-looking, inevitably No. 12 would turn out to be the individual she was confronting. If she wasn't, No. 12 would be off in a remote corner somewhere!

Another rich source of material were Billy Stead's diaries, which we tracked down at the Hocken Library in Dunedin. Stead, the vice captain from Southland and one of the team's most gifted players, handwrote 80,000 words on the art of rugby in seven days at the conclusion of the tour, for a UK publisher. He was paid the less than princely sum of £100, half of which he gave to Dave Gallaher, who assisted with the diagrams and photographs. The book, which ran to 322 pages, is today another collector's item.

The research would not have been complete without a visit to the New Zealand Rugby Union who gave us access to their dusty archives. Their minute books from 1902 provide a fascinating account of how the epic tour of 1905 unfolded. They also reveal that the NZRU initially intended funding the tour through debentures sold to its constituent unions. That concept was only partly successful and the team had to hike off to Sydney for three fixtures only weeks before sailing to the UK, to raise the balance of the money that allowed the tour to proceed.

It was a tour that helped shape a colony. To achieve what they did was truly astonishing — after all, rugby in the early 1900s was England's national game. But Dixon's heroic team fashioned a record of 34 victories from 35 outings with just the one (disputed) loss to Wales. They scored 976 points while conceding just 59. Twenty-three of their opponents failed to score.

They were the talk of society throughout England. There had never been a sporting team quite like them.

And the New Zealand Premier, Richard Seddon, didn't miss the opportunity to capitalise on the team's achievements. He went into print in the London *Daily Mail* extolling the virtues of his colony's healthy climate and extensive playing fields that produced the wonderful specimens who comprised the 1905 Originals.

We have derived immense delight in piecing this book together. It wouldn't surprise us if after reading of their amazing triumphs that, like us, you acknowledge them as the greatest ever New Zealand rugby touring team.

Bob Howitt
Dianne Haworth

Chapter 1

IN THE
BEGINNING

Minutes of
SPECIAL GENERAL
MEETING of the
NZRFU COUNCIL

HELD AT THE WELLINGTON CYCLING CLUB
ROOMS ON TUESDAY 5 JUNE 1902 AT 8 P.M.

MR G.F.C. CAMPBELL
(VICE PRESIDENT) IN THE CHAIR

The following Delegates were present: Messrs R.D. Isaacs, J.S. MacArthur, R.M. Falconer (Otago), D. McKenzie, N. Galbraith, G.C. Fache and A. Campbell (Wellington); A.W. Thomson, I. Hyams (Wanganui), G. Dixon (Auckland), W. Coffey (Canterbury), H. Kitching (Nelson), D.D. Weir (Hawke's Bay), R.C. Sim (Poverty Bay), A.C. Norris (Marlborough), N. McLean (Taranaki), J. Wesney (Southland), G.N. Goldie (Bush District) and A. Laurenson (Manawatu).

Purpose of meeting to consider several notices of motion relative to the simplifying of professionalism rules, with a view to the sending of a team to England at an early date.

The first notice of motion considered was one by Mr W. Coffey in the following terms: 'That, in the opinion of the delegates of the New Zealand Rugby Football Union, the time has arrived when definite steps should be taken to send a New Zealand representative football team to Great Britain; that it be a special instruction to the Management Committee to bring the matter about and to make the necessary arrangements to send a New Zealand representative football team to Great Britain not later than 1903.'

In speaking to motion Mr Coffey pointed out that the proposition he was making was no new one. The advisableness of sending a team Home had long been admitted. It was, though, absolutely impossible at present to send to England a team to represent New Zealand. The speaker believed that that difficulty could be overcome by asking the English Rugby Football Union to make special provisions for overcoming the difficulty.

The speaker had no doubt that the Home body would accede to such a request and also undertake the conduct of such a tour. 'The result of that would be a monetary gain to the English Union of £5000 or £6000. But to get a properly representative team we should allow players a living wage of £3 a week. It would be unfair to ask the men to go without wages, when many of them have relations dependent on them . . .' Mr Coffey then outlined his costings for the tour and added, 'The Government could be asked for a subscription to the cost of sending the team to England — it had been done similarly in the case of the Bisley riflemen.' He concluded that he was no advocate of professionalism but he hoped the English Union would meet the New Zealand body.

Mr D. McKenzie moved his amendment: 'That it be an instruction to the Management Committee to approach the English Rugby Football Union as to whether that body will waive its rules against professionalism to such an extent as to allow of a New Zealand representative football team being sent to Great Britain; and that the Management Committee be instructed to request a suitable person to interview the English Rugby Football Union on the matter.'

Mr Galbraith suggested that the best way would be to approach the English Rugby Football Union for permission to exercise discretionary powers in the way of allowances for travelling expenses and that the Management Committee be instructed to request a suitable person to interview the English Rugby Football Union on the matter. Mr G.C. Fache seconded this amendment which he deemed to be an improvement on the previous one.

Mr Isaacs moved on behalf of the Otago Union a further amendment asking the English Union to give the New Zealand body permission to raise money by public subscription. Money in that way could be given to the men as private citizens — not as footballers — as tokens of esteem.

Messrs Goldie and Galbraith considered the Otago proposal to be veiled professionalism of the worst sort. Mr Thomson agreed with the Otago amendment, because it asked the English Union the widest terms upon which — under the present rules — a team could be sent from New Zealand. Mr Hyams pointed out that presentations to players were equivalent to making them professional. Therefore the Otago proposition had no real weight. Mr Isaacs' amendment was lost on the voices.

A vote was next taken on the amendment moved by Mr Galbraith: ayes, 15; noes, 19.

Mr Dixon moved as a further amendment: 'That it be an instruction to the Management Committee to enter into communication with the English Rugby Football Union with a view to arranging for a visit of a New Zealand team to England at as early a date as possible.' That would, the mover pointed out, not bind the union to anything definite.

Mr Galbraith seconded the amendment, Mr Coffey accepted the amendment, the motion was then carried on the voices and thus the preliminary steps to the matter of sending a team to England was disposed of.

ORTUNATELY FOR NEW ZEALAND and its subsequent rugby fortunes, it was the shrewd and moderating counsel of George Dixon — a man who would almost single-handedly ensure the later financial security of the New Zealand Rugby Football Union — that prevailed at that Special General Meeting. The proposed New Zealand trip 'Home' could proceed without running aground on the controversial issues of professionalism and payment to players.

There was nothing new in planning a New Zealand rugby tour to the 'Mother Country' or 'Home', as England was familiarly called at the time. After all, in 1888–89 a predominantly Maori New Zealand Native Football Team toured Britain and Australia, where their dashing style of play excited much comment. They were away from New Zealand for a staggering 14-month period, during which time they played 107 matches — plus a further 17 matches against New Zealand sides in 1888–89, both before and after the grand tour.

From the late 19th century rugby was firmly entrenched as New Zealand's national game. The New Zealand Rugby Football Union was formed in 1892 and a year later the first team took the field under its auspices, when ten matches were played on a tour of Australia. One decade on, New Zealand's formidable reputation on the field was enhanced when it comprehensively won its first full-scale test match — against Australia — by 22-3 at the Sydney Cricket Ground on 15 August 1903. With the growing reputation of New Zealand rugby it was time to progress the NZRFU's proposal of the previous year that a representative team should travel to Britain.

Minutes *of* NZRFU MANAGEMENT COMMITTEE

HELD AT TROCADERO CAFE, WELLINGTON, ON FRIDAY 18 SEPTEMBER 1903

PROPOSED TOUR OF NEW ZEALAND TEAM TO ENGLAND

On the motion of Dr Newman, a subcommittee consisting of Messrs Campbell, Norris, Fache and the mover, was appointed to submit a report relating to the proposed tour to England.

Nine months later, significant progress could be reported:

NZRFU 12th ANNUAL REPORT & BALANCE SHEET

HELD AT THE WELLINGTON CYCLING CLUB ROOMS ON FRIDAY 6 MAY 1904 AT 7.30 P.M.

(G.H. DIXON, AUCKLAND DELEGATE, ELECTED TO MANAGEMENT COMMITTEE)

Chairman G.F.C. Campbell (Wellington) Report: 'The question of sending a team to Great Britain next year would come up for consideration and he felt sure the Council would give this important matter its fullest attention.'

Mr W. Coffey (Canterbury) proposed and Mr D.D. Weir (Hawke's Bay) seconded that 'in the opinion of this Committee it is desirable that a football team should be sent to Great Britain in 1905 and that the Management Committee be empowered to take the necessary steps to bring this about.' Carried, Otago voting against the motion.

IN AUGUST 1904 A TEAM from Great Britain arrived in New Zealand and attracted huge crowds to its matches against Canterbury-West Coast combined, Otago-Southland, Taranaki-Wanganui-Manawatu, Auckland and for the sole test, played at Wellington on 13 August 1904.

On that day New Zealand was captained by Southland's Billy Stead, who would later star in the 1905 tour. Duncan McGregor, also destined for 1905 glory, was the hero of the hour, being carried shoulder-high from the field by the crowd at the final whistle, having scored two tries to enable New Zealand to record a historic win against Great Britain 9–3.

Wellington's *Evening Post* exulted in a series of banner headlines:

BRITAIN v. NEW ZEALAND

MONSTER ATTENDANCE

TRIUMPH OF THE NEW ZEALANDERS!

The New Zealand team's first major victory on home soil was hailed the length of the land and the country's Post Offices were swamped with telegrams for 'their boys' in Wellington. One from a Jimmy Henderson in Sydney was simply addressed 'Stead Wellington' and carried the message 'Hoorah Hoorah'; from Pretoria, South Africa came 'Congratulations Maorilanders'; there was a telegraph in Maori, with a pencilled English translation underneath, and congratulatory telegraphs from every major union in the land addressed to 'Captain, New Zealand Football Team, Wellington'. The telegraph from the captain's excited brother, John Stead of Invercargill, entirely omitted a message, containing just the words 'Captain N.Z. Team. W. Stead.'

That evening, writing on crested notepaper, New Zealand's future prime minister, Sir Joseph Ward, added his plaudits:

Dear Mr Stead

I heartily congratulate you and your splendid team on your victory. Bravo New Zealand.

Yours sincerely

J.G. Ward

The mood was buoyant and the win had paved the way for the team's tour of Britain the following year. But money had to be found to finance such an ambitious undertaking. The coffers of the New Zealand Rugby Football Union held just £2000 and tour costs were estimated at more than £6000, leaving a shortfall of £4000. The NZRFU resolved to have debentures drawn up to help finance the tour to Great Britain, and that private individuals also be approached in regard to debentures.

Minutes *of the* NZRFU MANAGEMENT COMMITTEE

HELD AT THE TROCADERO CAFE, WELLINGTON, ON WEDNESDAY 14 SEPTEMBER 1904

ENGLISH TOUR

In reply to a cablegram from Mr Wray Palliser [a former Wellington player living in London, and appointed the New Zealand representative in England for the tour] re playing first match of New Zealand tour at Plymouth on 16 September 1905 it was decided to agree to the date mentioned and to notify the ERFU that their playing tour would not exceed three months in England. The Secretary was instructed to set out in detail the reasons and also to ask that the list of fixtures be forwarded to this union as early as possible.

The Finance Committee (Messrs Galbraith, Fache and Dixon) was directed to go fully into the financial question of the English tour, regarding routes etc., and to report within a month. It was resolved 'That the various Unions be asked to institute a canvass of those willing to take up debentures at the earliest possible date and that this Committee be advised from time to time what progress is being made.'

It was resolved that the local unions be asked if they can suggest suitable gentlemen as manager of the New Zealand Team to England, the gentleman's sanction to be obtained before his name is submitted to this union ...

Mr Galbraith proposed that Mr G. Fache (Wellington) be asked to act as sole selector of the New Zealand team. Mr Isaacs' amendment: 'That Messrs Fache, Evans, Murray and Harris be asked to select the New Zealand Team and to submit the names of 50 players as a preliminary selection by 1 November 1904.' Carried.

Minutes *of the* NZRFU MANAGEMENT COMMITTEE

HELD AT THE WELLINGTON CYCLING CLUB ROOMS ON FRIDAY NOVEMBER 11, 1904

DEBENTURES

It was decided to inform the larger unions that this committee wish debentures to be placed outside the number guaranteed by the various unions, and would ask that gentlemen interested be approached with the object of placing debentures with them.

A similar circular to be sent to all other unions. It was resolved that all monies received for debentures be placed at fixed deposit in a separate account. The Treasurer to make the best arrangement in this connection.

Mr G.C. Fache for the Selection Committee submitted the names of 50 players from whom the New Zealand team to tour Great Britain will be chosen.

BACKS (including wing forwards)
Dr Fookes, Deans, Gerard, Erekana, Booth, Harvey, Wallace, Hislop, Harper, Roberts, McGregor, Kiernan, Hay-McKenzie, Gallaher, Hunter, Porteous, Gilray, Guy, Wilson, King, Thomson, Bishop, Furrie, Stead, Mynott.

FORWARDS
Tyler, McMinn, Casey, Seeling, Whisker, McDonald, Nicholson, Smith, Hughes, Cross, Fanning, Stuart, Watkins, Newton, Dodd, Learmont, Glenn, Corbett, Glasgow, Cooke, O'Sullivan, Horgan, Thompson, Johnston (Otago), Johnston (Wairarapa).

Willis (Napier), Mackrell (Auckland) and Driscoll (Wellington) were also recommended for inclusion in the list. Carried.

It was decided to ask the various unions interested to submit to this union a confidential report on the character and general conduct of players representing their district whose name appears in the list submitted by the selectors.

It was also resolved to notify individual players of their nomination, replies to be in the hand of the Secretary not later than 31 December next. It was also decided to publish the list of the players.

Minutes *of the* NZRFU MANAGEMENT COMMITTEE

HELD AT THE WELLINGTON CYCLING CLUB ROOMS ON FRIDAY 9 DECEMBER 1904

It was decided that a team of twenty-four players be picked for the English tour, in the final week of January next, and that the selectors be asked to meet in Wellington at that time for the purpose stated. It was decided that every member selected for the tour to Great Britain shall undergo a medical examination before leaving the Colony.

ON 27 JANUARY 1905, the NZRFU's selectors submitted to Council the names of 24 players for inclusion in the team to tour Britain:

BACKS:
Booth (Otago), Wallace, McGregor, Roberts (Wellington), McKenzie (Auckland), Thomson (Wanganui), Harper, Deans, Harvey (Canterbury), Hunter, Mynott (Taranaki), Stead (Southland).

FORWARDS:
Tyler, Seeling, Nicholson (Auckland), Watkins, Cross (Wellington), Casey, Johnstone, Stuart (Otago), Glenn, O'Sullivan (Taranaki), Whisker (Manawatu), Corbett (West Coast).

The union's decision not to publish these players' names, opting to first study their form during the 1905 domestic season, met with council's approval. A further recommendation of the selectors that an additional back and forward be taken on tour, making 26 players in all, was carried.

After discussion as to whether one or two managers should accompany the New Zealand team to Great Britain, it was decided to appoint 'a' manager forthwith. Mr George Dixon of Wellington was unanimously appointed to the position. The question of a second appointment was deferred.

The debenture money only trickled in; a short tour of Australia could help the coffers. The New South Wales Rugby Union wrote offering 50 per cent of the net proceeds for two matches played by the New Zealand team, prior to the tour of England, stating 'Hotel expenses to be borne by the NSW Union and the steamer expenses to be charged against the NZRFU'. However, the New Zealand Rugby Football Union instructed its secretary that the NSW Union be informed that the 'terms offered were not considered satisfactory . . .'

It was decided that a leaflet be printed setting out particulars for issue to all prospective debenture holders, thus:

Estimates in connection with Tour of N.Z. Team in Great Britain	
Estimated total cost of tour	£6000
Cash in hand	£2000
Balance to be raised	£4000
Estimated gate receipts from matches (under ordinary circumstances)	£4000
Amount actually guaranteed by English Rugby Union	£2500

On the balance of £4000 to be raised, it is proposed to issue, before the team leaves the Colony, the sum of £2000 in debentures. This will enable the Union to land the team in England, and keep the team in funds pending receipts from the various matches being available.

It was decided to award the secretary £15 15s for his services in connection with the visit of the British team.

Minutes *of the*
NZRFU MANAGEMENT COMMITTEE

HELD AT THE TROCADERO CAFE, WELLINGTON, ON THURSDAY 23 FEBRUARY 1905

The finance committee, to whom the question of insurance against loss in connection with the proposed tour to Great Britain was referred for a report, reported that they were not in favour of the scheme outlined by the Union's representative in London, namely, that of insuring up to the amount guaranteed by the English Rugby Union for each match jointly with the body or club concerned.

They, however, recommended that the question of insuring the Union against loss be left in the hands of the Manager of the team to be dealt with on arrival in England; and that he (the Manager) shall have power to expend a sum not exceeding £100 in obtaining a policy to cover the difference between the estimated expenses of the tour (£6000) after deducting cash in hand (£2000) and the amount guaranteed by the English Rugby Union (£2500). Recommendation adopted. It was decided in the meantime to ask the Union's representative in London [Wray Palliser] to make enquiry as to the possibility of such a risk being obtainable.

A WELL-HEELED GROUP of Hawke's Bay graziers and businessmen responded generously to the debenture scheme. Two letters were received by the Union from a Mr Logan of Napier, informing the NZRFU that 'the following gentlemen had agreed to take up debentures in connection with the tour to Great Britain': R.W.W. McLean £50; J.H. Coleman £50; F. Logan £50; G.P. Donnelly £50; J.W. Williams £50; T.H. Lowry £20; Hon. J.W. Ormond £50. The donations amounted to £320, which was the highest individual commitment from any province in the country.

Minutes *of the*
NZRFU MANAGEMENT COMMITTEE

HELD AT THE WELLINGTON CYCLING CLUB ROOMS ON WEDNESDAY 10 MAY 1905

Medical unfavourable to D. Stuart. Secretary instructed to write to Mr Stuart conveying the committee's regret that he was unable to pass one of the required tests.

Mr W.R.P. Woodward wrote from Vancouver asking that the New Zealand team play matches in British Columbia on their return journey, namely in March 1906. It was decided to reply that the tour could not be extended.

A letter was received from J.W. Stead asking if the management committee intended making any provision for married men beyond 3s per diem and if 3s was to be paid for Sundays. Secretary to reply 'no' and 'yes', respectively.

THE MANAGEMENT COMMITTEE OF THE NEW ZEALAND RUGBY UNION, 1905. Back row: R.M. Isaacs, D.D. Weir, W. Coffey. Front row: G. Laurenson, E. Wylie (secretary), G.H. Dixon (chairman), N. Galbraith (treasurer), G.C. Fache.

DEBENTURES

Secretary Taranaki union wrote that his union had voted the sum of £10 and would endeavour to arrange match towards funds for team to Britain and it would also endeavour to place some debentures but did not anticipate any success; Poverty Bay Union agreeing to take up £20 debenture and covering cheque for same, a letter from A.P. Donnelly covering cheque for £50 debenture money; a letter from Auckland Union covering cheque for £250 being guarantee £100 and debenture £150; a letter from Wanganui Union that in event of loss on tour they would stand in pro rata with other unions for £150. A letter from Otago Union that its boundaries are those of the Province of Otago and stating that cheque for £100 would be sent on receipt of debenture. Secy replied with debenture and asked if this was additional to £250 previously promised. From the Secy Southland acknowledging receipt of debentures, four of £5 and 30 of £1 and hoping he would be able to dispose of them and asking whether guarantee or debentures take precedence in repayment and whether Union's debentures rank with those taken up by private persons. Secy instructed to reply debentures take precedence to guarantee.

TOUR FOR BRITAIN

Team to leave on morning of 30 July by *Rimutaka* arriving at Plymouth 8 September.

Jerseys: a letter from Wallace & Gibson submitting sample jerseys and knickers and caps. The Secretary was instructed to make arrangements for outfits for Sydney and for British Isles.

H.R. Woon wrote offering his services as trainer for tour to Britain — resolved to adhere to former decision not to take a trainer. Letter from Private Secretary to Lord Plunket that His Excellency had much pleasure in accepting office of Patron.

Following the North-South match at Wellington (won 26-nil by North), the selectors named 25 players to undertake the tour of the UK.

Gone from the original squad were Stuart, who had failed a fitness test, Hay-McKenzie, Harvey, Watkins, Cross and Whisker. The newcomers were Gillett (who had returned from Australia), Smith (who had come out of retirement), Gallaher, Glasgow, Mackrell, McDonald and Newton.

Criticism was voiced at the omission of 'confirmed' team members Hay-McKenzie and Whisker, especially as they had featured in North's crushing victory over South.

THE APPEAL FOR DEBENTURES had fallen well short of the sum sought by the Union and so it was decided to take up the offer of the Australian 'tour' and send 19 of the New Zealand players to Sydney, two weeks before sailing to Britain, to bring in extra funds. They would be accompanied on the three-match series in New South Wales for the week of 8–15 July by Mr Galbraith of the NZRFU, who would act as the manager. As a sweetener for the players, it was decided to pay the men going to Sydney a daily allowance from the time of their departure from Auckland.

Additional pre-England tour matches were also scheduled: 'Subject to support of the various unions it was decided to play the New Zealand team in Auckland on 1 July and on their return from Sydney in Dunedin on 22, in Christchurch on 27, and in Wellington on 29 July.'

Then a huge row between the unions erupted, almost without warning.

At the centre of the storm was the decision of the NZRFU to appoint Jimmy Duncan of Otago as coach for the upcoming tour of Britain. Jimmy Duncan had captained New Zealand in its first international test against Australia in 1903, and been invited by the NZRFU in 1904 to come to Wellington as coach for the 1904 team and was considered a brilliant tactician. The New Zealand team did not need a coach, the Auckland Union protested; his place would be better taken by an extra player on tour.

The Auckland Union wired its objection to the NZRFU, asking for a special meeting of council to obtain expressions of opposition to the matter and receiving support from Hawke's Bay, Taranaki and Southland over its request for a 'special meeting on the action of council in appointing a coach'.

Three weeks before the team was due to leave the country on the SS *Rimutaka* an informal meeting of the NZRFU Management Committee was called to consider the advisability of issuing an explanatory circular to affiliated unions as to the position taken up by the committee re the appointment of a coach.

A draft letter was submitted which, after some amendments, was ordered to be sent to affiliated unions: the NZRFU secretary was also instructed to procure a legal opinion on the various questions arising out of the appointment of a coach and the movement to upset it.

The letter did little to dampen the controversy, and just twelve days before the team was to depart, a special general meeting of the NZRFU Council, chaired by George Dixon, was called. It took place on 18 July 1905 at the request of Auckland, Hawke's Bay and Taranaki Unions 'for the object of considering and expressing the opinion of the Council upon the action of the management committee in appointing a Coach to accompany the New Zealand Team.'

Both sides in the dispute lobbied hard for support on their stance.

The Canterbury Rugby Union, who had received letters from Auckland and the NZRFU on the issue, decided to remain aloof from the fray, instructing their delegates instead to support the NZRFU management committee at the meeting but to express an opinion that their action in sending Duncan was ill-advised.

At the Wellington meeting the NZRFU minutes recorded: 'Mr McCormack, Secretary of the Auckland Union moved, on behalf of his union, that the appointment of a coach was a grave error, and in the opinion of the meeting ought to be cancelled. "The players as a whole resented the idea of a coach and the 'coach' appointed was not popular." Mr A.H. Holland (Taranaki) seconded the motion, saying that his union thought it would be more advantageous if an active player was sent in place of the "coach." Mr T. Hunter (Otago) did not see how the delegates could go behind the committee now that the appointment had been made. He had his own personal opinion on the matter, but no good could now be done by discussing the appointment. The motion was put to the meeting and lost.'

The following day, 19 July, the NZRFU voted to send two extra men to England, a lock forward and a back, announcing that these two men were to be selected without delay.

In their three matches in Sydney, New Zealand beat New South Wales 19-0, beat Sydney Metropolitan 22-3 and drew with New South Wales 8-8.

Minutes *of the*
NZRFU MANAGEMENT COMMITTEE

HELD AT THE WELLINGTON CYCLING ROOMS ON TUESDAY 25 JULY 1905

It was decided to vote the sum of 10 pence per diem from 30 July until return to Colony for personal expenses of Mr Dixon, Manager of the team to tour Great Britain.

Mr Fache reported that it was decided to play both Abbott and Logan in Saturday's match against Wellington with a view to final selection of extra back. Cunningham (Auckland) had been selected as extra lock forward. The appointment of referees for matches in the Old Country was left to the manager of the team.

The committee decided to appoint Captain, Vice-Captain and Selection Committee for the tour and the following were appointed: Captain, D. Gallaher, Vice-Captain, W.J. Stead. Selection committee: The Captain, Vice-Captain, the manager, J. Duncan and W.J. Wallace.

THE NEXT 'TOUR' ROW to blow up had more far-reaching repercussions, resulting in Canterbury being suspended from the NZRFU.

The Otago Union had written to the NZRFU at the end of June, querying whether the NZRFU had any recommendation to make regarding entertainment of the New Zealand team on its pre-tour matches in Dunedin, Canterbury and Wellington, before the team's departure for Britain. A starchy reply was delivered from the Union, stating that it was 'not in a position to sanction expenditure for the entertainment of the New Zealand team in any centre'.

History does not record how, or whether, Otago entertained its illustrious guests, but Canterbury was, as ever, hospitable. Its entertainment committee overspent the budget by £4 6s when the New Zealand team played Canterbury on 27 July, four days prior to going on tour to Britain. The Union said Canterbury had overspent and should pay up. Canterbury said that as this was an NZRFU game, with profits going to the national body, the cost should be borne by them.

NAMES OF PLAYERS
—IN—
NEW ZEALAND TEAM.

BACKS.		st.	lb.
G. Gillett, Canterbury	...	12	8
E. E. Booth, Otago...	...	11	10
W. J. Wallace, Wellington	...	11	12
D. McGregor, Wellington	...	12	2
H. D. Thomson, Wanganui	...	10	12
G. W. Smith, Auckland	...	11	4
E. T. Harper, Canterbury	...	12	6
H. J. Mynott, Taranaki	...	11	4
R. G. Deans, Canterbury	...	13	10
J. Hunter, Taranaki	...	11	4
J. W. Stead, Southland	...	10	0
F. Roberts, Wellington	...	12	4
FORWARDS.			
S. Casey, Otago	...	12	1
G. Tyler, Auckland	...	12	12
D. Gallaher, Auckland	...	12	8
W. H. Mackrell, Auckland	...	12	8
F. Glasgow, Taranaki	...	13	0
J. Corbett, West Coast	...	13	5
William Johnstone, Otago	...	13	6
A. McDonald, Otago	...	12	12
F. Newton, Canterbury	...	14	6
A. Seeling, Auckland	...	13	7
W. Nicholson, Auckland	...	13	10
J. O'Sullivan, Taranaki	...	13	7
W. S. Glenn, Taranaki	...	12	7

J. DUNCAN, Coach for Team in England.

New Zealand Rugby Union.

OFFICIAL ...
SOUVENIR .

.. OF ..

NEW ZEALAND TEAM.

Published by
LINLEY & CO., Wellington.

G. H. DIXON,
Manager of N.Z. Team.
Chairman Management Committee, N.Z.R.U.

NEW ZEALAND TEAM
LIST OF FIXTURES
—IN—
AUSTRALIA AND NEW ZEALAND.

AUCKLAND PROVINCE—
1st July, won by 9 points to 3.

IN AUSTRALIA—
8th July, N.S.W.; won by 19 to 3.
12th July, Metropolitan Union, won 22 to 3.
15th July, N.S.W.; drawn, 8 to 8.

OTAGO PROVINCE—
At Dunedin, on 22nd Jul.

CANTERBURY PROVINCE—
At Christchurch, on 27th Jul.

WELLINGTON PROVINCE—
At Wellington, on 29th Ju'.

Leaving Wellington for England on 30th July.

Thirty Matches will be played in England, dates not yet finally fixed for same.

A SOUVENIR BROCHURE produced prior to the team's warm-up matches in Dunedin, Christchurch and Wellington. 'Bunny' Abbott and Bill Cunningham were still to be added to the touring party.

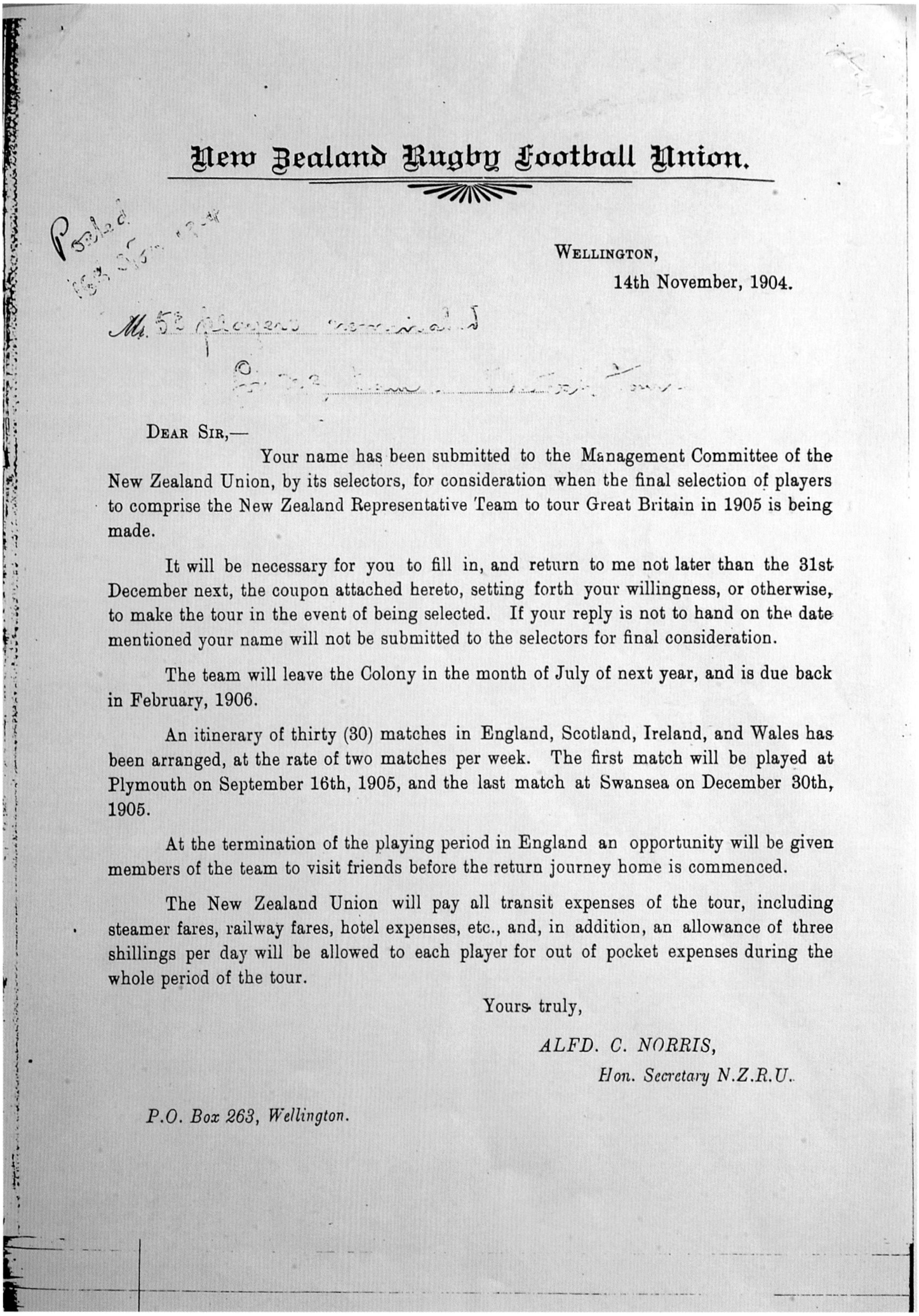

New Zealand Rugby Football Union.

WELLINGTON,

14th November, 1904.

M̲r̲. ....

DEAR SIR,—

Your name has been submitted to the Management Committee of the New Zealand Union, by its selectors, for consideration when the final selection of players to comprise the New Zealand Representative Team to tour Great Britain in 1905 is being made.

It will be necessary for you to fill in, and return to me not later than the 31st December next, the coupon attached hereto, setting forth your willingness, or otherwise, to make the tour in the event of being selected. If your reply is not to hand on the date mentioned your name will not be submitted to the selectors for final consideration.

The team will leave the Colony in the month of July of next year, and is due back in February, 1906.

An itinerary of thirty (30) matches in England, Scotland, Ireland, and Wales has been arranged, at the rate of two matches per week. The first match will be played at Plymouth on September 16th, 1905, and the last match at Swansea on December 30th, 1905.

At the termination of the playing period in England an opportunity will be given members of the team to visit friends before the return journey home is commenced.

The New Zealand Union will pay all transit expenses of the tour, including steamer fares, railway fares, hotel expenses, etc., and, in addition, an allowance of three shillings per day will be allowed to each player for out of pocket expenses during the whole period of the tour.

Yours truly,

ALFD. C. NORRIS,

Hon. Secretary N.Z.R.U.

P.O. Box 263, Wellington.

IN 1904 A LETTER went to 53 players, advising them they were under consideration for the Great Britain tour.

The row rumbled on long after the team's departure. In September 1905 the NZRFU gave Canterbury a seven-day ultimatum to pay up or be suspended from the Union. The Cantabrians, who had over-imbibed on 'liquid refreshments' in entertaining the national team, refused — recording in their minutes of 5 September 1905, '. . . it was decided that the committee of the CRFU strongly objects to the refusal of the New Zealand Rugby Union to refund the £4 6s expended by members of this executive on the entertainment of the New Zealand representatives on behalf of the governing body; but that in the event of the New Zealand Rugby Union committee adhering to their refusal to pay this cost, the Committee declines to in any way entertain in the future any team visiting Christchurch under the auspices of the NZRFU . . .'

Canterbury's suspension stood until the CRFU's Annual General Meeting on 30 March 1906, when the Canterbury All Blacks had returned home and the union was forced to back down, stating: 'This action of the NZRFU placed the Canterbury members of the New Zealand team at a most anomalous position, which was naturally resented by your committee. In view of the near approach of Easter when several clubs have important engagements with visiting teams, the sum has been paid under protest much sooner than it otherwise would in order that the suspension may be removed. It is hoped that your representatives at the Annual Meeting of the NZRFU will have the matter thoroughly ventilated.' Canterbury posted its cheque for £4 6s and was promptly reinstated by the NZRFU.

Meanwhile, two days after its match against Canterbury, New Zealand had its final pre-tour game against Wellington on 29 July. An *Evening Post* reporter braved the elements, along with 3000 diehard rugby enthusiasts:

'The New Zealand representative team played its final match against a Wellington provincial fifteen in wind and rain and mud, before embarking on its long voyage on the *Rimutaka* for Home. The elements were just about as unkind as they possibly could have been and the ground was thoroughly soaked, so much so that the game resolved itself into a hotly-contested mud scramble.

The result cannot be taken as indicative of the relative merits of the team and the fact that the picked men of the colony were beaten by 3 points by the provincials need not occasion any undue concern about the chances of the losers at Home. Wellington went on to win (3-0) and it was a little surprising that the crowd barracked vigorously and consistently for the province. A crowd of about three thousand witnessed the match.'

Despite the newspaper's reassurance, this was not the best of results for a team about to embark on the most expensive and ambitious tour in the Colony's history.

On the following day, Sunday 30 July 1905, the New Zealand team, along with coach and manager departed from Wellington for England on the SS *Rimutaka*.

FROM OUR LONDON CORRESPONDENT

FAREWELL TO THE COLONY'S REPRESENTATIVES

THE TEAM CONSISTING of twenty-seven players, a coach (Mr James Duncan of Otago) with Mr G.H. Dixon as manager, was generally regarded as the best that could be chosen in the colony and an infinitely stronger combination all round than the New Zealand native team which visited Great Britain in 1888–89.

It was selected by Messrs Bayly (Auckland), Fache (Wellington), Evans (Canterbury) and Harris (Otago). Certain men were left out who for their football qualifications would have been of the party, but for other reasons were not considered.

Each member had to pass a severe medical examination, and by this means players of supreme physical gifts were assured — players in the full vigour of youth, sound in wind and limb. In order to get some combination a short tour was undertaken in New South Wales, and matches were also played at home against the provinces of Canterbury, Otago and Wellington. One of these was lost and another drawn, thus illustrating the wealth of football talent in New Zealand.

Chapter 2

THE
TEAM

THIS FIRST TEAM PICTURE — taken by a local photographer at Newton Abbot — before the New Zealanders' opening match on tour proved hugely popular with the public. Within hours of being printed, the photograph, with its picturesque backdrop of an old ivy-clad home, went on sale as a postcard and sold freely at Exter at the first match.

Thousands of copies of this postcard were distributed throughout the country and many were sent with messages back to family and friends in New Zealand. For reasons unknown, Billy Glenn is absent from the photograph.

GEORGE DIXON'S DIARIES

Newton Abbot — Stay at Globe Hotel, old-fashioned rambling house. Kept best table — no fancy French dishes but good wholesome British fare. Beautiful fresh rolls, fish very nice indeed, plenty of Devonshire cream and junket.

Boys anxious but fairly confident, expect them to put up a big game for this first match on tour. This morning we are to have team photograph taken . . .

THE TEAM PHOTOGRAPH

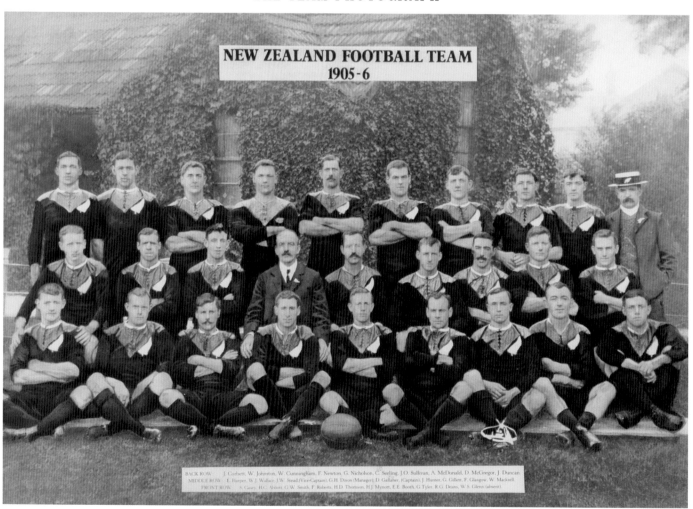

BACK ROW: J. Corbett, W. Johnston, W. Cunningham, F. Newton, G. Nicholson, C. Seeling, J. O'Sullivan, A. McDonald, D. McGregor, J. Duncan (coach)
MIDDLE ROW: E. Harper, W. Wallace, W. Stead, G. Dixon (manager), D. Gallaher, J. Hunter, G. Gillett, F. Glasgow, W. Mackrell
FRONT ROW: S. Casey, H. Abbott, G. Smith, F. Roberts, H. Thomson, S. Mynott, E. Booth, G. Tyler, R. Deans
ABSENT: W. Glenn

HAROLD ABBOTT

TARANAKI

wing
23
5ft 10in
13st 1lb

ERNEST BOOTH

OTAGO

fullback/wing
29
5ft 7½in
11st 10lb

STEVE CASEY

OTAGO

hooker
22
5ft 10in
12st 4lb

JOHN CORBETT

WEST COAST

lock
25
5ft 11in
13st 9lb

BILL CUNNINGHAM

AUCKLAND

lock
31
5ft 11in
14st 6lb

BOB DEANS

CANTERBURY

centre
21
6ft
13st 4lb

DAVE GALLAHER

AUCKLAND

wing forward
29
6ft
13st

GEORGE GILLETT

CANTERBURY

fullback
28
6ft
12st 8lb

FRANK GLASGOW

TARANAKI

loose forward
25
5ft 10in
13st 3lb

BILLY GLENN

TARANAKI

loose forward
27
5ft 11in
12st 12lb

ERIC HARPER

CANTERBURY

centre
27
5ft 11in
12st 7lb

JIMMY HUNTER

TARANAKI

second-five
26
5ft 6in
11st 8lb

WILLIAM JOHNSTON

OTAGO

loose forward
23
6ft
13st 6lb

ALEX McDONALD

OTAGO

loose forward
22
5ft 10in
12st 12lb

DUNCAN McGREGOR

WELLINGTON

wing threequarter
23
5ft 9in
11st 3lb

BILLY MACKRELL

AUCKLAND

hooker
23
5ft 10in
12st 8lb

SIMON MYNOTT

TARANAKI

first-five
29
5ft 7in
11st 9lb

FRED NEWTON

CANTERBURY

lock
23
6ft
15st

GEORGE NICHOLSON

AUCKLAND

lock
27
6ft 3in
13st 10lb

JIM O'SULLIVAN

TARANAKI

loose forward
22
5ft 10in
13st 7lb

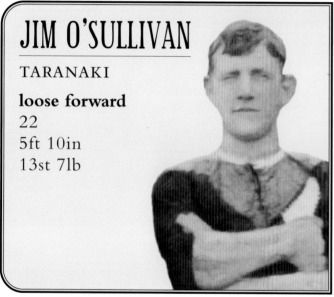

FRED ROBERTS

WELLINGTON

halfback
23
5ft 7in
12st 4lb

CHARLIE SEELING

AUCKLAND

loose forward
22
6ft
13st 7lb

GEORGE SMITH

AUCKLAND

wing
31
5ft 7in
11st 12lb

BILLY STEAD

SOUTHLAND

five-eighth
28
5ft 8in
10st 9lb

HECTOR THOMSON

WANGANUI

wing
24
5ft 8in
10st 12lb

GEORGE TYLER

AUCKLAND

hooker
26
5ft 10in
12st 12lb

BILLY WALLACE

WELLINGTON

fullback
27
5ft 8in
12st

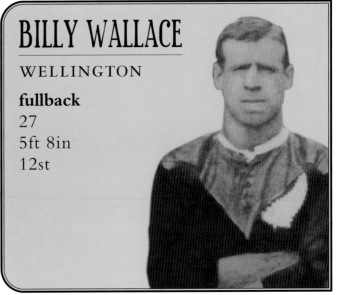

GEORGE DIXON

WELLINGTON

manager
46

JIMMY DUNCAN

OTAGO

coach
35

Chapter 3

THE ITINERARY

THE NEW ZEALAND TEAM'S ITINERARY, 1905–06

SEPT 16	v	DEVON COUNTY,	Exeter
SEPT 21	v	CORNWALL,	Camborne
SEPT 23	v	BRISTOL,	Bristol
SEPT 28	v	NORTHAMPTON,	Northampton
SEPT 30	v	LEICESTER,	Leicester
OCT 4	v	MIDDLESEX,	London
OCT 7	v	DURHAM COUNTY,	Durham
OCT 11	v	HARTLEPOOL CLUBS,	Hartlepool
OCT 14	v	NORTHUMBERLAND,	North Shields
OCT 19	v	GLOUCESTER,	Gloucester
OCT 21	v	SOMERSET COUNTY,	Taunton
OCT 25	v	DEVONPORT ALBION,	Devonport
OCT 28	v	MIDLAND COUNTIES,	Leicester
NOV 1	v	SURREY,	London
NOV 4	v	BLACKHEATH,	London
NOV 7	v	OXFORD UNIVERSITY,	Oxford
NOV 9	v	CAMBRIDGE UNIVERSITY,	Cambridge
NOV 11	v	RICHMOND,	London
NOV 15	v	BEDFORD,	Bedford
NOV 18	v	**SCOTLAND,**	Edinburgh
NOV 22	v	WEST OF SCOTLAND,	Glasgow
NOV 25	v	**IRELAND,**	Dublin
NOV 28	v	MUNSTER,	Limerick
DEC 2	v	**ENGLAND,**	London
DEC 6	v	CHELTENHAM,	Cheltenham
DEC 9	v	CHESHIRE,	Birkenhead
DEC 13	v	YORKSHIRE,	Headingley
DEC 16	v	**WALES,**	Cardiff
DEC 21	v	GLAMORGAN COUNTY,	Swansea
DEC 23	v	NEWPORT,	Newport
DEC 26	v	CARDIFF,	Cardiff
DEC 30	v	SWANSEA,	Swansea
JAN 1	v	**FRANCE,**	Paris
FEB 10	v	BRITISH COLUMBIA,	Berkeley
FEB 13	v	BRITISH COLUMBIA,	San Francisco

NOTE: The final three matches, in Paris, Berkeley and San Francisco were arranged after the team departed New Zealand.

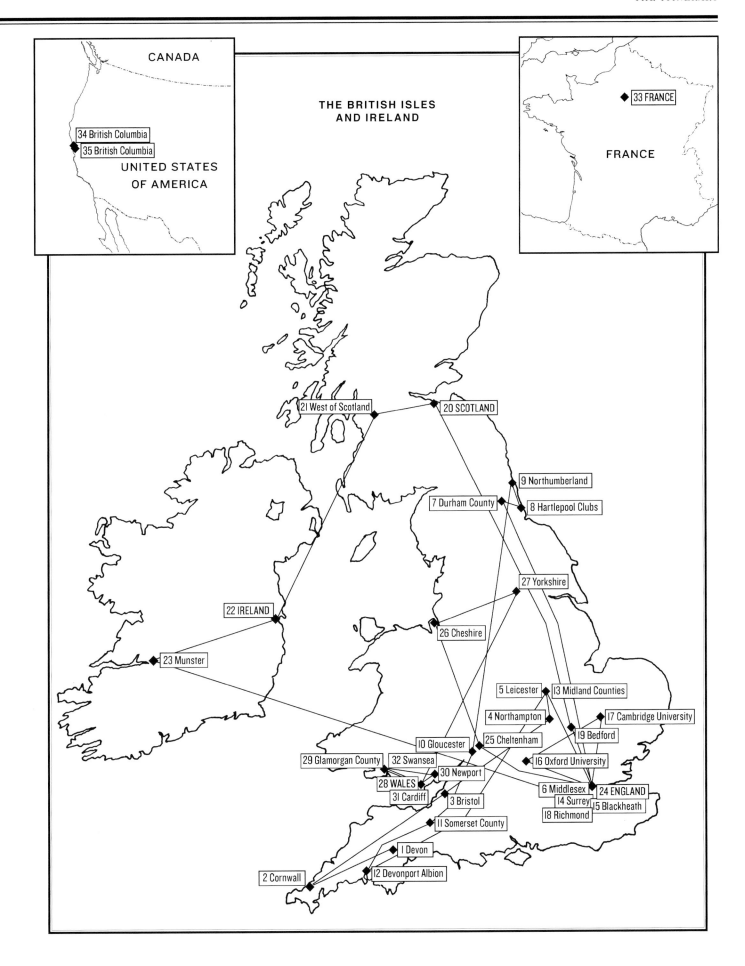

CANADA

UNITED STATES
OF AMERICA

34 British Columbia

35 British Columbia

THE BRITISH ISLES
AND IRELAND

33 FRANCE

FRANCE

21 West of Scotland

20 SCOTLAND

9 Northumberland

7 Durham County

8 Hartlepool Clubs

27 Yorkshire

22 IRELAND

26 Cheshire

23 Munster

5 Leicester

13 Midland Counties

4 Northampton

17 Cambridge University

19 Bedford

10 Gloucester

25 Cheltenham

29 Glamorgan County

32 Swansea

30 Newport

16 Oxford University

28 WALES

6 Middlesex

24 ENGLAND

31 Cardiff

3 Bristol

14 Surrey

15 Blackheath

18 Richmond

11 Somerset County

1 Devon

2 Cornwall

12 Devonport Albion

Chapter 4

THE
GRAND TOUR

TO BE RETURNED TO THE HON. SECRETARY, NEW ZEALAND RUGBY UNION,
WELLINGTON, NOT LATER THAN DECEMBER 31st, 1904.

HON. SECRETARY,
NEW ZEALAND RUGBY UNION,
P.O. Box 263, WELLINGTON.

DEAR SIR,— I will be able to make the tour to Great Britain, if selected, under the conditions mentioned in your letter.

Name in full

Address

Age   Weight

Married :   YES.   NO.

DEAR SIR,— I will NOT be able to make the tour to Great Britain.

Name in full

Address

Free Lance Print.

FROM THE PRIVATE DIARIES OF
GEORGE DIXON
MANAGER OF THE NEW ZEALAND TEAM

SUNDAY 30 JULY 1905

Strange how sudden the whole business of embarkation appeared. Last impression, last view of Emma wearing hat, little Zillah's face at the window. Emma's handkerchief fluttering at the window, then for the first time realizing wouldn't see dear ones for months.

Duncan appears quite happy with rest of team and gives impression of being shrewd and a leader — decent fellow — don't anticipate any trouble in this direction. Duncan, Gallaher, Stead and Smith already talking about arrangements for training and all seem thoroughly impressed with importance of undertaking.

Since leaving Wellington wind and seas steadily getting up and ship is pitching. Noticed cockroaches in cabin — hope not plentiful. Very comfortably fixed in 2-berth cabin by self.

Not given to mal-de-mer, wonder how long I can last, nice to pull through successfully (wonder what Emma and kiddies are doing now? If she was with me would be perfectly contented).

Almost forgotten about the inevitable stowaways turned up this morning . . . ran out of food. Miserably cold and pinched, they looked by no means abashed — their adventure seemed to be taken as a matter of course.

FROM THE DIARY OF BILLY STEAD

The appearance of three stowaways, who had stowed away in Wellington and passed three nights and two days in the boat on the upper boat deck, exposed to hail and rain for the whole of the previous night. Despite their abject starved appearance one could not resist the laugh which was accorded them. They proved to be Auckland lads who stowed away in coasters to Wellington, and tempted by the success which attended this, their first venture, boarded the ship with the intention of barracking for us in the Home Country. They were given work to do and as Montevideo, our first port of call, refuses to take stowaways, they will have to be taken on to Plymouth.

In the early days of the voyage a poker school was organised for afternoons in the first saloon. It seemed innocent enough, with penny stakes, but soon the amounts being wagered began to increase. And it wasn't long before the mug players were beginning to lose sizeable amounts to the 'sharks'.

Once the situation was brought to manager Dixon's attention, he ordered the poker school to be closed down.

Boys very jolly and enjoying themselves thoroughly — marching on deck, boxing gloves, punching ball, wrestling is keeping them fairly occupied. Some first-class humorists. Very funny wrestling bout between Tyler and Thompson, latter by reason of his slight build has been christened Sandow after the famous bodybuilder. After tea arranged for use of piano on deck and had first-rate concert — Glasgow plays really well and Newton, Nicholson and one or two others sing really well. Singing and dancing fills up the evening.

One D . . . fool in saloon — immeasurably round-shouldered white-faced dude who stood about with a big pipe and a supercilious air — remarked to someone 'Wouldn't like my people to know that I travelled in an old tramp like this.'

All the ship's company heard him and he has been christened 'the Insect', which in our part of the ship has been promptly transposed to 'the worm'. This is the kind of fellow who comes out to the colony and from whom many people gather an altogether erroneous impression of the average Britisher.

'Uncle Jimmy' Duncan is making himself very useful and appears to be well liked by everybody.

First thing on reaching the deck this morning was a cry of 'whales' and sure enough we were passing through a school of whales. Committee organised for entertainment. Boys had good run around deck covering fully 2 miles. Cricket and then football on deck until Glasgow with a rousing kick lost ball overboard.

A party of us taken through engine room. Very interesting. Cricket, boxing and various forms of exercise fills up the afternoons. The majority of the boys take plenty of exercise, one or two, notably Deans and to a lesser degree Newton, seem disinclined to exertion — both are inclined to flesh and really require it more than the others — must continue to get both going.

None of the team shows signs of sickness, even Wallace (a notoriously bad sailor) is regular at meals. Today noticed a number of lady passengers on deck who had not previously made an appearance.

THE WOODEN DECKS of the S.S. *Rimutaka* permitted a daily workout.

FACING PAGE, TOP: New Zealand's leading players needed to advise the NZRFU of their availability.

FACING PAGE, BOTTOM: The S.S. *Rimutaka* was home to the Originals for six weeks on their voyage from Wellington to Plymouth.

PILLOW FIGHTS helped keep players entertained and sharpened their competitiveness.

CALLISTHENICS and deck games provided entertainment for fellow passengers.

FROM THE DIARY OF BILLY STEAD

Another good form of keeping condition is down in the stoke-hole and coal bunkers. Four of us took a shift stoking and went the two hours with good results.

The match committee have drafted out the following regulations: physical drill, 7.45 a.m., bath, 8.15 a.m., breakfast 8.30 a.m., running and sprints (backs), scrum formations (forwards) 10 a.m., every alternate afternoon 3 p.m., physical exercises, boxing, Sandow developers, 5 p.m. discussion of rules.

Number of boys took a turn at fuelling and wheeling baskets of coal to the bunkers — Casey, McGregor, Tyler, Cunningham, Glasgow, Stead, Mackrell and Duncan all taking part. Deans seems to have rooted objection to training in that direction — Seeling indulges in very little exercise also. Chatted him with a good deal of earnestness on this. He replied, 'I didn't come on board this ship to work.' Corbett is another who doesn't go looking for work . . .

Find it difficult to read on board, seem unable to concentrate on books . . .

Evening entertainment. Cunningham as usual really funny — got up in borrowed dresscoat, white waistcoat, green silk handkerchief, pince-nez. It made me laugh only to look at him. At supper adjournment he paraded the deck to the intense amusement of the captain and first-class passengers.

7TH DAY. FRIDAY 4 AUGUST

Boys this morning for first time commenced talking football. Later found boys in groups extending discussions. Good sign this . . .

Slept badly last night. Dreamt saw Emma in some uncommon kind of wrapper or dress and wearing red hat. Thought she sat on my knee. On rising learned that snow fell during night — boys got fun out of snowballing. Huge storm. Must have been a tremendous sea that struck us last night. Ship damaged — the Doctor got a ducking and the chief officer was capsized head-first into the bath. Decks covered with frozen snow, temperatures down to -7 degrees. Whole of upper frames forced out. All the boys were up to breakfast save Wallace and Glasgow. Many unable to sleep . . .

Church service, captain preached little sermon on selfishness. In fact, the best sermon I've heard for many a long day . . .

Strange being cut off from the world. One doesn't miss the papers nor feel a keen desire for newspapers. Bitterly cold. Slept badly . . .

D'Augmier asked for passengers to drink with him it being his little girl's Ist birthday. We gave silver fern and sang 'For he's a jolly good fellow' in Maori to delight of other passengers, who afterwards were anxious to secure the words. I secured them from Cunningham who seems to have a good knowledge of Maori. Gillett slipped and inflicted cut over eye.

Eight days into the voyage a crisis situation arose when Gallaher announced at a team meeting that he was resigning the captaincy. Immediately, Stead declared that he was standing down as vice-captain. Gallaher, speaking to the assembly, said that it had become apparent, following the team's departure from Auckland, that the players wished to appoint their own captain.

I intervened, advising the gathering that the appointments made by the New Zealand Rugby Union had to stand, that they could not be varied at the whim of a group of players. I felt that the position was awkward.

Frank Glasgow, after weighing the comments from all sides, put forward a motion, that 'this meeting heartily endorses the appointments made by the (New Zealand) management committee'.

I decided to accept the motion which, mercifully for the good of the demanding tour ahead, was carried, seventeen of the twenty-nine persons present supporting it.

16TH DAY 13 AUGUST

Land in sight. Expect to pass Horn about midday. Captain took us very close (about ¼ mile), we had very good view of southernmost point of Terra del Fuego; the appearance of this portion of the earth's surface is very uninviting. Still very cold . . .

Corbett seems to have very vague idea of scrum work and generally doesn't appear to have the same keen interest in games as other members . . .

Complaints about late noise. Quite certain not fault of our boys . . . who but a cantankerous beggar would complain?

MONTEVIDEO

Few hours ashore. Footpaths of flagstones, some very fine buildings. Stairs of marble. Most persistent feature of city: smell — what it must be in summer. Lunch very tedious process, no one seems in a hurry in this part of the world. Only decent dish I partook of was fish.

Found on return fellow cabin mate. On my dressing table talc powder, one bottle scent, one bottle dentifrice, one bottle containing I don't know what — quite sufficient to inform me my room mate was a foreigner (Spanish gentleman); quite sufficient also to arouse that insular prejudice with which all Britishers are cursed — later got moved after one night.

FROM THE DIARY OF BILLY STEAD

Our first call in Montevideo was the cathedral, the beauty of which held us in speechless wonder, though even there you can't entirely get rid of the smell of garlic. Thence we crossed over to Teatro Solis (the Theatre of the Sun) and in whatever way you look at it from the outside you see the representation of the rays of the sun. It has five tiers of boxes encircling the hall, and an immense stage. The staircases are of marble, with beautiful inlaid tiles and at every turning a lifesize statue of some of their deceased statesmen, holding an electric globe. These are exquisite specimens of art.

Dinner: At the hotel our manager had to pay 4s 6d per head for dinner to take 'a la Spanish', which takes two hours. The peculiar thing being that both men and women smoke cigarettes between the various courses. We all lamented our own corned beef and cabbage.

SIXTEEN DAYS out from Wellington, the S.S. *Rimutaka* rounded Cape Horn.

BILLY WALLACE'S RECOLLECTIONS

When we left New Zealand Jimmy Duncan, being a staunch Dunedin man, had taken a case of Speight's beer with him and smuggled it into his cabin.

Of course the knowledge of such splendid refreshments got to the ears of the boys and at odd moments they used to sneak down to Jimmy's cabin and broach the precious cargo, filling the empty bottle with water and carefully replacing the cork and wire and silver paper so that the bottle seemed untouched. It was then carefully placed at the bottom of the case. A guard was always posted on these occasions and so Jimmy never suspected his larder was getting lower.

When we arrived at Montevideo a fresh crowd of visitors arrived aboard and one of them gave Jimmy a very attentive hearing.

Jimmy talked about football and Dunedin and its attractions, and referred to the fact that it made 'the best beer in the world' and to prove this he invited his new friend down to 'have a taste'.

He took up a bottle, held it up proudly and taking out the cork poured out a glass. It was water! Greatly puzzled he took out another. It was water again! So was the next and the next.

Then Jimmy guessed what had happened. There was not a drop of beer left. And didn't Jimmy hit the roof!

Now very hot. Officers and captain in white ducks — team in football gear . . .

Hurdles race on deck. Had I known would have prohibited it. Too dangerous. Captain took it, however, a number of boys jibbed on their own account . . .

Consulted Dr re McGregor still looking very unwell — heat bothering him. Sneak thief in one of the cabins, boys keeping guard tonight. Beastly hot . . .

Sighted Tenerife, 36th day. From our anchorage we were immediately surrounded by a number of roving boats filled with eager, gesticulating Spaniards. Went to Hotel Victoria for dinner. This meal consisted of four or five courses, none of which I could eat. Everything was oil and of very distasteful flavour. An electric tram exists and more English spoken. Very little sleep for anybody tonight . . .

Fancy costume ball in 1st class saloon, who have invited 2nd class as their guests.

Newton dresses as a disreputable-looking woman, Nicholson as a tramp, Thompson as Sandow. At supper when get message O'Sullivan ill. Found him in high fever — temperature 105 degrees. Dr put to work. Got to bed 2 a.m. Smith staying with O'S. and promising to call me when he wanted a spell. Heard Nicholson was awarded winner by a large majority . . .

THURSDAY 7 SEPTEMBER
End of voyage. Sports and competition day. Harper won men's potato race, Thomson obstacle and egg and spoon.

Final concert. Held meeting of team today and congratulated them on record up to date and expressed hope that record would be as good on tour. Informed them that every individual member responsible for keeping himself in form and that if anyone by his own act rendered himself unfit, then the consequences whatever they might be would be on his own head.

A MERCURY REPRESENTATIVE had a chat with a gentleman who left New Zealand by the same steamer that brought the Colonials to this country:

'This Briton declared there was no doubt, that they meant business. They were triers — there was no mistake about that. "We found out to the cost of our comfort on the way across. They had the deck netted pretty well all round and were out every day and all day in their football dress for practice."

THE FIRST–CLASS PASSENGERS watch on as a group of players gather for a photo.

BILLY WALLACE'S RECOLLECTIONS

At Tenerife the boys bought boxes of quality cigars very cheaply and only when we got back on board did we find that under the top layer, there was just packing.

'They played football, perhaps a little too much for his liking as they came across and novel as the experience was of being a witness at sea of the latest tricks in dodging and passing, this spectator was not anxious to renew the experience.

'Asked if the Colonials added much to the social gaiety of life on board, he says they were not much in that line. A few of them sang songs occasionally at night in the smoke-room: but on the whole they simply contented themselves with their football practice from early morn till what corresponds on the ocean to dewy eve.

'Before quitting the subject he mentioned an interesting circumstance in connection with the silver fern worn by the New Zealand players. This emblem was presented to them, he said, by a Maori girl, who is rather a personage in her way.

'She came down to Wellington to see the players off and personally decorated them with the Maori leaf. She is the same lady that the Prince and Princess of Wales honoured with a call on their visit to the colony.'

42ND DAY FRIDAY 8 SEPTEMBER

Arrived Plymouth Sound. Woke up by a loud knocking at cabin door shortly after 4 a.m. and on opening found Wray Palliser, Donne (Somerset County,) Pring (Devon County). Dressed hastily — on going into saloon met by big parcel of letters (one from Emma but containing newspaper clippings only).

Barely managed to get a cup of tea before being bustled away. Reaching gangway we found all passengers and officers assembled to say goodbye. After hasty but general handshaking got aboard tug and as she cast off ship's people cheered us heartily — we responded just as heartily and finishing with a war-cry, much to amusement of Englishmen on tug.

Plymouth looked very pretty in the early morning but so closely was I kept in conversation that I only gathered in the general impression and beauty. Plymouth very clean, English-looking town and very pleasant to our eyes after Montevideo and Tenerife.

◆

CHRISTCHURCH PRESS'
UK CORRESPONDENT

THE NEW ZEALAND FOOTBALL TEAM'S long sea voyage is at an end. The good ship *Rimutaka* arrived off Plymouth Sound at daybreak yesterday and by six o'clock a score or so of stalwart young colonials were taking their first stroll on English soil in the deserted streets of the sleeping town.

There was no mistaking their country of origin. The silver fern-leaf proclaimed it on seven-and-twenty hatbands and in seven-and-twenty buttonholes. But for the time being there were none to read the signal and spread the tidings. The New Zealanders had succeeded where the Spanish Armada failed; they had caught Plymouth napping.

Mr C. Palliser, accountant to the High Commissioner's Department, went out to the *Rimutaka* in the tender at 5 a.m., accompanied by Messrs Pring and Donne of the English Rugby Union, and by these gentlemen the team were officially received and welcomed to England.

Mr Palliser represents the NZRFU in England and has carried out all the preliminary arrangements in connection with the tour.

Mr Pring, a Devon man, is vice-president of the English Rugby Union and Mr Donne represents Somerset on the ERU. Their courtesy in coming to Plymouth to meet the steamer was much appreciated by the team.

The weather was perfect. Whether or not this was a lucky omen for the tour, it certainly made all the difference in the newcomers' first impressions of the Mother Country.

With the exception of George Smith and Jimmy Hunter, all the members of the team are, I fancy, on their first visit to this side of the world and the introduction to Old England could not have been made under happier auspices.

From this point of view, it was fortunate that the team's plans enabled them to land in picturesque Plymouth and travel through one of the most beautiful of the English counties, instead of coming in by the 'back door' of London, with its grimy docks and its mile after mile of mean streets and smoking chimney pots.

In the brilliant sunshine of yesterday beautiful Devon had put on its fairest dress, all the fresher and the brighter for the heavy weather of the day before.

Looking out upon the famous view seaward from Plymouth Hoe, and then speeding inland through a smiling landscape of green hill and dale and silver stream, he would be a dull dog indeed who failed to respond to the vivid yet reposeful beauty of the scene.

In Plymouth, the New Zealanders had time only for a brief stroll round before breakfasting and entraining for their destination, Newton Abbot.

Their first view of an English town, with its rows of stone dwellings, was an experience in itself.

Said one of the team, 'It's a strange sight to colonial eyes — no verandahs, no gardens, no wooden buildings . . . well, well!'

Mr Dixon said all his men were well and that he hoped to have them perfectly fit in time for the opening match next Saturday.

Apart from a fortnight of rough weather, up to the time of rounding Cape Horn, the voyage had been a good one, and all the team had proved to be good sailors; seasickness had troubled them not at all.

Practice had been kept up systematically during the voyage and there was but little superfluous weight to get rid of.

After breakfast the team left by the 9.50 a.m. train for their training quarters at Newton Abbot, a small Devonshire town pleasantly situated near Teignmouth Estuary on line between Exeter and Plymouth.

They will prepare there for the first match, versus Devon County, which takes place on Saturday 16 September at Exeter (not Torquay as originally arranged).

They are not due in London until 4 October. The travelling arrangements are in the hands of Messrs Thomas Cook and Son.

Chapter 5

THE
MATCHES

GAME 1 — SATURDAY 16 SEPTEMBER 1905 — At County Ground, Exeter

NEW ZEALAND DEVON COUNTY

55

4

FOR NEW ZEALAND
Tries by Smith 4, Wallace 3, Hunter 2,
Glasgow, Nicholson, Stead; 8 conversions,
1 penalty goal by Wallace.

NEW ZEALAND
Gillett, Thomson, Smith, Hunter, Wallace,
Stead, Roberts; Gallaher (captain), Glasgow,
Seeling, O'Sullivan, Cunningham,
Nicholson, Tyler, Casey.

FOR DEVON COUNTY
Dropped goal by Lillicrap.

DEVON COUNTY
F. Lillicrap (Devonport Albion), Lt Moir
(Albion), A.J.R. Roberts (Barnstaple),
E.J. Vivyan (Albion), F. Dean (Albion), R. Jago
(Albion), J. Peters (Plymouth),
M. Kelly (Exeter), J. Tucker (Torquay
Athletic), T. Willocks (Plymouth),
G. Williams (Albion), W. Spiers (Albion,
captain), W. Mills (Albion), W. Roberts
(Albion), A. Knight (Albion).

Weather: Sunny, ground firm
Referee: Percy Coles (England)
Crowd: 6000

KICK OFF
From a scrum, Roberts to Stead to Hunter who scored. Wallace converted: 5-0.
Wallace a penalty goal: 8-0.
Smith scored after slick passing among the backs. Wallace missed: 11-0.
Wallace regathered a punt by Roberts to score and convert: 16-0.
Nicholson scored after a surge by the forwards. Wallace missed: 19-0.
Smith used his explosive pace to score from broken play. Wallace converted: 24-0.
Wallace crossed from an attacking scrum. Gillett missed.

HALFTIME
New Zealand 27, Devon County 0

Glasgow scored following a forward rush. Wallace converted: 32-0.
Smith scored after slicing through in dazzling fashion. Wallace converted: 37-0.
Wallace and Hunter nonplussed the defence, Hunter scoring. Wallace missed: 40-0.
Smith's startling pace secured another try that Wallace converted: 45-0.
Stead went in from another backline attack. Wallace converted: 50-0.
Lillicrap, the Devon fullback, landed a brilliant left-footed dropped goal: 50-4.
Wallace had the last say, racing through the entire opposition to score and convert.

FULLTIME
New Zealand 55, Devon County 4

FROM THE SIDELINES

E.D.H. SEWELL

I F A TEAM OF RUGBY PLAYERS, the members of which are locked into their rooms after lunch for an hour's rest before going down to the ground, does not mean strict business, I should like to know what it does mean.

That is what the assiduous trainer of the New Zealand team did with his men before they turned out to score 50-odd points to 4 against Devon County at Exeter.

Such an arrangement cannot conveniently be carried out on every occasion. But its advantages are too obvious to need further comment here.

This rule is typical of the regularity, which is almost drastic, that governs the actions of this fine, well-set-up, hard-grafted set of athletes from over the sea.

You will see them go springily on to the field of play, and will wonder how they can, without pain, put up with the rather thin-soled boots and lengthy knobs which they wear. But by barefooted exercise they have toughened their feet, and the knobs do not hurt.

More system! You will, I doubt not, observe the almost uncanny silence in which they play. Still further evidence of a system which must make for victory. There is a complete absence of all that noise with which habitués of London football grounds are only too well acquainted.

The men do not need to be told where the ball is, for the simple reason that each is watching it. So much breath and foot pounds of energy are thus put by towards expenditure on the common end — that is, the crossing of the opponents' goalline.

It is easy to say, on the strength of its opening display, that the team will win all its matches, and I am not so sure that it will not do so. If it returns unbeaten I shall not be surprised.

From what I saw of rugby in the four Home Unions last season, I must confess I felt none too sanguine, as I saw several movements in the New Zealanders' play which I do not believe it possible for human agency to improve.

THE EXPRESS AND ECHO

T HE VISITING TEAM were the first to make their appearance, and, as they filed on to the ground, they received an enthusiastic ovation.

The 'All Blacks' as they are styled, by reason of their sable and unrelieved costume, were under the guidance of their captain (Mr Gallaher), and their fine physique favourably impressed the spectators.

Spiers quickly followed with his Devon men, who wore the Exeter City Club jerseys, in consequence of the new Devon outfit not being to hand.

SPORTING DRAMATICS

O F RECENT EVENTS in the football world, the most notable has been the opening match of the New Zealand rugby players in England.

There was an impression that they would defeat Devonshire, but nobody anticipated the complete rout which befell the famous Western county.

On paper, they had a very good side; on the field, they were helpless.

Seven New Zealand forwards pushed the Devonshire eight anywhere and everywhere and the few loopholes for opening up the attack which were presented to the Devon halves were invariably closed in double quick time by the 'winger' on the opposing side.

This player, professedly the eighth forward, made no effort to do what we regard as a forward's work. His duty was to obstruct the opposing half, and he gave R. Jago a bad time.

Still, we must see the New Zealanders far more severely tested ere we form definite opinions as to their merits.

They are undoubtedly a splendid body of athletes, a team of tall, powerful and speedy young men who may show us a combination of Irish dash and Welsh science.

Billy Wallace is, judging by his opening display, a back of the highest class. His passing is perfect, and he is about the best place-kick seen in this country since W.L. Rogers was in the Oxford fifteen. Whether he is another Bancroft remains to be seen.

PROGRAMME FOR THE tour's opening match.

GEORGE GILLETT, wearing a hat, attempts a conversion against Devon County at Exeter.

WESTERN MORNING NEWS

THE NEW ZEALANDERS HAVE STARTED their tour with a glorious win at the expense of Devonshire and the result no doubt has come as a great surprise to followers of the handling code all over the country.

In many quarters it was hardly expected Devon would win, but few, if any, expected the Western County to be defeated by such an enormous margin.

The first few minutes served to show what form the Colonials were in.

The home side seemed to be quite overwhelmed by the superior pace and tactics of the New Zealanders.

The peculiar formation of the Colonials evidently confounded the Devon outside men, who quite failed to mark their opponents successfully.

Several of the tries were scored through the ball being sent out to an unmarked man, who had only to run over to plant the ball where he liked.

It was expected that the Dumplings would at least hold the Colonials in the scrum, but the Colonials proved themselves superior both in scrum work and the loose. Their rushes were irresistible, the five-eighths and halfbacks joining the forwards in making dashes for the home line.

The Devon defenders had practically 11 forwards to stop and no wonder they failed.

Gallaher, the Colonials' captain, who is the 'winging' forward of the team, quite upset the Devon halfbacks as no sooner had he put the ball in the scrum than he was after it again, repeatedly securing the oval after it had been heeled by the home forwards.

On the whole, the game was very exciting, the tremendous pace at which it was fought out being surprising on such a hot day. Although Devon were outclassed, play never got monotonous.

HAMISH STUART, ATHLETIC NEWS

THOSE WHO EXPECTED TO SEE something from the New Zealanders altogether different from anything they had ever seen before must have been rather disappointed.

What they saw was nothing new in rugby football, but it was such a vigorous display of dashing forward play as the best Irish and Scottish packs have often shown, backed up by clever and speedy backs, whose individual excellence was far in front of their collective merit. The passing of the backs was, in other words, far below the Welsh standard and, broadly speaking, the rout of Devon in the first half was not a triumph for the New Zealand system but was due to the superiority of the New Zealand forwards as a pack and of the New Zealand backs individually.

The New Zealand forwards struck me as being one of the best

BILLY WALLACE'S RECOLLECTIONS

That result was as great a sensation in England as I believe it was in New Zealand. Some papers when they got the result assumed that a mistake had been made in transmitting the scores and put them the other way round! They had to contradict the result on the Monday morning.

When the dinner was over we took the train back to Newton Abbot and it was almost midnight when we got back to the station. We were quite unprepared for the wonderful reception that awaited us. I don't think there was a soul in the village who had gone to bed!

They met us at the station with a drag and a band and cheered us to the echo. There was an enormous crowd and their excitement was intense. The reception took us by surprise and our manager had to make a speech from the balcony before they would let us go to bed.

trained and most vigorous set of forwards we have ever seen.

In point of cleverness as a combination, the New Zealand backs fall a good deal short of the best Welsh standard, but they are so excellent individually that if their forwards can show more superiority, the New Zealanders will win most of their matches.

BILLY STEAD IN HIS MEMOIRS

Wearing hats or caps during games was quite unknown at Home. Billy (Wallace), looking into the sun for a conversion in the opening game, borrowed a sunhat.

Later, in a carefully rehearsed move he went outside his winger to score. The try was at first disallowed. Seeing a hatted figure racing down the side, the ref naturally assumed some clown on the sideline had joined in.

NEW ZEALAND TIMES' UK CORRESPONDENT

THE NEW ZEALAND FULLBACK George Gillett wore a hat throughout the game, and might have added a sunshade for all the inconvenience it would have caused in his play.

He touched the ball just twice in the course of the match! Only on two occasions were the Devonians in the least dangerous. The first time hesitation on Vivyan's part threw away a chance of scoring, but towards the end of the game Devon got within a few yards of their opponents' line and Lillicrap dropped a beautiful goal.

That was the home team's one and only score, and New Zealand promptly avenged the check by scoring another converted try before the call of time.

It was indeed a startling triumph, but as a test the game must be pronounced a failure. In saying this, one does not depreciate the very fine form shown by the men from Maoriland. Their brilliant win was thoroughly deserved. Moreover, it has served a very useful purpose in attracting a great amount of attention and arousing public interest in the New Zealanders' tour.

A sensational success like that of Saturday is the best possible commencement from the popular point of view.

The general chorus of praise of the New Zealanders' game at Exeter was marred by one discordant note. With startling unanimity the critics discovered and fastened firmly on one 'blot' in the game as played by the New Zealanders, one, we are told, that is 'against every canon in rugby union football'.

This blot is, of course, the work allotted to the wing forward.

According to C.B. Fry's 'Magazine' my old friend Tom Ellison claimed to have invented this personage in a rugby team and held that the 'winger' need never transgress the rules if he knows his business.

Our English critics, however, condemn the wing forward utterly. They ban him by bell, book and candle, goalposts and referee's whistle.

He is 'no forward at all' but 'an extra halfback' whose duty is to 'loaf on the outside of the scrum and obstruct', either passively or actively, the opposing half whose game may thereby be ruined.

We are further informed that 'the moment the ball is heeled he becomes off-side' and liable to the penalty for obstruction.

Not a single critic at Exeter whose writings I have seen fails to curse the 'winger' — in parliamentary language, of course — and most of them suggest that the penalties he will incur when the team is engaged in important matches and playing under the nose of strict referees will bring the New Zealanders to grief.

Whether the English clubs will seek to combat the New Zealanders' innovation by indulging in 'winger' tactics themselves or will be content to rely on the rigid administration of the off-side rule for an equitable solution of the matter remains to be seen.

From many quarters, referees have been told that the 'winger' is really a person worthy of all discouragement — a player who can only be really useful to his side if he can keep on the referee's blind side.

GEORGE DIXON'S DIARIES

The dinner (following the match against Devon County) was attended by Mr Rowland Hill, president of the English union, who spoke with great feeling and earnestness, and completely carried the audience with him.

◆

After dinner, we attended a performance of Maritana and, as illustrating the smallness of world nowadays, found that Mr St Clair, well known in New Zealand as advance for Williamson and Musgrove, was business manager of the company, and that Mr Carter, late of Pollards, was leading tenor.

On returning to Newton Abbot at 11.45 p.m. we found an immense crowd waiting outside the station.

We were driven to our hotel at a walking pace, preceded by a brass band, and accompanied by the crowd cheering and shouting congratulations the whole way.

Such a welcome I have never before experienced, and it speaks volumes for the sportsmanlike qualities of the Newton Abbot people that they should so welcome a team who had just defeated the pick of their county.

Evidently, the Newton Abbot people had adopted the team and certainly on our side the friendliest possible feelings were entertained towards them.

◆

Wallace tried to take the hat off at halftime but the crowd wouldn't let him.

'BRONCO' SEELING leads the forward charge against Devon County.

GAME 2 — THURSDAY 21 SEPTEMBER 1905 — at Recreation Ground, Camborne

NEW ZEALAND
CORNWALL

41
0

FOR NEW ZEALAND
Tries by Hunter 3, Smith 2, Abbott, Deans, McDonald, Mynott, Nicholson, Wallace; 4 conversions by Wallace.

NEW ZEALAND
Wallace, Abbott, Smith, Hunter, Deans, Mynott, Roberts, Gallaher (captain), Johnston, Seeling, McDonald, Cunningham, Nicholson, Tyler, Casey.

CORNWALL
J. Jackett (Falmouth), E. Bennetts (Camborne), C.H. Milton (Mining Students), H. Bodily (Camborne), B. Bennetts (Richmond), Wedge (St Ives), F. Garter (Exeter), J.G. Milton (Mining Students), Gore (Mining Students), Edmunds (Mining Students), R. Jackett (Falmouth), Bishop (Falmouth), Trevaskis (St Ives), Tregurtha (St Ives), Peters (Camborne).

Weather: Fine, ground firm
Referee: D.H. Bowen (Wales)
Crowd: 6500

KICK OFF
Wallace, wearing a hat, scored the first try, outside winger Abbott. His kick missed: 3-0.
Hunter scored from a long pass from Roberts. Wallace, kicking into a gale, missed: 6-0.
Smith used his pace from a scrum to run in a try. Wallace missed: 9-0.
Hunter swooped on a loose ball and set up Mynott for a try. Wallace missed again.

HALFTIME
New Zealand 12, Cornwall 0

Nicholson scored from a passing rush, Wallace converted: 17-0.
Abbott beat five opponents to score in the corner. Wallace missed: 20-0.
Deans showed pace to score in the corner. Wallace missed: 23-0.
Roberts used his skill to put Hunter across for a try, Wallace converted: 28-0.
Hunter was in again moments later, Wallace missing the conversion: 31-0.
Wallace went close, a quick throw-in giving McDonald a try that was converted: 36-0.
Smith snapped up a loose ball and sprinted through to score. Wallace converted.

FULLTIME
New Zealand 41, Cornwall 0

FROM THE SIDELINES

EVENING STANDARD

THE CAMBORNE GROUND, upon which the second match of the New Zealanders' tour was played, is rather undersized and occupies a very exposed position, which does not tend to reduce the strength of a high wind, such as that which prevailed on this occasion and which blew right down the ground.

The deadball line behind the goals is short and at each corner takes the slope of the corner of the cycle track which surrounds the playing area.

Indeed, this cost the New Zealand speedster George Smith a try early in the second half. Smith, not realising that the cycle track constituted the deadball line, was ruled by the referee to have run the ball dead.

The turf was in grand order and brilliant weather prevailed when New Zealand kicked off against the wind.

Much of the New Zealanders' play in the first half was ragged. Perhaps the lively ball handicapped them and there was, if anything, too much herbage on the ground.

Billy Wallace, who played throughout in a sunhat which gave him a quaint appearance, had difficulty kicking for goal into the wind but is one of the surest-handed backs ever seen.

The New Zealanders have opened their tour with two hollow victories.

That the New Zealanders possess all the elements which make for a high-class team is certain. They have combination, great power, unerring tackling and passing power and play the finer points of the game admirably.

Of their vigour, there is no doubt whatever, but as a team they must, if they want to be popular, guard against roughness due to the heat of the moment. Good, solid tackling none of their opponents will object to, but the foul play involved in hindering opponents who are not in possession of the ball can be carried to excess.

Above all, their absolute fitness is splendid. The probability is that they will find greater difficulty in defeating good clubs than county or even international teams which are not so together.

How their rather loose formation will be able to cope with Irish and Scottish forward rushes remains to be seen. The team as it stands affords the most likely combination I know of to beat Wales at her own deft passing game.

One or two of the team were in the Boer war and, if looks are to be believed, every one of the team certainly answers to the description — fit to go anywhere and do anything.

The gate for the Cornwall game amounted to £156.

◆

WESTERN MORNING NEWS

THE NEW ZEALANDERS have started their tour in Great Britain in no half-hearted manner, having badly defeated the two south-westernmost shires.

They walked over the Devon team to the tune of 55 points to 4

and they went down to Camborne yesterday and trounced Cornwall nearly as badly, pulling up a score of four goals and seven tries with not a single point against them. Present record: Played 2 matches, won 2; points for 96, against 4. Truly a great performance against no mean opponents.

It was anticipated in Cornwall that New Zealand would never score 55 points against 'Pasties' and 30 points were generally accepted as the price Cornwall would pay.

The selection committee of the county had the advantage after the Devon debacle of meeting and deciding upon the style of play that should be adopted against the New Zealanders but, as was the case against the sister county, the Colonials overwhelmed the home team.

The New Zealanders made five changes from the team which defeated Devonshire, placing the versatile Wallace back and bringing in Abbott, a burly and speedy player, to the threequarter line. There were two alterations forward and Mynott came in as five-eighth in place of Stead.

Cornwall placed in the field the originally selected team and on the whole they did well but they could not stand the pace and the whole of the second half they had to settle down in their own twenty-five and defend.

Wallace played back, with a sunhat which he never lost from his head, and proved his versatility by coming up into the quarter line as a useful factor and scoring from the hands of the threequarters.

When the final whistle went, the New Zealanders were heartily cheered and upon returning to the Commercial Hotel they gave a Maori chorus.

Cornwall football enthusiasts will remember the New Zealand team for some time to come.

CROQUET AT REDRUTH: (from left) Smith, Stead, Mynott, McGregor, McDonald.

IMPERIAL HOTEL,
CLIFTON.

Manageress .. .. Miss Teek.

A POSTCARD home from Billy Wallace.

DENIS LAWRY, SECRETARY OF CORNWALL

THE MUCH-DISCUSSED WING-FORWARD (Dave) Gallaher was closely watched. His play was by no means of the off-side nature we had been led to expect.

Few free kicks were given against him; certainly nothing like the number one often sees given against halves in keen club games.

As a factor in the attacking abilities of a team, the wing forward is of undoubted value, if only for the fact that he is an extra man outside the scrum, and to this and to the admirable wedge formation adopted by the visiting flyhalf, five-eighths and three-equarters, in a large measure their success was due.

The New Zealanders' success was due to tactics as intelligent as they are original — superior in every way to anything witnessed in English football. Backed up as they are by running, passing and kicking of the highest class, it is indeed difficult to say what British team will check their victorious career.

STEVE CASEY

Otago — hooker
22, 5ft 10in, 12st 4lb

Educated at the Christian Brothers School in Dunedin, Casey first represented Otago in 1903 as a 20-year-old, playing alongside his brother Mick. He was in the South Island team in 1904 and was an early selection for the Originals tour. A brilliant hooker, Casey's combination with George Tyler on the 1905 tour — the pair played in the Scotland, Ireland, England and Wales internationals — was one of the potent weapons of the All Blacks' success.

GEORGE DIXON'S DIARIES

Redruth — not a bad ground but rough. In fact, all the grounds we have seen so far are on rough side. Visited Dolcoath Mine — oldest mine in the world. Since 1785 working on tin, lowest level 3380ft, employs 1159 persons. Saw a few women working, mostly the reverse of young — their earnings don't exceed 25s per month. Fortunately with the introduction of machinery the employment of women is falling off. Some eight of team went on excursion underground and came back very hot and very dirty. Harper not quite well yet. McGregor seems to be slowly improving.

Post match: Big crowd for Cornwall — a record gate £156 10s and very proud of it they were.

Gallaher very clever on wing and also made a number of fine openings and only once or twice penalised in game — afraid newspaper reporters here one-eyed — they started off with preconceived notion that winger was offside abomination and are allowing this judgement to run away with them — as a matter of fact Cornish half and winger (they brought a man out of scrum) were more frequently at fault than Davey. I saw several cases of deliberate obstruction by Cornwall which was not mentioned even in reports. Great fault of English forwards so far as we have seen it is want of pace, indifferent tackling, weak follow-up and want of initiative. Our share of gate close on £100.

AN UNUSUAL SIGHT for the Kiwis — women engaged in manual work.

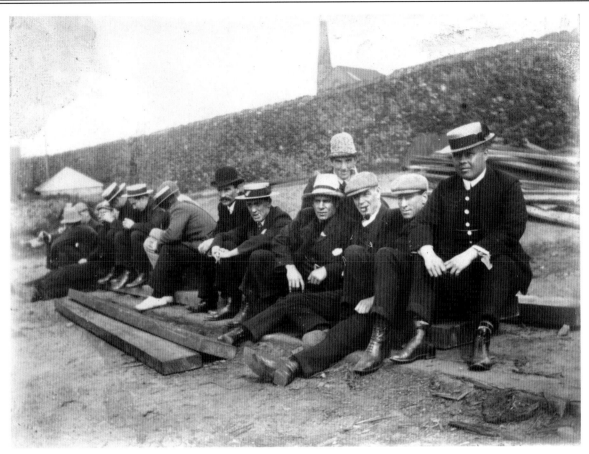

NEW ZEALAND PLAYERS mingle with locals on a visit to the Dolcoath tin mines.

THE SPORTSMAN

THE GREAT INNOVATION in the New Zealanders' game is the winging forward. As a matter of fact, he is not a forward, and is a wolf in sheep's clothing.

He makes no pretence to do scrimmage work but claims the privilege of a forward. Apparently, his position has been invented to obstruct the opposing half, and the only thing that English clubs will have to do over here is to play 'diamond cut diamond' and throw out from this scrimmage a player to fulfil the same duties.

But is this 'winging' football? We think not. And referees have the rules to support them in a constant application of the offside penalty. We can see trouble ahead when this 'winger' finds himself opposed to certain class halves that we can call to mind.

DAILY EXPRESS

ENOUGH WAS SEEN of Gallaher's methods to convince the most latitudinarian that the 'winger' is not a person to be encouraged, but to be vigorously penalised, for he was offside most of the game, and is almost amusing, so frank is his disregard for the rules as to passive and active obstruction.

THE LONDON TIMES

THE WING FORWARD of which the New Zealanders throw out of the scrimmage is rather a startling innovation. As seen on Sunday, he is no forward at all, merely skirmishing on the fringe of the pack.

BILLY WALLACE'S RECOLLECTIONS

The first try was a beauty. From a scrum the ball went to Freddy Roberts and then through the hands of Mynott, Hunter, Smith and Abbott, and I came up from the fullback position to receive the final pass and cross the line. This caused a bit of a sensation as it was an unheard-of thing for a fullback to score.

The try had a very interesting result on the football fans who tried their hands at picking the outcome. Most of the papers were running football coupons. The football fiends had to pick the first scorer in each of the six matches of which ours was one. There were thousands of entries, but nobody thought of putting down the fullback as the first scorer in the New Zealanders match, and nobody got the result right that week!

After the match there was a big banquet with plenty of champagne flying round. About halfway through the evening we noticed our poor old manager was wearing a very worried look as some of the boys were getting merry and so word was passed round to make the most of it as it seemed likely we wouldn't get another chance.

GAME 3 — SATURDAY 23 SEPTEMBER 1905 — at Memorial Ground, Bristol

NEW ZEALAND
BRISTOL

41
0

FOR NEW ZEALAND
Tries by Hunter 2, Smith 2,
Thomson 2, Roberts, Seeling, Stead;
7 conversions by Wallace.

NEW ZEALAND
Booth, Smith, Thomson, Hunter, Wallace,
Stead, Roberts, Gallaher (captain), Nicholson,
Corbett, Johnston, Cunningham, Seeling,
Glasgow, Casey.

BRISTOL
J. Oates (captain), C. Phillips, H. Shrewring,
F.S. Scott, H. Leonard, J. Spoors, J. Larcombe,
J.L. Mathias, T. Webb, N. Moore, A. Manning,
H. Thomas, W. Cooper, W. Meads, W. Hosken.

Weather: Fine, ground firm
Referee: D.H. Bowen (Wales)
Crowd: 6500

KICK OFF
Smith took an inside pass from Wallace to score, Wallace converted: 5-0.
Smith broke upfield, Roberts finishing off a spectacular try. Wallace converted: 10-0.
Smith ran through the whole Bristol backline to score. Wallace missed: 13-0.
Hunter and Smith combined brilliantly for Hunter to score. Wallace converted.

HALFTIME
New Zealand 18, Bristol 0

Wallace broke through, setting up Hunter for a try. Wallace converted: 23-0.
Oates failed to gather a rolling ball, allowing Seeling to score. Wallace missed: 26-0.
Thomson scored after a great solo run from halfway. Wallace converted: 31-0.
Thomson was in again after fielding a flykick from Glasgow. Wallace converted: 36-0.
A classic passing rush resulted in Stead scoring, Wallace converted.

FULLTIME
New Zealand 41, Bristol 0

FROM THE SIDELINES

WESTERN DAILY PRESS

THE MATCH BETWEEN the Bristol team and the New Zealand combination, which had been anticipated with such exceptional interest, took place at the County Ground on Saturday under conditions that were favourable in every respect.

Any doubts that might have been entertained as to their remarkable form were dispelled before the play had half run its course.

No rugby event locally had possessed such elements of attraction as this one, and it was not at all surprising to learn that for a club engagement the receipts exceeded previous records, the returns working out to £230.

It must, however, be remembered that the admittance fee, except for those who purchased their tickets before the day of the match, was a shilling and, moreover, the usual custom of admitting ladies to the ground free was suspended.

It will thus be seen that the number of persons who were present did not reach the proportions some sanguine enthusiasts anticipated, and it will probably be found the crowd was made up of between 6000 and 7000 spectators.

The visitors were well satisfied with the support accorded them, the receipts exceeding those of the Devon match by about £30 and the Cornwall game by about £80.

◆ ❖ ◆

One of the pleasantest features of the visit of the Colonials was the interest taken by the leading citizens of Bristol.

The Lord Mayor, the Lady Mayoress and the High Sheriff not only graced the proceedings by their presence but personally welcomed the team from New Zealand.

At a quarter past three the teams and officials of the Bristol club assembled in the pavilion and Mr J.W. Arrowsmith introduced

GEORGE DIXON'S DIARIES

FRIDAY 22 SEPTEMBER.

Picked team. Corbett very pleased at getting in — has been training hard — wish Newton would take the same view. Find I shall have to provide coaches again to take us to ground tomorrow. English teams never seem to do this. Saw in local paper Llewellyn [Welsh threequarter] has been asked to play for Bristol — wonder what are his qualifications?

Learnt that referees' constant stopping of the scrum was owing to the interpretation, common in England, that ball must be put past second man in front row — how it could be put past our second man and yet be in scrum is a mystery.

Fast trip up to London on the train. We timed several miles each done in 57 seconds. Saw Mother a couple of times, brother Jack.

Game against Bristol: The forwards also were all backs when occasion required.

Dave Gallaher, the New Zealand captain, and James Oates, the popular captain of the city fifteen, to the distinguished visitors.

The Lord Mayor took the opportunity of expressing sentiments which must have been very acceptable to the Colonial players. He assured them of the keen pleasure which it afforded him to welcome them to Bristol on behalf of the citizens and it was the hope of himself and the Lady Mayoress and the High Sheriff that they would return to their far-off homes carrying with them a happy remembrance of their visit to the ancient city.

Mr Gallaher briefly but sincerely acknowledged the Lord Mayor's kind greeting.

Afterwards, the civic representatives watched the game from the grandstand, the seats usually occupied by members of the press being placed at their disposal.

GEORGE SMITH and Billy Stead enjoy life in the West Country.

It is generally admitted that the exhibition given by the New Zealanders surpassed in individual and collective merit anything previously seen at the County Ground and expectations formed as a result of the crushing defeats of Devon and Cornwall were fully realised.

Their play, in fact, was a revelation to the majority of those present.

We have for many years past been accustomed to exceptional skill in handling the ball when Swansea, Newport or Cardiff have appeared on the ground, but in many respects even these famous Welsh teams have yet much to learn before their play reaches the standard of the New Zealand fifteen.

The Colonials have realised the possibilities of open play as it has never yet been realised by British footballers. Their all-prevailing idea is to handle the ball and make full use of their speed.

BILLY WALLACE'S RECOLLECTIONS

The day following the second match we left by train for Bristol. When we were on the train the manager called us together and on his suggestion it was agreed to cut out all intoxicating drinks for dinner.

On Saturday morning we were shown over the great tobacco factory of W.D. and H.O. Wills. After inspection of the factory we were invited to morning tea and then we were allowed to take away as much tobacco and cigarettes and cigars as we could put in our pockets. Needless to say we crammed our pockets as full as possible and many of the boys were lamenting the fact that they hadn't brought their handbags!

When we went to the ground we were given a great reception by the Mayor of Bristol and his daughter. They both shook hands with every member of the team and as she was an extremely good-looking young lady, I fear quite a number of us held her hand a good deal longer than was actually necessary.

There was the usual dinner after the match, but this time we had to drink the toasts in tea and lemonade.

The remarkable feature of their play was that no matter how or where the ball was thrown there was always a colleague in position for acceptance.

Foot play has no part in the visitors' scheme of attack except as regards high punting. And it was curious to note that the touch-line was generally ignored.

◆ ❖ ◆

On the morning of the match, the New Zealand team were shown over the Imperial Tobacco Company's factory and after the match they were entertained at dinner at the Imperial Hotel.

This latter gathering was a particularly interesting one. Mr E.W. Ball, who played in first-class football before many of the men who had taken part in the game in the afternoon were born, proved a popular chairman and the music supplied by Mr Percy Smith's Bric-a-Brac Company delighted everyone.

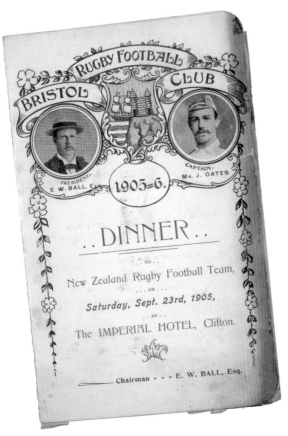

TICKET FOR THE official dinner for the Bristol match.

BRISTOL TIMES AND MIRROR

WE ARE USED TO SEEING the best Welsh teams on the county ground, and have witnessed some magnificent struggles, yet in no case have we had such an exhibition of all-round excellence in a side.

The New Zealanders have a style of their own, or rather, to be more correct, they appear to have adopted all the best points from the game as played in Great Britain.

Their threequarters have all the skill and dash of a Welsh back division, with the advantage that they have five players where those in the Principality have four.

HAROLD ABBOTT

Taranaki — wing
23, 5ft 10in, 13st 1lb

Abbott was introduced to rugby in South Africa during the Boer War, when his commanding officer, disbelieving that a New Zealander possessed of great speed did not know the rules of rugby, ordered him onto the field of play. 'What do I do?' asked Abbott. 'I come from the Taranaki bush and I have never played before.'

'Look at this,' his officer ordered, pointing to his jersey. 'We're the goodies. Those jerseys,' waving his hand towards the opposing team, 'belong to the baddies. Don't let the bastards past us and I'll talk to you again at halftime.' Abbott was added to the Originals tour party just days before the team sailed for Britain.

Billy Stead recalls how Bunny Abbott got his nickname: 'He was keen to try out body swerves taught him by Billy Wallace on board ship on the voyage over, and took off twisting and turning at the team's first practice at Newton Abbot.

'This prompted Mona Thomson, seeing Abbott at the far end of the field, to ask, "Who is that darting and diving around like a bloody startled rabbit?" The name stuck.'

Their passing is as clever as Swansea's, and they possess one characteristic which is common to all the team — there is no hesitancy in going for the line. Their forwards unite the solidity and tackling power of the best English pack, with the dash in the loose of the typical Irish or Scotch forward.

The secret of their great scoring power is the perfect understanding which exists among every member of the team and the versatility of their attack. On Saturday, there were tries scored in a manner almost unknown to English football.

◆ ❖ ◆

It was a great day for Bristol rugby, for the match attracted the record gate of £230; but as a shilling was charged for admission on Saturday instead of the usual sixpence it is a record in money only, and not in attendance. The association record is £754.

The New Zealanders will render great service to English rugby football if they convince the players that the game is worthy of more careful personal study than they have hitherto given it.

England's many failures in international matches in recent years have been mainly traceable to the clumsy, slipshod style into which even some of our leading teams have fallen.

DAILY TELEGRAPH

M R ROWLAND HILL PRESIDED over a special meeting of the Rugby Football Union yesterday, at the Inns of Court Hotel, held for the purpose of considering the alterations to the laws submitted to be approved by the International Board. There was a large attendance and the proposals were carried en bloc.

At first there was a disposition on the part of members to criticise the letter and spirit of some of the proposals, and Mr H. Green, of the Eastern Counties, moved a resolution to negative the alteration to the rule proposing to fix the distance for scrummage when a throw-in is not straight, to ten yards from touch instead of between five to fifteen as heretofore.

The chairman explained that most of the new proposals came from New South Wales, Queensland, and New Zealand, and were too late to submit to the union. They were therefore submitted to the International Board as a matter of courtesy to the Colonials.

No one was more anxious than he was that the International Board should not dictate on points of law to the various countries, but he thought they might adopt the proposals that evening, and if they did not work well bring up the matter again.

THE OTAGO ORIGINALS. (Back) Ernest Booth, Jimmy Duncan, Steve Casey, Massa Johnston, (front) Alex McDonald.

GAME 4 — THURSDAY 28 SEPTEMBER 1905 — at Franklin's Gardens, Northampton

NEW ZEALAND
NORTHAMPTON

32
0

FOR NEW ZEALAND
Tries by Harper 2, Hunter 2, Mynott 2, Stead, Tyler; 4 conversions by Wallace.

NEW ZEALAND
Wallace, Abbott, Stead (captain), Hunter, Harper, Mynott, Roberts, Gillett, O'Sullivan, Seeling, Corbett, Cunningham, Nicholson, Glasgow, Tyler.

NORTHAMPTON
C. Leigh, J.H. Miles, H.C. Palmer, F. Coles, J.L. Malkin, T.H. Preston, C.F. Malkin, H.B. Follitt (captain), A.J. Hobbs, L. Johnson, C. Franklin, H. B. Grandidge, G. Burke, A. Chalmers, J. W. Warren.

Weather: Fine, ground firm
Referee: D.H. Bowen (Wales)
Crowd: 6500

KICK OFF
Mynott broke from a scrum and Hunter weaved his way over. Wallace missed: 3-0.
Roberts and Mynott combined from a scrum for Hunter to score. Wallace missed: 6-0.
Stead scored from a break by Mynott, Wallace converted: 11-0.
Hunter attacked from a scrum setting up a try for Harper. Wallace converted: 16-0.
Hunter ran 50 metres, breaking several tackles to score. Wallace converted.

HALFTIME
New Zealand 21, Northampton 0

Gillett regathered his own high kick, creating a try for Tyler. Wallace converted: 26-0.
Roberts probed the blindside from a scrum and Mynott scored. Wallace missed: 29-0.
Forwards and backs combined from a lineout, Harper scoring. Wallace missed.

FULLTIME
New Zealand 32, Northampton 0

FROM THE SIDELINES

DAILY TELEGRAPH

BY ORDINARY, THAT IS TO SAY extraordinary, superiority rather than because of the speciality of their formation, the New Zealanders conquered Northampton at Franklin's Gardens. The score of 32 points is the lowest of the tour but while giving Northampton the credit for stubborn resistance — their line was crossed only three times in the second half — it is difficult to resist the conclusion that the Colonials kept plenty in hand in view of future responsibilities.

As it was, they pressed fairly continuously from end to end and, without achieving a pronounced spectacular triumph, impressed their abilities on all who cared to see.

There is animation about these New Zealanders that electrifies the atmosphere. They vary in size but where they are not tall they are broad and massive, and without exception they are clever.

No doubt the chief factors in the superiority of the New Zealanders are great pace, magnificent physique and apparently inexhaustible stamina, but their excellence is not merely physical, for they have the intelligence to economise their strength and the rapidity of thought which enables them to make order out of chaos.

Among the many features of this game which, though more or less an exhibition, was thoroughly interesting and enjoyable, were the certainty with which the Colonials found touch, their quick adaptability to the distinct requirements of the styles individual and combined, the emphatic strength of their tackling and, above all else, the celerity of recovery and backing-up.

Big, square athletes, actuated by the vim and enthusiasm which in some respects recalled the characteristics of Australian cricketers, the New Zealanders dominated this game to such an extent that the field seemed full of black jerseys relieved by the white fern just over the heart.

BILL CUNNINGHAM poised to receive a throw against Northampton.

While for the most part their strength is suggestive of the bear or the lion, there is something vividly panther-like in their sudden springs and cat-like in the manner in which they dive for a tackle.

Somehow, we do not appear to breed such types of muscular manhood who exploit their strength too well to be clumsy.

NORTHAMPTON GAZETTE

THE SIZE OF THE NEW ZEALANDERS WILL appeal to the general public, for there are half a dozen players in the team who are real giants.

The average weight is 12 stone and the young gentleman who 'locks the scrum' tips the beam at 15 stone, so that although they play one man less in the pack than we do, the total weight is quite enough for their purpose.

We, too, have big, weighty scrummagers in this country, but I daresay none so fast as the New Zealand forwards. The speed of the whole team is little short of marvellous, and it is this quality rather than the high degree of combination which they have attained which makes them so dangerous and such prolific scorers.

Northampton gave them a very good game, up to a certain point. They tackled with as much vigour as the opposition and made them go all the way, but their fight was all more or less of a defensive character.

Once in the first half they made the New Zealand fullback touch down and, in the second half, Miles, the sturdy ex-Leicester flier, made one or two runs that sent local enthusiasm up to fever heat.

One could not, however, reasonably say that the visitors were ever in danger of being scored against.

Whenever the Northampton pack got too near for their liking the New Zealanders simply found touch well down the field and relieved the situation. Better touchfinding I have rarely seen, not even by Welsh teams.

The New Zealanders seem to be always attacking, and if by any chance they happen to be on the defence they also appear to be bobbing up everywhere — the whole team resolved into one big human octopus with myriads of arms ready to embrace the enemy in a deadly grip and bring him to the ground.

Passing is only a mere detail with the New Zealander and it is the individual running, the sprint straight through the backs, the bird-like swoop and swerve, the feint and dodge that will commend themselves to the respect and fear of English teams.

Not since the days of Stoddart have I seen this art of individual effort so finely illustrated. We have 'combined' the individual player out of existence nowadays but the New Zealanders have happily preserved the two qualities, making combination and individualism one happy, productive blend.

The New Zealanders played Gillett, whose first appearance had been at fullback, as wing forward in place of Gallaher, who having injured his knee against Bristol, acted as touch judge.

◆ ❖ ◆

The Bristol Rugby Club have appointed a sub-committee with the object of seeing if it is possible to model their teams on New Zealand lines.

YORKSHIRE POST

THE NEW ZEALANDERS are in splendid condition and they surprised the Northampton people by going to the field at seven o'clock on the morning of the game for practice. Can you imagine the young, steady-going, plodding Jack Bull doing likewise?

The players, dressed in black, with just a white fern worked in the left breast of their jerseys, have a rather sombre appearance, but this quality does not extend to their prospects.

The jerseys are interwoven across the shoulders and chest with a silken cloth, which renders tackling rather difficult, but then, of course, the proper way is to collar low.

Northampton were outclassed. I hear that England are going to meet all France at the rugby game in Paris on 1 April next. I wonder if they will beat the Frenchmen by more points than the New Zealanders will beat them by in December!

I had almost forgotten to say that about 6000 spectators were present, including the Leicester team who meet the New Zealanders on Saturday.

W. PICKFORD IN THE SPORTSMAN

THAT DEAR OLD INSTITUTION the 'scrummage' has, I think, almost vanished. In the seventies when I was a rugger enthusiast and adored the name of Leonard Stokes, our 'scrums' used to be most tremendous in their duration.

You went into the pack on a frosty winter afternoon, cold and chilly. You came out of it — were hurled out, crawled out, or fell out, sometimes on your head and sometimes on your feet — all on fire with the generating of an intense heat from 20 struggling bodies shoving like madmen, struggling, clutching, butting, scrambling and tugging and the icy wind no longer gave you a shiver, but was welcomed as a cooler to the fever'd brow.

Five minutes in the centre of such a heaving scrum with your head shoved back, your chest bulged forward, one leg in one place and the other at right angles, anticipating at any second a collapse, with its direful consequences, was a lifetime of glorious joy.

But I believe that the 'scrum' is now an attenuated thing, although I did not set out to describe a rugby scrum of the seventies; what impelled me to revive such memories was the wonderful success of the New Zealand team.

How it is achieved I am not expert enough to say. All I know is that the colonials are credited with having introduced fearsome novelties into their methods, and that I have believed clubs

HOOKER GEORGE TYLER throws to the lineout against Northampton.

AT BREAKFAST, from left, Alex McDonald, Massa Johnston, Bronco Seeling and Steve Casey.

like Devon and Bristol to be pretty good at rugby, and it set me wondering whether some distant colony of Anglo-Saxons, introducing new plans of playing Association, would be able to make our best clubs look as silly as these West Country rugby friends of ours are looking.

ASTRAL IN THE SPORTSMAN

I N THE LIGHT OF THEIR PHENOMENAL SCORING, it may seem foolish to say so, but I fancy the Colonials' strongest point will be their defence. When they run up against really fine forwards, with good backs to support them as, say, in Wales, backs who have made a profound study of offensive tactics, this idea will be tested for what it is worth.

There may be weak points in their armour, but I confess that I could discover none at Northampton yesterday. The arrangement of the backs behind the scrum all makes for defence.

There is the wing forward who stands on the edge of the scrum and always puts the ball in for the halfback, who does what we usually call the donkey work close in. Behind these men are a pair of five-eighths and three threequarter backs, who more often than not form a line of five players extended right across the field with the fullback in the rear.

Each of these backs are big, weighty fellows, terribly fast demons at tackling, and who know exactly what each other are going to do. Imagine the difficulty of getting through a defence of this kind.

CHARLIE SEELING

**Auckland —
loose forward**
22, 6ft, 13st 7lb

The outstanding forward of the tour, operating in the back row or as a breakaway forward, Seeling possessed a huge onfield presence. He was considered a giant by the opposition and added to his robust physique with pace, natural athleticism and, as a tackler, complete fearlessness. Seeling originally came from Wanganui, but was enticed north to Auckland in 1903 and arrived in time to play in the first Ranfurly Shield defence. At just 21 he was selected for New Zealand against Great Britain in 1904. On the Originals tour he appeared in 25 matches, including all five tests, scoring eight tries. Noted British critic E.H.D. Sewell considered Seeling's contribution to be 'colossal', writing that 'this splendid specimen of manhood has everything necessary to the composition of a good forward'.

GAME 5 — SATURDAY 30 SEPTEMBER 1905 — at Welford Road, Leicester

NEW ZEALAND
LEICESTER

28
0

NEW ZEALAND
Tries by Abbott, Mynott, Nicholson, Smith, Tyler, Wallace; 5 conversions by Wallace.

NEW ZEALAND
Gillett, Abbott, Smith, Mynott, Wallace, Stead, Roberts, Gallaher (captain), O'Sullivan, Seeling, Glasgow, Cunningham, Nicholson, Tyler, Casey.

LEICESTER
A.O. Jones, A.O. Parsons, N. McFarlane, J.W. Bainbridge, A.E. Hind, J. Braithwaite, B. Hills, S. Matthews (captain), S. Penny, H.P. Atkins, T. Goodrich, A. Goodrich, R.F. Russell, F. Jackson, D.B. Atkins.

Weather: Fine, ground firm
Referee: Percy Coles (England)
Crowd: 16,000

KICK OFF
Swift passing from a lineout found Smith who scorched across. Wallace missed: 3-0.
In loose play, Nicholson and Roberts combined to put Wallace in. He converted: 8-0.
Mynott handled twice from a scrum before Abbott scored. Wallace converted.

HALFTIME
New Zealand 13, Leicester 0

Seeling led a forward rush from which Tyler scored. Wallace converted: 18-0.
Stead probed from a scrum and Mynott scored. Wallace converted: 23-0.
From a scrum near the line, Nicholson scored. Wallace converted.

FULLTIME
New Zealand 28, Leicester 0

FROM THE SIDELINES

EVENING STANDARD

THE PRESENCE OF A NEW ZEALAND football team in England this season has immensely added to the interest of the public in the rugby code.

There was abundant proof of this in Leicester when the Antipodeans were the guests of the Tigers. Large as have been many of the 'gates' which the Leicester club's fixtures have attracted to the well-appointed enclosure, the attendance today must have constituted a record. From far and near enthusiasts gathered, all desirous of reaping an acquaintance with the play of the famous athletes from 'down under'.

The visitors had played four matches previous to their appearance in Leicester and had caused a sensation by the emphatic manner in which they established supremacy over their opponents.

The gates had been thrown open for quite an hour before the kick-off and at three o'clock, half an hour before the ball was set in motion, there was an attendance of fully 10,000 people.

The throng increased until at 3.15 the company numbered 16,000 and the ground was fast assuming the appearance it wore on the occasion of the contest, England v Wales, two seasons ago.

BILLY WALLACE'S RECOLLECTIONS

One of the Leicester players to distinguish himself greatly was their fullback A.O. Jones, who represented England at cricket and rugby football. His line kicking was really splendid. Later he wrote an interesting article for one of the papers in which he reckoned we were the finest team he had seen, but he considered we would probably be stale before we got to the Welsh matches and on that account, Wales would probably win. Jones proved a very able tactician for the Tigers.

ATHLETIC NEWS

THERE IS NO QUESTIONING the superiority of the New Zealanders. It is evident in everything they do, and is a palpitating fact. Individually, they are brilliant, collectively they are irresistible.

If one section of the team stands out more than another by reason of its polished capacity, it is the threequarter line, and the man who shone pre-eminently in that line on Saturday was G.W. Smith.

But the perfect combination of the backs, the smartness with which they fielded the ball and the speed at which they darted away had a great deal to do with the success achieved.

When once the ball was sent to the rear division every member began moving in anticipation of being called upon the next second.

They seemed to be always at full speed and the moment they handled the leather they were going like champion sprinters.

The trio who acted as threequarters are certainly exceedingly

speedy but Smith combines with his sprinting powers an ability to swerve and dodge that is as bewildering to an opponent as it is delightful to witness. It was positively exhilarating to see this tall, clean-limbed athlete running with the ball. How he twisted and turned, eluding opponents on all sides, was simply marvellous and such an exhibition as he gave was worth going miles to see.

VETERAN, THE LEICESTER NEWS

WE WERE TOLD DOWN SOUTH,' said the New Zealand captain David Gallaher after the match, 'that when we came to Leicester we should know about it. 'Well, we do know about it. It was the hardest game we have had since we've been here.'

And yet, mark you, our Colonial friends won with the greatest possible ease by five goals and a try to nil. In five games they have now scored 197 points to 4.

It is not surprising that they are causing a flutter in the dovecotes of the mighty. Who, indeed, will be the little David to stop them? I don't think we shall do it by football; we may by hospitality.

And as for showing the versatility of the players, let me point to a few changes they made on Saturday. Gillett, who played admirably as their wing forward against Northampton, was transferred to the fullback position and Wallace, probably the surest goalkick in the world — he landed five goals out of six attempts in this game — and the recognised fullback played as right wing. Again, Stead, at centre on Thursday, took Hunter's place at five-eighth.

DAVE GALLAHER

Auckland — wing forward
29, 6ft, 13st

Billy Wallace said of Gallaher: 'Dave was a wonderful captain, immensely popular with the team and with the officials wherever he went. Always the welfare of the team and the honour of the country he represented were the first considerations. He was a very shrewd judge of a player and always endeavoured to be fair and just to every member of the team.' At the end of the tour a great and spontaneous friendship sprang up between the French captain Armand and Gallaher — a welcome change after the controversy his wing-forward play evoked in Britain. Gallaher, a tactical mastermind, led the New Zealanders on their first official tour, to Australia in 1903, playing as wing-forward in the inaugural test in Sydney. He was a Boer War veteran.

For fully thirty minutes Leicester held these giants of the game right manfully. During this period the forwards on both sides were magnificent.

In the closing stages Smith and Mynott ran brilliantly through the defence, and when eighty minutes were nearly completed the New Zealanders were going stronger than ever. They looked as though they could have gone on for another eighty minutes.

The pace throughout was terrific and it was this and the splendid backing up of the whole team, together with individual brilliancy, that led to Leicester's downfall.

I have not seen the local side play a better game, and I have seen them play many good ones, but they were as toys in the hands of these giants of football.

Whether we like their style or not, it is a winning style, and by it the Colonials will pierce the armour of the majority of their opponents. The game was pleasantly contested and well refereed by Mr Percy Coles. The gate realised £392.

Apart from their cleverness as footballers they are a splendid body of men, and we in Leicester are very fortunate that within a month they will visit us again and give us another example of their skills. That game will be played on a Saturday under the auspices of the Midland Counties Union and I wish it were possible for that body to advise as many players as possible to be present. They would see much that would be most helpful to them in trying to realise the possibilities before them.

NEW ZEALAND TIMES' UK CORRESPONDENT

THE NEW ZEALAND TEAM came up to town from Leicester last-Monday afternoon and had two practices on the Tuesday in preparation for the for the Middlesex match the next day.

The manager, Mr Dixon, discountenances entertainments and the team cordially back him up, as all realise that football and banquets do not mix well.

The men are thoroughly in earnest about the tour and are just as anxious as the manager that they may keep their condition.

'Do you think the team will find this programme of matches too heavy?' I asked one of the men.

'Not if they take it as seriously as I do,' was the prompt reply.

Undoubtedly they take it seriously, as the following example goes to show.

A caller at the Manchester Hotel on Tuesday afternoon found several of them resting in bed, in order to save their strength, when without any breach of discipline they might have been out seeing the sights of the metropolis, to which almost all of them are strangers. But no; they had felt a little tired after the morning's practice and so turned in for an hour or two's rest before practising again later in the day.

◆ ❖ ◆

THE NEW ZEALANDERS with their hosts at a Yorkshire beauty spot.

NEW ZEALAND team manager George Dixon.

The visit of Mr Dixon's team is naturally recalling to the minds of our press scribes the tour of the so-called 'Maori team' in 1888-89. Many of the writers of today evidently know nothing of Joe Warbrick and company, save from hearsay, and consequently accusations of rough play on the part of the 'Maoris' are frequent.

As one who saw most of the principal games, I must put in a good word for Warbrick's men. Some of them were several removes from being gentlemen, but this much I will say in their favour: they played the game as their opponents asked for it. If the opposing team played a clean game the 'Maoris' did so willingly, but if the other side opened the ball in the knockout fashion they very soon found that the New Zealanders were quite as good at giving as receiving rough treatment.

Some of the teams they met played the blackguardly game to perfection, and the consequences were that the spectators who had been previously prejudiced by hearsay against the 'Maoris' laid all the blame for the rough play on the New Zealanders.

Given a fair chance, the 'Maoris' played a real good game of fair football.

DAILY CHRONICLE

SOMEWHAT UNEXPECTEDLY, the visit of the New Zealanders has attained to the dignity of the tour of the Australian cricketers.

A year or so ago the suggestion that the supremacy of Great Britain and Ireland in football was immediately to be challenged as determinedly as the Australians challenge English cricket would have been laughed to scorn; yet here are some thirty New Zealanders who, though not playing the same fifteen in consecutive matches, are with a series of brilliant triumphs fully vindicating their right to the international trials which they claimed.

W.T.A. BEARE, DAILY EXPRESS

I WAS PRIVILEGED to see the match against Leicester on Saturday and shall remember it as the grandest game I have ever seen. It was an exhibition of the very finest forms of rugby play given by a magnificent team of athletes who played it in the thorough wholehearted way in which it should be played.

The winger George Smith is the greatest all round threequarter I have ever seen.

I notice that interviewers keep asking the New Zealand manager whether the team will adhere to its present style of play throughout the tour.

The question seems to be singularly inept, considering that the team has won every match up to date and never had its line crossed. Surely it is time to talk of altering tactics when the team is beaten, and not before.

◆ ❖ ◆

In a brilliant series of manoeuvres at Leicester one of the most remarkable episodes was a run by George Smith which, in its audacious cleverness, recalled the feats of A.E. Stoddart in his best days.

Getting possession outside the enemy's 25, Smith threaded his way like an eel through a swarm of Leicester men, swerving here, dodging there, outpacing a third, leaping over a fourth, wriggling through the arms of a fifth until he actually touched down.

The try was not allowed, the referee ruling that Smith had been held just outside the line; but though unsuccessful it was the most brilliant episode of the match and one of the greatest feats I have ever witnessed on a football field.

◆ ❖ ◆

BILLY WALLACE'S RECOLLECTIONS

On Monday afternoon we left for London and how excited we were! It was a wonderful drive for us through the traffic and the enormous crowd of people. We had never seen anything like it before.

The next day about half a dozen of us went to the Tower of London and spent a long time there listening to all the stories of wicked deeds and when we came out we were very thirsty. So we all adjourned to the hotel nearby for a 'spot'. We had our glasses of beer and saw a very fine counter lunch on the table, so we waded in to it in our very best style.

We noticed a chap in uniform standing up and taking notes and presently we were given a bill for sixteen shillings.

We protested that in New Zealand counter lunches were always provided free of charge, but that didn't cut any ice for we were told we were not in New Zealand. So we had to have a 'tarpaulin muster' amongst ourselves and with much difficulty we managed to square the account.

GAME 6 — WEDNESDAY 4 OCTOBER 1905 — at Stamford Bridge, London

NEW ZEALAND
MIDDLESEX

34
0

FOR NEW ZEALAND
Tries by Hunter 2, Smith 2, Deans, Johnston, Seeling, Wallace; 5 conversions by Wallace.

NEW ZEALAND
Gillett, Deans, Smith, Hunter, Wallace, Stead, Roberts, Gallaher (captain), Johnston, Seeling, McDonald, Cunningham, Glenn, Glasgow, Casey.

MIDDLESEX
E.M. Harrison, H. Hosken, H.T. Maddocks, R.E. Godfrey, F.H. Palmer, A.L. Wade, A.D. Stoop, C.E.L. Hammond (captain), H. Alexander, F. Turner, A.F. Harding, J.F. Williams, J.C. Jenkins, R.O.C. Ward, W.B. Grandage.

Weather: Fine, ground firm
Referee: Percy Coles (England)
Crowd: 10,000

KICK OFF

From the first scrum the backs attacked, Johnston scoring. Wallace converted: 5-0.
Wallace ran incisively, Smith carried on and Hunter scored. Wallace converted: 10-0.
Smith scored a beautiful solo try which Wallace could not convert: 13-0.
From a scrum, Smith broke through again and Wallace scored, and converted: 18-0.
Roberts probed from a scrum and Smith scored again. Wallace converted.

HALFTIME
New Zealand 23, Middlesex 0

Twenty minutes into the spell Seeling scored from a lineout. Wallace missed: 26-0
From a scrum, Hunter and Smith put Deans across. Wallace missed: 29-0.
Hunter finished off a magnificent movement with a try. Wallace converted.

FULLTIME
New Zealand 34, Middlesex 0

FROM THE SIDELINES

CAPTAIN THE HONORABLE SOUTHWELL FITZGERALD WRITING IN THE TELEGRAPH

THE FIRST APPEARANCE of our visitors in London attracted a large crowd to Stamford Bridge, there being quite 12,000 people present when the New Zealanders kicked off against the wind and with the sun in their faces.

I am certain that nobody on the ground could grumble at the game.

Middlesex was beaten, and well beaten, by the large margin of five goals and eight tries, but C.E.L. Hammond and his men may take this consolation to themselves — that they had to acknowledge defeat to the finest team of rugby players that have ever played the game in London.

A lot has been said and written on the wing forward, but I saw nothing in his play to bring down on him all the condemnation which is on all sides levelled at him.

He was in this match penalised twice, but how often in club matches does one see a half penalised many times more?

The New Zealanders do not go in for scrummaging as we over here understand that term. Their object is to get the ball, break up quickly and let the pace, finesse, swerving, feinting and passing of their backs generally, and the whole team if necessary, do the rest.

It must be acknowledged that Middlesex got the ball oftener than their visitors. But what a difference in their methods!

The pace and quickness with which the New Zealanders followed the ball was nearly always the means of preventing the Middlesex men from getting going.

In all their running the New Zealanders were using their thinking powers; they were constantly, as it were, thinking out an individual opening for themselves, and, failing this, they by cleverness and pace, made an opening for a combined movement.

What struck me most about their play was that they invariably turned a Middlesex attack into a Middlesex defence.

They take risks in order to score and they give passes which would be suicidal for an ordinary team to attempt. They are, however, justified in taking these risks, which nearly always come off, because of the pace and cleverness of the whole side.

What pleased the crowd was the life, go and verve of the whole New Zealand team. Nobody could say their exposition of rugby is any other than an invigorating one, and how rugby would hold sway all over England if teams of the calibre of the New Zealanders were to meet one another.

Their style of play is such that the games they take part in must of necessity be brimful of incidents and that, after all, in games is of paramount importance to the spectators.

GEORGE DIXON'S DIARIES

Got up early found N and T had not been home all night, latter had been out to visit friends and apologised for staying with them. Had very straight talk with N about staying out . . . general neglect of training and pointed out that he could not hope to play unless fit — contended that he was fit, but that is all nonsense.

AN ARTIST'S IMPRESSION of Bob Deans' spectacular try against Middlesex.

EVENING STANDARD

THE FOND HOPES CHERISHED by the chief rugby authorities in London that Middlesex would to some extent check the invincible New Zealanders were rudely dispelled at Chelsea.

The tourists met a very strong side but had no difficulty in winning by 34 points to nil. The brilliant exhibition of the winners was greatly appreciated by the crowd.

If only our own rugby clubs could play the game as they do we should not hear so much about rugby losing its hold on the public. Nothing like the performance against Middlesex had ever been seen in London, and it is safe to say that the form of the New Zealanders will be a revelation wherever they go.

The keynote of victory was struck in the first two minutes when Johnston ran through the opposition. He is a forward, but the distinction does not mean the same as we understand it in this country. With the New Zealanders, a forward is quite as much a scoring medium as the backs. In England, it is the exception rather than the rule for a forward to get over.

The visitors were far too quick on the ball for our men, and they kept up one unceasing attack. Smith, who is the fastest man in the team, was responsible for sending in Deans for the second try, but the scorer did a clever bit of dodging before he landed the ball under the posts.

Then Smith got the try of the match. He tricked the whole crowd of Middlesex men in front of the posts, making three or four eel-like swerves. Nobody could tackle him and then, with a straight dart through, he got the third try.

The New Zealanders dearly like to keep the game going, and this is why they so rarely attempt to find touch. Secure in the pace and readiness of their backs they invariably foot the ball into midfield and then follow up like demons.

It is quite like the Welsh game. Meanwhile, it is curious that the Zealanders themselves should claim that they merely play the old English style of football.

There was plenty of trick play in the game. The dodging of the backs made a rare appeal to the crowd and as public entertainers our visitors are a huge success.

Acrobatic feats stimulate the imagination, you know, and there is a good deal of the circus quality — using the phrase without disrespect — in their play.

Wallace on one occasion was being swung around in the air by a couple of men. His arm holding the ball was free and while his Middlesex friends were conducting him on a circular tour he got his kick in and found touch 40 yards upfield.

BILLY WALLACE'S RECOLLECTIONS

On Tuesday morning we had a run and practice on the Stamford Bridge ground where we were to play the match. It was a ground of happy recollections for George Smith for, on this same ground about three years earlier, he had broken the world's record for 120 yards hurdling when he had been sent over to represent New Zealand at athletics.

BRONCO SEELING'S aggressive defence against Middlesex.

THE SPORTSMAN

THERE IS A NOTE of what might almost be called desperation, or, better still, desperateness, in the play of the New Zealanders.

Somebody said of Lord Beaconsfield as a debater, 'He talks like a horse racing — he talks all over.' That is how the New Zealanders play, as if their hopes of eternal welfare depend upon success, every nerve and sinew braced all but to snapping point.

They are as persistent as a lot of wasps; as clever and alert as a crowd of monkeys. Their organisation, their apparently instinctive knowledge of what is going to happen next, their acquaintance with each other's pace and method, is truly marvellous. They work together like the parts of a well-constructed watch.

DAILY CHRONICLE

THE CERTAINTY with which the New Zealanders build order out of chaos, the consummate ability displayed in reversing an attack, the supreme subtlety of feinting, the inexhaustible stamina, the perfect application of strength as well as the economy of it, the automatic regularity of backing up — all these and many other qualities were left vividly impressed on the mind of the spectator as he went away from the Middlesex game.

Whatever be the virtues of the special formation which the New Zealanders affect, there is no doubt that the primary cause of success is individual cleverness and the ordinary properties of combination.

These Middlesex cracks, who certainly are not without honour in their own country, faded away into abject nothingness. All the cleverness they possess in attack was stifled at birth.

GEORGE DIXON'S DIARIES

A goodly number of New Zealanders present from the *Rimutaka*, including Captain Greenstreet. Stamford Bridge is a very fine ground with magnificent stand accommodation. Like other teams met [Middlesex] lacked pace forward. No initiative in attacks. Followed practice of screwing scrums before ball goes in.

Awful nuisance both coming and going from ground by underground — took long time — very late for dinner. Saw Crabtree re returning via London and Gloucester but decided to ask for a decision to dodge London.

NEW ZEALAND TIMES' UK CORRESPONDENT

AT THE MOMENT I cannot make up my mind whether the uninterrupted triumphal march of the New Zealand footballers is becoming really a fire tragedy or a diverting comedy.

There cannot have ever been anything like it since quasi-international athletic contests first began. Assuredly, there has been nothing in cricket history at all to approach it, nor can there have been in football history either.

The New Zealand scrum still remains an impregnable stone castle to their English assailants while the New Zealanders, when attacking, 'Goes through our scrum, Lor-bless-yer, just as if we was a sheet of paper!'

English ruggers are at a loss for words that will adequately express their feelings.

It has been the same story throughout, with variations merely in detail. Not a single point has been scored against the New Zealanders since the Devonians piled up that famous four, to the New Zealanders' 55, of which the former were at the time so heartily ashamed.

They are the only team to have scored anything at all against the Antipodean raiders. It has been the same tale match by match. 'Oh, they may have licked Devon, but wait till they tackle Cornwall; the Cornishmen will get them a doing!'

But the Cornishmen didn't. They could not score even a unit. And the same was predicted successively about Bristol and Northampton and Leicester and Middlesex.

'Ah well,' said one observer, 'those country teams may not be able to beat 'em, but just you wait till they meet a real London lot, like Middlesex at Stamford Bridge. You'll see a jolly different show then, or I'll eat my hat.'

That man must now be suffering the pangs, either of dyspepsia, as the result of fulfilling his rash vow, or of remorse for his perjury in breaking it.

Some people in this country — perhaps even one per million, I shouldn't wonder — are beginning to understand that New Zealand isn't a little town in West Australia or New South Wales, but is a country as large as Britain. That's something to the good, at any rate.

MORNING LEADER

DURING THE MIDDLESEX MATCH an enterprising camera fiend anxious to secure snapshot titbits had a couple of narrow escapes of having his machine wrecked.

Once, from a huge punt skyward by Gillett, the ball after bouncing on the grandstand roof dropped right on the snapshotter's bowler, 'bonnetting' him beautifully, to the great amusement of the crowd, and nearly causing him to drop his camera.

On another occasion an ill-directed kick into touch by the Middlesex fullback ricocheted off the pavilion rails and nearly knocked the camera out of the photographer's hands.

JOHN CORBETT

West Coast — lock
25, 5ft 11in, 13st 9lb

Corbett was a national representative before being called on to play for his West Coast union. A strong lock who worked as a baker in Reefton, his first major game came for the combined Canterbury-West Coast-South Canterbury team which lost 5-3 to the touring Great Britain side of 1904. From his standout performance in this match he was selected for the South Island team in 1904 and eventually for the Originals.

BILLY WALLACE'S RECOLLECTIONS

When we came off the ground into the dressing shed we found warm plunge baths ready for us. There were about twenty of them all in a row and we just peeled off our togs and plunged in. Then the soccer trainer and his assistants were waiting to give us all a good rub-down and so we came out after the match almost as fresh as when we stepped on to the field.

By this time we had created quite a reputation and the people were beginning to take a deal of notice of us. We were easily recognised by our straw hats with the black band and silver fern.

We left on the Thursday morning for the North of England and as we left the hotel, all the servants lined up in a row for their tips. This was a rather unusual experience for us, as we were not used to tipping, nor had we the money to do it. But we had our bit of fun out of it, for as we filed down the row of outstretched hats we filled them up with cigarette butts, visiting cards and any other rubbish we could dig out of our pockets.

One of the chaps told them to see the manager as he had all the money. I think George Dixon must have treated them well because they greeted us with smiling faces on our return to London.

GAME 7 — SATURDAY 7 OCTOBER 1905 — at Hollow Drift Ground, Durham

NEW ZEALAND
DURHAM COUNTY

16
3

FOR NEW ZEALAND
Tries by Wallace 2, Hunter, Stead;
2 conversions by Wallace.

NEW ZEALAND
Booth, Thomson, Smith, Hunter, Wallace,
Stead (captain), Roberts, Gillett, Glenn,
McDonald, Nicholson, Cunningham,
Johnston, Glasgow, Casey.

FOR DURHAM COUNTY
Try by Clarkson.

DURHAM COUNTY
S. Horsley (Hartlepool Rovers), P. Clarkson
(Sunderland), J. T. Taylor (West Hartlepool),
C. Adamson (Durham City), H. Imrie
(Durham City), T. Wallace (West Hartlepool),
J. Knaggs (Hartlepool Rovers), Dr West
(West Hartlepool), G. Carter (Hartlepool
Rovers), T. Hogarth (Hartlepool Rovers),
G. Summerscales (Durham City), R. Elliott
(Durham City), J. Elliott (Durham City),
E. F. Stock (Sunderland), H. Havelock
(Hartlepool Old Boys).

Weather: Overcast and cold, ground muddy
Referee: Adam Turnbull (Hawick)
Crowd: 8000

KICK OFF
Wallace probed the blindside from a scrum and Hunter scored. Wallace missed: 3-0.
From a lineout Hunter and Smith combined to put Wallace over. His kick missed: 6-0.
From a scrum, Adamson threw a long pass to Clarkson, who scored. Adamson missed.

HALFTIME
New Zealand 6, Durham County 3

Roberts broke from a scrum, sending Stead for the posts. Wallace converted: 11-3.
Stead attacked from broken play, Johnston putting Wallace across. He converted.

FULLTIME
New Zealand 16, Durham County 3

FROM THE SIDELINES

EVENING STANDARD

THE NEW ZEALAND TEAM has more than fulfilled expectations. On Saturday afternoon, on the Hollow Drift Ground, they met the champion county in the first of their matches in the north and, in a rousing game, defeated them by 16 points to 3.

Notwithstanding Durham's pre-eminence among the counties, the New Zealanders had made so great an impression on the rugby world since their arrival, the result became a matter of speculation as to how many points the Colonials would win by.

The New Zealanders, and everybody else at the field, were in for a surprise, for not only did Durham stubbornly contest every inch of ground but the visitors crossed their line only four times.

Durham rose to the occasion and there would doubtless be many who felt that the Dunelmians had not played as well before.

The match aroused considerable interest and had the morning not been so unpleasantly wet many more spectators would have been present, the heavy rain in Newcastle and neighbourhood undoubtedly limiting the attendance.

There was a delay of a quarter of an hour in starting, Knaggs and Boylen being delayed at Ferryhill in their journey from Hartlepool and Durham was compelled to start the game with 13 men.

It was when their opponents were short-handed that New Zealand scored the first try. Meanwhile, R. Elliott of Durham City had been found and he took Boylen's place in the forwards, and then Knaggs and Boylen arrived, the halfback taking his place while Boylen became an enforced spectator.

NEW ZEALAND TIMES' UK CORRESPONDENT

IT HAS COME TO BE REGARDED as 'the wonder of the season' how the New Zealanders came to concede a try against Durham.

Because no one had hitherto crossed their line, Phil Clarkson, who did so, will doubtless be immortalised.

By keeping the Colonials' score to reasonable limits, Durham will have done something toward producing equanimity in rugby circles.

So utterly had the New Zealanders' spirited and beautifully executed attacks demoralised other teams that the defence had hardly been seriously called upon.

Not only did Durham make New Zealand battle hard for a

comparatively small number of points, but they actually overcame their defence.

To Clarkson had fallen the honour of being the first Englishman to cross the Colonials' line, and his success will do more to encourage the teams to take the field subsequently against the New Zealanders than anything else.

GEORGE DIXON'S DIARIES

Arriving at Durham on Thursday night we found the weather very much colder, and the members of the team were only too pleased to hug the fires provided in that old-fashioned hostelry, the Three Tuns.

In the early morning of match day it unfortunately commenced to rain and continued until shortly before the play began.

The ground was situated in a hollow, and was very rough and high in the centre, with a slope towards each touchline and a regular hog back.

The accommodation for spectators was very poor, there being only two small stands on each side, and no terraces. Even so, from seven to eight thousand spectators attended.

PHIL CLARKSON — the first to score a try against the Originals.

BILLY WALLACE'S RECOLLECTIONS

We were put up at the Three Tuns Hotel in Durham, a nice comfortable place run by two old maids. The weather was very cold and, while we were waiting for tea, some of the boys went for a brisk walk while others sat round the fire. When the gong went for dinner the chaps in front of the fire got there first

and when they had finished so was the food!

The old maids hadn't experienced the appetites of New Zealand footballers. You can imagine the looks on the faces of those who had gone for a long walk and returned with healthy appetites to find the food gone. However, the two old ladies got to work and

brought in a great bucketful of hard-boiled eggs. I think we broke all records in the egg-eating line that night! Our two hostesses were in a great state and one of them remarked in a rather sad voice that they had taken us too cheaply and they wouldn't make any money out of us.

Certainly, the improvement is gratifying; but it must not be forgotten that last season Durham were the best fifteen in England, and it was only to be expected that they would do better than the six teams which in turn had fared so disastrously.

In one respect the New Zealanders were at a disadvantage. Gallaher, their captain, whose presence as wing forward has done so much to disturb the work of the UK halfbacks, stood down, in company with Seeling and Deans, both of whom scored tries against Middlesex.

ATHLETIC NEWS

IN HOLDING THE NEW ZEALANDERS to 16 points to 3, Durham had the distinction of becoming the first team to cross their line. The first man in Great Britain to pierce the New Zealanders' line was Phil Clarkson of Sunderland.

We trust that such a good example will be followed by others. Clarkson has played the game for a long while now and is equally at home as a half or threequarter back. In the latter position he has frequently played for his county and at his best no county could desire a stronger or more resolute player.

Durham can take credit for making a very fine show against our Colonial brethren and this despite their misfortunes.

In the first 15 minutes, they were short of two of their players owing to trains missing connections. Then Horsley had to play in his ordinary boots for a quarter of an hour, in consequence of his regular coverings having gone astray.

All things considered, therefore, it may be said that the champion county players worthily sustained their reputation.

◆ ❖ ◆

When the New Zealanders come to Manchester is as yet undecided. The Lancashire Country Club did not make arrangements at the proper time but are now exerting themselves to get a fixture with the Colonials.

Mr Rowland Hill, the president of the English union, is using his persuasive powers and it might be suggested to the New Zealanders that if they dropped say, any one of the matches with Devonport Albion, Bedford or Cheltenham, room could be made for a game in Manchester.

It may be mentioned that the directors of the Manchester City ground have offered their splendid enclosure as a venue for a match between Lancashire Rugbeians and the New Zealanders, and if any efforts of ours will be of service in bringing the Colonials to Manchester we of the *Athletic News* shall be only too glad to give assistance.

Perhaps Mr George Dixon will listen to reason and and consider whether it would not be advisable to let his men come and see the beauties of Manchester.

◆ ❖ ◆

GEORGE DIXON'S DIARIES

This was our hardest game so far as ground was uneven and ball greasy — Durham forwards played hard, solid game. Referee Adam Turnbull of Scotland was not a great presence and allowed a lot of offside in the loose. In evening attended 'Smoker' in Town Hall — High Sherriff of County was in chair and quite a number of notables present. Splendid programme of songs provided by local Glee Club, many were members of Cathedral Choir. Although good singing find it very tedious work filling these functions out — majority of boys don't. On returning found Mynott in bed all day with a cold, very feverish so went out and got a Doctor. Found he has got attack of influenza and will probably for some days be laid up.

A SILVER FERN

Dame Fortune entered a florist's shop,
And all around was a lovely crop
Of Roses and Leeks and Shamrocks green,
And the finest Thistles ever seen;
But none of these emblems pleased the Dame.
To her their beauty seemed but tame,
She treated them all with a lofty spurn,
For she'd set her heart on a Silver Fern
A Silver Fern,
A Silver Fern
Her most aesthetic,
Very coquettic
Fancy took this turn —
'Some like red roses
To make their posies
But give me a Silver Fern!'

And Rose, with her petals all ablaze,
At Dame Fortune's choice expressed amaze,
And, oh, what a look of surprise and pique
Came to the face of the Cymric leek.
The Thistles in anger pricked themselves,
And danced in rage upon the shelves,
While the Dame walked out of the shop quite gay,
So pleased with herself and her Fern bouquet.
A Fern bouquet!
A Fern bouquet!
These very splenetic,
Unenergetic
Roots all came to learn
The curious riddle;
That second fiddle
They'd to play to a Silver Fern.

H.B.

DAILY EXPRESS

NEVER IN THEIR PALMIEST DAYS did the Australian cricketers create half the sensation that has been caused by the New Zealand footballers.

The tour of the footballers through the British islands is more than a margin of triumph, it is a devastation. They have played

BILLY WALLACE'S RECOLLECTIONS

That night it started to rain and it poured in torrents right through the night and up to the start of the game. We had to dress in a small tin shed about 14 feet by 12 feet. Punctually at 3 o'clock we were sent on to the ground but the Durham team did not follow. We hung around there waiting for them to come out, but it was half an hour before they appeared.

You can well imagine that we were wet through and shivering with the cold and were not in a condition to give of our best. The ground too was in bad order. The grass was long and there were big tussocks all over the ground. I am not exaggerating when I say that sometimes when the ball came out of the scrum it would get stuck in a tussock.

Then came the sensation of the match. Durham, by good line-kicking, had managed to reach our twenty-five. A scrum was formed and Durham hooked. Their halfback passed to one of the centres, Adamson, and he kicked high towards the wing. Clarkson, the Durham wing, and Mona Thomson both raced for it, but the ball bounced right away from Mona and into Clarkson's hands and he had merely to gather it in cleanly and go over the line to score near the corner flag. It was the first time our line had been crossed and you can imagine the cheering of the crowd and certainly the try was a clever piece of work.

---

seven matches against some of the crack counties of England and won them all as easily as John Roberts would beat the champion marker of a provincial town.

They have scored 247 points against a miserable total of 7 by their opponents, and of the 7 British points, 4 came from that fortuitous visitation of luck, a dropped goal.

They played Durham on Saturday and Durham are esteemed a good team. Yet the Durham committee allowed it to be known that so long as the New Zealanders did not win by more than 20 points, they would be satisfied.

This is probably the most striking compliment the visitors have received.

There is no mystery about this wonderful brilliance of the New Zealanders. Efficiency is the sole secret.

Individually, the men are as good as any that can be found; they have reduced combination to a science without refining it into a tangle, and they play with understanding and resource, quite indifferent to the hoary and respectable teachings of tradition.

That is how the Japanese defeated the hordes of Russia; that is how the New Zealanders are overwhelming the picked teams of Great Britain.

There is one gleam of hope. Within the next five weeks the Colonials play the chosen national teams of Scotland, Ireland, England and Wales and it may be that a victory will at last console our wounded honour.

But it will not diminish the fame of the New Zealanders who in this small matter of football stand for the growing ability and effectiveness of the Colonials.

There are still male grandmothers in England who patronise the colonies, their products and their men and tacitly suggest that the chief use of a colony is to act as an asylum for 'remittance men'.

They will soon have as rude a shock as the British footballers have received.

◆

ATHLETIC NEWS

GeORGE SMITH, THE NEW ZEALAND wing threequarter, has become a convert to the general superstitious dislike of the number 13.

Against Durham, he wore the number on the back of his jersey, in accordance with the system of identification common in the colonies, and brought over here by the New Zealanders, but had terribly bad luck throughout the afternoon.

'Nothing came off for me,' he afterwards explained, and forthwith proceeded to tear the offending numerals from his jersey. He says he will never wear 13 again.

Previous to the match, he laughed when a friend recalled the popular superstition regarding the number and suggested that he should change it.

Strange as it may seem to New Zealanders, the Colonial system of attaching numbers to the players' jerseys, with corresponding numbers on the programme, is quite an innovation in this country.

This simple method of identifying the members of a visiting team is warmly approved and will probably be permanently adopted by the English unions.

Another novelty introduced by the New Zealanders is the leather 'yoke' on the jersey which not only prevents the garment from tearing but renders if difficult for an opponent to grip his man by the jersey.

ERIC HARPER

Canterbury — centre
27, 5ft 11in, 12st 7lb

Harper first played for New Zealand against Britain in 1904 by which time he had already made a name for himself as a track athlete, winning the New Zealand 440-yard hurdles and 880-yard titles. He was a notable cricketer and a keen mountaineer who made a number of discoveries in the Southern Alps, including a pass to the West Coast.

A fine centre from a distinguished Canterbury pioneering family, Harper had a breezy disposition and was always eager to join in any fun that was going. Despite being dogged by injuries on tour, he emerged as a leader of men and was extremely popular among his teammates.

GAME 8 — WEDNESDAY 11 OCTOBER 1905 — at Friarage Field, Hartlepool

NEW ZEALAND
HARTLEPOOL CLUBS

63

0

FOR NEW ZEALAND
Tries by Hunter 4, Abbott 3, Roberts 2,
Smith 2, Deans, O'Sullivan, Stead, Wallace;
conversions by Wallace 8, Glasgow.

NEW ZEALAND
Wallace, Abbott, Deans, Hunter, Smith, Stead
(captain), Roberts, Gillett, Johnston, Seeling,
O'Sullivan, Cunningham, Newton, Glasgow,
McDonald.

HARTLEPOOL CLUBS
D. Ellwood (Rovers), B. Wellock (West
Hartlepool), J. T. Taylor (West Hartlepool),
G. Wass (West Hartlepool), J. Knaggs
(Rovers), H. Wallace (West Hartlepool),
J. Thompson (Rovers), S. Brittain (Rovers),
T. Hogarth (Rovers), F. Boylen (Rovers),
G.E. Carter (Rovers), A. Scott (West
Hartlepool), R. Moule (West Hartlepool),
I. Metcalfe (West Hartlepool),
Dr West (West Hartlepool).

Weather: Fine, ground firm
Referee: Robin Welsh (Scotland)
Crowd: 13,000

KICK OFF
Stead and Hunter combined from a scrum and Smith scored. Wallace converted: 5-0.
Hunter probed from a lineout and Deans scored. Wallace converted: 10-0.
Roberts scampered through from a lineout to score. Wallace missed: 13-0.
Stead scythed through from a lineout to score. Wallace converted: 18-0.
Stead probed again and Hunter scored. Wallace converted: 23-0.
Hunter and Deans combined to put Smith across. Wallace converted: 28-0.
Hunter and Deans were at it again and Abbott scored. Wallace converted.

HALFTIME
New Zealand 33, Hartlepool Clubs 0

O'Sullivan broke from a lineout and Hunter scored. Wallace converted: 38-0.
Wallace joined the backline to put Abbott across. Wallace converted: 43-0.
Wallace was involved again for another Abbott try. Wallace missed: 46-0.
Roberts broke from a scrum and Stead put Hunter in. Wallace missed: 49-0.
Stead and Smith combined to put O'Sullivan over. Wallace missed: 52-0.
Roberts darted through from a scrum to score. Wallace missed: 55-0.
Wallace sprinted 50 metres from loose play to score. Gillett missed: 58-0.
Stead broke from a scrum and Hunter scored. Glasgow converted.

FULLTIME
New Zealand 63, Hartlepool Clubs 0

FROM THE SIDELINES

DAILY MAIL

OLD INTERNATIONALS WHO HAD SEEN and taken part in many a stirring struggle stood and watched the New Zealanders' amazing exhibition of speed, strength and cleverness with sparkling eyes and bated breath, with an occasional gasp of supreme wonderment at some more than usually daring or novel achievement.

The game from beginning to end was a succession of football pyrotechnics, so brilliant, so clever, so varied, as to defy description. Only those who saw them could possibly conceive the heights which they reached.

At the end of five minutes Smith, the champion hurdler 'down under', hopped over, as it were, the Hartlepool line and from that moment the fun, if it could be called fun from the Hartlepool point of view, began.

Try after try, goal after goal followed with the most disconcerting regularity.

The crowd gradually grew mute with astonishment.

Such speed, such feinting, such daring, such strength, such skill they had not conceived possible as they saw unfolded by this aggregation of perfect human machinery from overseas.

It was bewildering and the crowd stood as one man, entranced.

The New Zealanders were not playing rugby football as we know it.

Surely they were playing some other game entirely, some game hitherto unknown to the Hartlepools, but they were breaking none of the rugby laws, though nearly all its conventions.

It was a refinement of rugby, rugby intellectualised, rugby metamorphosed.

Concerning (Billy) Wallace, two old England internationals watching the game and comparing notes agreed that he is absolutely the finest fullback who ever wore shoe leather.

His comrades call him Kill Danger because danger to the side ceases to be when he is in the breach.

He is as strong as a lion, quick as lightning, cool as a cucumber and the most wonderful of kicks into touch or goal, while he never fails to grass his man.

BILLY WALLACE

Wellington — fullback
27, 5ft 8in, 12st

Wallace scored the first points in New Zealand test match history when he slotted a goal against Australia in Sydney in 1903. A towering presence on the field on the Originals tour, Wallace was the team colossus both as a goalkicker and for his pace around the field. He scored 28 points in the opening match against Devonshire, when he wore a sunhat, and he went on to accumulate 246 points on tour, including 27 tries (in an era when fullbacks rarely scored tries). Possessed of a sparkling personality and a noted lover of fun, Wallace was one of the most popular members of the team. He was nicknamed Carbine after the great racehorse of the same name, and on tour Wallace met his namesake (by then retired to stud duties) and was presented with one of the hairs from Carbine's tail.

ATHLETIC NEWS

THE FIXTURE ATTRACTED a larger rugby crowd than has been seen for many a long day in the seaport town.

All the roads led to Hartlepool, even the Association centres, where it is heresy to talk 'rugger', sending their contingents of curious spectators.

The gates were closed before the start of the game, every window in the houses which surround the ground was framed with faces and even the balcony of a neighbouring lighthouse had its ring of spectators.

It is computed by one writer that the crowd numbered nearly

BILLY WALLACE'S RECOLLECTIONS

Freddy Roberts and I were standing on the steps of our hotel when a couple of gentlemen came up and asked us if we were coming to the Masonic gathering that night. We replied, 'Too right, if it's any good, we'll be there!'

Then they asked us if we would like to look over the Temple and we said 'Rather!'

We had inspected the Master's chair and were passing on to other things when we made a mistake in our conversation and asked what something was for and at once one of the chaps said: 'You are Masons, aren't you?' Then we had to confess we were not and in a surprisingly short time we were outside again!

The weather was foggy and cold, therefore we did not go out at night much, but preferred to spend the time in the warm rooms of the hotel. Billiards was a great craze with us just then and we had several tournaments amongst ourselves. George Smith and Bunny Abbott were our best players.

The game was remarkable in one respect — seven times in succession the Hartlepool team did not handle the ball, except to kick-off after a try had been scored. Again the critics had to change their opinions and we were dubbed 'The Terrible All Blacks' by the *Daily Mail*.

20,000. The match is said to have thrown the town of Hartlepool entirely out of its industrial habits; shops and schools were closed, nothing was done at the shipyards or factories and business was at a standstill.

It seems now to be acknowledged that there is no longer any room for doubt as to the position of the colonists, viz 'They are the finest rugby team that ever played in the British Islands and if any British team is to defeat them,' says one authority, 'it can only be done by a careful study of the visitors' methods and incessant practice of them by the best men that can be found.'

NEW ZEALAND TIMES' UK CORRESPONDENT

THE *DAILY MAIL* seems to have taken the New Zealand team under its wing and the momentous question 'Why do the New Zealanders win?' has been started as a subject of correspondences by that weighty organ.

One is glad to see the *Mail* giving so much prominence to the New Zealanders in its crowded columns, but it would be even more satisfactory if the scribe who chronicles their achievements knew at the least the rudiments of rugby football.

The *Mail* man seems to think that rugby is played between teams of eleven for, in the course of a lengthy disquisition, he says, 'The New Zealanders are much better than the best English

THE TOURISTS enjoy a visit to the Hartlepool Municipal Gardens.

ERIC HARPER, IN A LETTER HOME

We were loath to leave London after our round of excitements and gaieties in that great city. As many as possible of the chief places of interest were visited by us, besides the numerous places of amusement which London provides.

Our journey from London to Durham reminded us once more of the New Zealand railways, for we left at 10.30 a.m. and did not arrive until 6.30 p.m. However, we had a most enjoyable hour's break at York and most of us visited the famous cathedral.

We found Durham, so far as the town was concerned, rather dull; but the people were kindness itself, and could not do enough for us. Nearly all of us found our way to the ancient cathedral and castle, over which we were kindly escorted by guides.

We expected a good hard tussle with the Durham team, and we had one. This team is by far the best we have met so far, both in forwards and backs.

The ground was very wet and in consequence the ball was difficult to handle. I can confidently say that if it had been a drier day the score would have been larger on our side.

There are no serious accidents to report but minor ones are preventing some of our men from playing. Tyler has a slightly sprained ankle, Gallaher a bad knee and Casey a bruised shoulder. Mynott has had a bad attack of influenza but is now recovering and we hope to see Mackrell, whom we left in London with influenza, with us this week.

We arrived in West Hartlepool on Monday. Mynott and Casey stayed behind at Durham . . . Both have now joined us again and will be fit to play again next week.

West Hartlepool is a large shipbuilding centre and we had a most interesting inspection of Gray's Shipbuilding Yards, the largest, we were informed, in the world.

Great interest was taken in the match and all the dockyard and shipbuilding hands were given a half holiday for the occasion. A record gate for Hartlepool was the result.

Our backs played brilliantly against Hartlepool and this was the most brilliant display they have given during the tour. Of course, the opposition was feeble but, nonetheless, our passing was faultless and we rattled up 33 points in the first spell. In the second spell we put on another 30.

county sides in every respect, and there seems little probability of a picked English eleven overcoming them.'

If the writer had ever seen a rugby game in his life he would know that . . . but there! A rugby 'expert' who thinks the game is played eleven a side is past praying for.

The day after this memorable statement appeared, the *Mail* again distinguished itself by informing a wondering world that George Smith, the speedy New Zealand threequarter 'holds several Antipodean records, including the Australian 100 yards in nine and a quarter seconds'.

The paper naively adds, 'It may thus easily be conceived that when he has full steam on he takes some catching.'

I should think so, indeed. When our friend George or anyone else succeeds in covering a hundred yards, Australian or otherwise, in nine and a quarter seconds, I should believe that the age of miracles is not yet dead.

◆ ❖ ◆

BILLY WALLACE'S RECOLLECTIONS

We left for Tynemouth where we arrived late in the afternoon. Early in the tour we used to catch trains at 6 a.m., but we soon knocked that on the head for we couldn't get the fellows out of bed. We liked to have a lie-in in the morning after the match but we all liked to be down for breakfast together for this was the most enjoyable meal of the day. It was then that we were free and easy and we had our fun, barracking one another over the many little humorous incidents that happened day by day.

A rather comical illustration of the estimation in which the New Zealanders are held came under my notice when I was present at a lecture given to an engineering society.

The lecturer, who formerly lived in New Zealand, but who does not wish his name mentioned, had a tremendously enthusiastic reception, and subsequently the president, in putting a vote of thanks, remarked that the meeting would cease to be surprised at the quality of the lecture when they remembered that the lecturer came from the same colony that had produced the marvellous footballers who were now engaged in successfully demolishing all the best British teams.

He suggested that, according to present appearances, before the end of the football season they might possibly see a British team, formed from the two best international fifteens, playing against a selected team of five or seven of the New Zealand players, and he professed considerable doubt as to what the result would be even then. It struck me that, to quote Sam Weller, that was 'piling it up rayther mountaynious'. But I simply quote it as uttered. Still, it did seem a large order.

◆ ❖ ◆

The New Zealand footballers are the topic of the day. Little more than a month ago their existence as a team was practically unknown over here. Today all England is talking of their exploits.

They have played eight matches, achieved eight decisive victories and scored 310 points against a miserable seven.

Their success has been sensational and for that reason they have captured the imagination of the British public.

The fact is that the newspapers, finding first-rate 'copy' in these dashing footballers, have given an amount of space and discussion to their doings which the promoters of the tour could never, even in their most roseate dreams, have hoped for; and the result is that hundreds of thousands of people who have hitherto taken no interest in rugby football, in addition to every follower of the game, know all about the doughty visitors, and are keenly following the progress of their tour.

The New Zealanders are drawing record crowds at every ground which proves conclusively that thousands of people who have seldom or never attended the ordinary rugby matches have made a point of seeing the 'Invincibles'.

They are, in short, the heroes of the day and have won general admiration not only by their prowess but also by their modest demeanour in the hour of victory.

Deeds not words has been their motto. Swelled head and over-confidence are conspicuously absent.

The team steer clear of banquets wherever possible and fight shy of interviewers. If one of them has to make a speech in reply to a public welcome, it is almost apologetic in its reference to the day's match, and the inevitable victory.

The vice-captain greatly amused the Durham folk at the smoke concert in that city by saying that the team had come to England to learn. I have no doubt he meant it seriously.

The 'Blacks' have also created a favourable impression upon the English by the spirit in which they play the game. They are 'willing' without being rough and their methods are open and above board.

Said one famous English international at the close of the Hartlepool match on Wednesday, 'I cannot understand how anyone can charge the New Zealanders with being rough. I never saw a team play a more perfectly proper game.'

GEORGE DIXON'S DIARIES

Decided to leave Mynott behind. Left for Hartlepool after lunch. Hartlepool people delighted with exhibition. No official dinner, thank goodness.

◆

PRESS ASSOCIATION

THE NEW ZEALAND Rugby Football Union has received letters from Mr George Dixon saying the attendances so far were considered very good and in several instances they were records, but only sixpence was charged for admission, which was the recognised amount for county matches.

He mentioned a point which has been attracting notice lately, namely, the matches interposed between the international games and asked for authority to drop some if it appeared desirable.

It was decided to send the following cable to him: 'Authorise you to postpone, cancel or add any matches. Congratulations.'

The team has received an invitation to play in France after its tour at Home and the union has given Mr Dixon authority to accept the invitation as the team will have a margin of some three weeks after its last match in England.

◆

EVENING STANDARD

MR J. ALLAN THOMSON, New Zealand's first Rhodes Scholar, describes the points of difference between the New Zealand and the English styles of playing rugby football.

He believes that in the scrum work and in five-eighths play the New Zealand style is superior to the English but holds that the wonderful success of the present New Zealand team is 'due very largely to the individual physique and excellence of the members of the team' — a conclusion that cannot be gainsaid.

'It will be a splendid thing for rugby, both in this country and in New Zealand, if these visits can be made regularly,' says Mr Thomson. 'The New Zealand team is no better this year than it has been any time in the past ten years, so there is every hope of a sufficiently even contest to keep up the interest.'

GAME 9 — SATURDAY 14 OCTOBER 1905 — at Preston Avenue, North Shields

NEW ZEALAND　　　31

NORTHUMBERLAND　　0

FOR NEW ZEALAND
Tries by Hunter 5, Deans, Gillett, Harper, Seeling; 2 conversions by Cunningham.

NEW ZEALAND
Booth, Harper, Deans, Hunter, Smith, Stead (captain), Roberts, Gillett, Corbett, Seeling, O'Sullivan, Cunningham, Newton, Glasgow, Glenn.

NORTHUMBERLAND
C.F. Stanger-Leathes (Northern), J.E. Hutchinson (Durham City), J.E. Scott (Percy Park), J. Harrison (Rockliff), T. Simpson (Rockliff), E. Averill (Rockliff), W. Maddison (Percy Park), C. Russell (Percy Park), R. Stedman (Rockliff), J. Kyle (Rockliff), A. Kewney (Rockliff), W.G. Hepple (Northern), A. Emerson (Tynedale), F.R. Cumberlege (Northern), H. Beckerson (Percy Park).

Weather: Wet and windy, ground muddy
Referee: F. Nicholls (Midland Counties)
Crowd: 12,000

KICK OFF
Gillett chased his own kick and scored. Glasgow missed: 3-0.
Hunter picked up a loose ball and scored handy. Cunningham converted: 8-0.
Stead put Hunter in for a try from a scrum. Booth missed: 11-0.
Deans stole a wild pass and raced away to score. Booth missed: 14-0.
Hunter was in again from a scrum, set up by Smith. Gillett missed: 17-0.
When the locals dropped a high kick, Seeling scored. Cunningham converted.

HALFTIME
New Zealand 22, Northumberland 0

Stead put Hunter across from a scrum. Cunningham missed: 25-0.
Another scrum, another Stead burst, another Hunter try. Cunningham missed: 28-0.
Again from a scrum, Deans put Harper across. Glasgow missed.

FULLTIME
New Zealand 31, Northumberland 0

FROM THE SIDELINES

ATHLETIC NEWS

SHORT OF SNOW AND FROST, it would be difficult to imagine more unfavourable atmospheric conditions than those which prevailed at North Shields for New Zealand's game against Northumberland.

A hurricane of wind and rain was blowing athwart and half down the field during the whole game and made it difficult, almost impossible, to play good football.

Northumberland, it seems, reckons to have done well to get off with a 31-point beating and certainly after the beanfest of points at Hartlepool one anticipated that the New Zealanders would inflict something like a three-figure beating on the Northumbrians, for last year (1904) the county team was one of the weakest in the North Country.

◆

DAILY MAIL

ALTHOUGH THE ALL-CONQUERING New Zealand footballers experienced no difficulty in vanquishing Northumberland by the comfortable margin of 31 points to nothing, the 12,000 or so Tynesiders who witnessed the match scarcely saw them to their best advantage.

The weather conditions were most unpleasant for players and spectators alike. The New Zealanders do not shine under these conditions so brightly as when the ball is dry and the foothold secure.

Their scientific methods have been so well thought out and are so mathematically exact that adverse meteorological conditions such as prevailed on Saturday are apt to upset the perfect working of the machinery.

It is, for example, impossible in a high wind to pass the ball with absolute accuracy at no matter how short a range if the wind, playing the part of a ubiquitous extra threequarter, cuts in when least expected and with exasperating frolic carries the leather forward or lifts it out of reach over the head of the bewildered player.

Needless to say, the 'All Blacks' do not like the wind and the rain, and if they are fated to receive a bad beating or a beating at all during their tour it will probably happen when their machinery gets blown out of order.

What strikes one most about the 'All Blacks', apart from their homogeneity on the field, is their comradeship in private life.

The team of 27 players is composed of men of different social grades but no one would imagine it judging from the camaraderie which prevails.

Ability to play football and the intense desire to win is their standard of comradeship and this is largely due their perfect understanding on the field.

Of course every man likes to score a try but with the New Zealanders they never attempt to do so if by passing to a comrade the chance of getting over the line is enhanced.

Several times against Northumberland, Smith and Deans might have crossed themselves had they not decided in a flash that there was a better chance of scoring by passing at the last second.

Thus it is that not too much should be made of the appended list of tryscorers as it often happens that the actual scorer has done far less to bring about the desired result than one or two others who made the opening or gave the pass that led to the conquest.

As Gallaher, their captain, points out: 'We reckon that every man of the fifteen has had a hand in every try.' That is the spirit that wins matches and that is the spirit that makes the 'All Blacks' so formidable.

There are, however, occasions on which an 'All Black' will throw conventions to the wind and utterly ignore his comrades. And into this category must be placed the five extraordinary tries made by Hunter on Saturday afternoon.

Even the 'All Blacks' themselves, accustomed as they are to flashes of individual brilliancy, were amazed as what their brilliant little five-eighth did.

He is only five foot six, but sturdy and well knit, with determination writ on every line of his strong, aquiline face. Five times getting the ball behind the scrum he forged his way at lightning speed through the opposition backs and safely grounded the ball over the line.

A more meteoric display would be inconceivable. He cut and wriggled his way through an almost solid phalanx of opponents, feinting, dodging, swerving but all the time scarcely deviating from a straight line.

◆

EVENING STANDARD

THOUGH NORTHUMBERLAND suffered a heavy defeat, it was far from humiliating when the fact is taken into consideration that only Durham and Leicester of the earlier opponents have had less points scored against them.

ROBERTS AND WALLACE pose with a local W. Campbell (centre).

The New Zealanders have so pleased, nay, astounded the critics and public alike since arriving in the mother country that it seems almost superfluous to say that their exposition of the handling game was wonderful.

Safe it is to say that the like has never been witnessed in the North Country.

If there was a fault and, in spite of the score one feels bound to point it out, it was the repeated failure to improve upon the advantage gained from tries.

In this respect, the Colonials missed the services of Wallace, who previously had so distinguished himself in this particular department of the game.

NEW ZEALAND TIMES' UK CORRESPONDENT

THE NEW ZEALAND PLAY is a particularly happy mixture of combination and individualism, and they are consequently constantly doing those things which their combination-ridden opponents least expect them to do.

They violate the canons of rugby football as seemingly understood by our players in a manner most shocking.

Last Saturday, for instance, Hunter, playing five-eighths, got over the Northumbrian line five times. On each occasion he ought, according to the rules of the game as understood by a majority of our players, to have passed out to his threequarters.

Instead of doing so, he feinted, and having put the opposing backs off the scent, dodged through himself.

An English half who did such a thing might possibly find himself the hero of the crowd and receive the plaudits of the irresponsible halfpenny press, but he would certainly receive a lecture for such 'selfish' play. I wonder how Hunter fared at the hands of his captain and the team. Was he beaten with sticks, or patted on the back and called 'good boy'?

BILLY WALLACE'S RECOLLECTIONS

Mr Buttery of the *Daily Mail* accompanied us for a great part of the tour and was a very fair critic indeed. Incidentally, he told me how it was that one critic, Mr Hamish Stuart, in particular, gave us a very bad spin.

It seems that this critic saw some of the boys before the first match and, trying to get a 'scoop', asked them the names of the selected team. The boys played a joke on him and gave him a team of has-beens who were 13,000 miles away in New Zealand. That team was published as given to him and it was a huge joke, but he never forgave us.

HAMISH STUART, ATHLETIC NEWS

IT WOULD BE A VERY EASY MATTER to name certain sides of the past that would probably inflict decisive defeats on the New Zealanders, even without enjoying the same opportunity of playing together, etc, as the Colonials have enjoyed.

A few seasons ago the rugby world agreed practically to a man

ERIC HARPER, IN A LETTER HOME

Very cold, wintry weather greeted us at Tynemouth, which is about a mile from North Shields, where we played Northumberland.

On Saturday the weather was really bad. A very strong and bitterly cold wind blew all the day and heavy rain fell during the match. This may account for the score of 31 to nil, which is rather below our average.

An experiment was tried with the position of our backs, Smith being played on the wing, Deans in the centre and Harper on the wing. The experiment was very successful, the combination working well. Hunter scored five brilliant tries.

Our front rankers Tyler and Casey were unable to play, Tyler on account of a slight sprain and Casey from the injuries to his shoulder. Glenn and Glasgow went into the front instead and worked well.

Gallaher's bad knee has now almost recovered and he expects to be able to play next week. Abbott is laid up with a bad knee. He had the misfortune to poison it but after being lanced, it is recovering rapidly.

Mackrell has recovered from his severe cold and has joined us again.

that the Scottish fifteen of 1901 were the finest side and played the most perfect football ever seen.

I do not quite share this view, simply because the said side were only proved to be a really great side under certain conditions — a dry ball, a fast ground and a windless day.

In any case, it is safe to say that under such conditions the 1901 Scottish fifteen would certainly have beaten all the sides the New Zealanders have met with equal ease and by equally large margins.

The team combination, both in defence and in attack, of that fifteen was almost perfect. They had pace fore and aft and they played a most distinctive game.

Then take the Welsh team of 1903, when at full strength. I refer here to the fifteen that beat Ireland, at Cardiff, by 6 tries to 0 on a mudheap. That side played on that day the finest football under the conditions obtaining — a heavy ball and a field that was literally a mudheap.

Would that Welsh side have beaten the New Zealanders? I have no hesitation in saying they would have done so, and that too by a pretty big margin.

Let me add that I am in no way surprised at the success of the New Zealanders. It is perfectly natural, and ought to have been anticipated, because every New Zealander, of any note identified with English rugby, has been a first-class player (Fell, Ritchie, O'Brien and McEvedy are examples), while the New Zealand schools (Nelson, Wanganui, Christchurch, etc) have long been quite as fine nurseries as Fettes, Loretto and any of our public schools.

Then rugby is essentially the national pastime, as distinct from a popular spectacle, in New Zealand; while some years ago a New Zealander, who had got his Scottish cap, assured me that a representative New Zealand side were quite as good and would hold their own with any of our national fifteens.

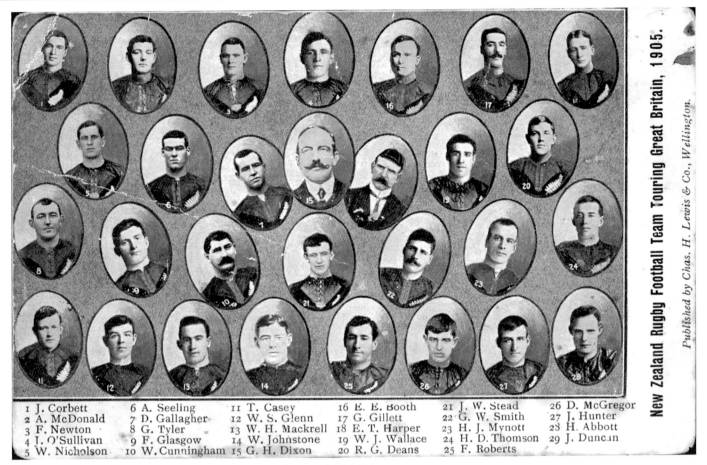

New Zealand Rugby Football Team Touring Great Britain, 1905.

Published by Chas. H. Lewis & Co., Wellington.

1 J. Corbett	6 A. Seeling	11 T. Casey	16 E. E. Booth	21 J. W. Stead	26 D. McGregor
2 A. McDonald	7 D. Gallagher	12 W. S. Glenn	17 G. Gillett	22 G. W. Smith	27 J. Hunter
3 F. Newton	8 G. Tyler	13 W. H. Mackrell	18 E. T. Harper	23 H. J. Mynott	28 H. Abbott
4 I. O'Sullivan	9 F. Glasgow	14 W. Johnstone	19 W. J. Wallace	24 H. D. Thomson	29 J. Duncan
5 W. Nicholson	10 W. Cunningham	15 G. H. Dixon	20 R. G. Deans	25 F. Roberts	

ONE OF MANY POSTCARDS produced in the UK of the stunningly successful Originals.

NORTHERN DAILY MAIL

THE LANCASHIRE UNION is feeling very sorry for its mistake in refusing the offer of a New Zealand match when making up the season's programme.

Now that the Colonials are proving such a 'draw' Lancashire is endeavouring to get another union to transfer its New Zealand fixture.

Mr W. Sawyer, the secretary of the Cheltenham Rugby Club, has received a letter from the president of the Lancashire Rugby Union, asking if the Cheltenham Club is willing, in return for compensation, to give up its match with the New Zealanders, in order that the latter may play a game with Lancashire.

The idea of agreeing to such an offer is ridiculed in Cheltenham, and it may be taken for granted that if the officials, players or supporters at Cheltenham have any say in the matter, the fixture arranged for 9 December will be duly kept.

JUDEX IN THE SPORTING LIFE

A SUGGESTION WAS MADE to a contemporary that New Zealand should meet a team picked from England, Ireland, Scotland and Wales, that the King be asked to be present and that the proceeds be given to the King's Hospital Fund.

Our contemporary suggests as the venue Crystal Palace, and the date January 6. If I may be allowed to say so, I think the idea an excellent one. A rugby football match has never been honoured by the King's presence since he came to the throne, and I doubt very much if His Majesty ever witnessed a match whilst he was Prince of Wales.

BILLY GLENN

Taranaki — loose forward
27, 5ft 11in, 12st 12lb

Glenn played 19 matches for Taranaki from 1901 to 1904 and was selected to play for New Zealand against the touring British team in 1904 in what was the first official test match staged in New Zealand. Injuries prevented him being selected for the Originals in the early part of the tour and he made only 13 appearances. Possessed of a fine singing voice, he was a great 'hit' on stage when he appeared at a Devon concert in combination with Bubs Tyler.

GAME 10 — THURSDAY 19 OCTOBER 1905 — at Kingsholm, Gloucester

NEW ZEALAND
GLOUCESTER

44
0

FOR NEW ZEALAND
Tries by Deans 3, Hunter 2, Wallace 2,
Glasgow, Seeling, Smith; conversions by
Wallace 6, Gillett.

NEW ZEALAND
Gillett, Smith, Deans, Hunter, Wallace,
Stead, Roberts, Gallaher (captain), Johnston,
Seeling, Nicholson, Cunningham, O'Sullivan,
Glasgow, Glenn.

GLOUCESTER
L. Vears, C. Smith, E. Hall, J. Harrison,
A. Hudson, J. Stephens, A. Wood, D.R. Gent,
W. Johns (captain), A. Hawker, B. Parham,
F. Pegler, G. Vears, B.H. Collins, G. Matthews.

Weather: Fine, ground firm
Referee: F. Nicholls (Leicester)
Crowd: 15,000

KICK OFF
From a lineout, Glasgow and Roberts put Hunter across. Wallace converted: 5-0.
From a scrum, Deans ran hard and Smith scored. Wallace missed: 8-0.
Nicholson broke through a lineout and Deans scored. Wallace missed: 11-0.
Glasgow scored from loose play near the line. Wallace converted: 16-0.
Wallace joined the backline from a scrum and scored, adding the conversion: 21-0.
Smith was pushed into touch but a quick throw-in gave Smith a try. Gillett converted.

HALFTIME
New Zealand 26, Gloucester 0

Stead and Hunter combined to put Deans across. Wallace converted: 31-0.
Wallace took Hunter's pass from a scrum and scored, adding the conversion: 36-0.
Cunningham broke through a lineout, setting up a Seeling try. Wallace missed: 39-0.
Roberts cross-kicked from a scrum, Deans winning the sprint. Wallace converted.

FULLTIME
New Zealand 44, Gloucester 0

FROM THE SIDELINES

NEW ZEALAND TIMES' UK CORRESPONDENT

FOR SEVERAL DAYS during the current week the ancient city of Gloucester gave itself over to hero worship of the New Zealand football team who arrived there on Monday.

The Gloucester City team has for years been in the forefront of the Western Rugby clubs but never in the history of the game there had such enthusiasm been shown as that aroused by the visit of the colonists.

And this extraordinary interest in the match was excited not only in the county of Gloucester itself but throughout all the neighbouring counties.

Even so far afield as Swindon (Wilts) the Great Western Railway Co closed their vast works for the day in order that their employees might witness the game, and the same concession was granted by the colliery owners in the Forest of Dean.

Excursion trains were run from all parts of South Wales, where of course interest in the formidable 'Blacks' is particularly keen.

Factories and works and elementary schools all were closed in Gloucester City in order that the men and boys might be present at the contest.

The ground, which is not a large one, was packed long before the time of starting; indeed, so great was the crush that the gates had to be closed and money refused before the players had arrived, the gate receipts amounting to over £550, a sum which has only once been exceeded there — when England and Wales played at Gloucester, but on that occasion the charges for admission were considerably higher.

The record also constitutes a record for the New Zealanders, the previous highest gate being £410 at the Middlesex match.

The play of the visitors was a revelation to the onlookers. At first, their brilliant efforts were received in silence, but soon their great cleverness called forth round upon round of applause.

Overwhelming as was their triumph, it is remarked by one authority that the actual play was by no means so one-sided as one would infer from the fact the Gloucester team's line was crossed ten times. The whole of the New Zealanders' scoring took place during two periods, amounting to half an hour, while Gloucester were a man short.

Unfortunately, in a collision with Gillett, Hudson, Gloucester's best threequarter, was so badly stunned he had to retire. Handicapped in this way, the home team were soon overwhelmed.

◆ ❖ ◆

It is always recognised as a special compliment to be caricatured on cartooned in *Punch* magazine.

This compliment had been paid to the New Zealand footballers, to whom is devoted a full-page cartoon by Bernard Partridge. It shows New Zealand as a lion cub struggling at football with the parent lion, and the legend is 'The Un-licked Cub'.

Under the heading, 'How to Beat the New Zealanders', *Punch* has the following droll correspondence:

Dear Sir,

All this hysterical outcry about new methods and reorganisation of our rugby football teams is sheer feeble-minded nonsense. Our players are good enough for any country under the sun, New Zealand included.

The present trouble is merely caused by that immoral innovation of the wing forward who, being neither flesh, fowl nor good red herring, can only be stigmatised as a tweeny.

The way to meet the difficulty and stop the contagion from spreading in our own country is to produce a referee who will systematically penalise the methods of this tricky gentleman until he is forced to resume his proper place in the pack, being glad, in fact, to hide his head anywhere.

If heroic measures of this sort are practised it will be unnecessary to adopt the suggestion that New Zealand tries count only two points.

Yours truly, Durham Lad.

Dear Sir,

In consequence of the representations of a great nephew, I recently attended a football match at Torquay and was much shocked at the conduct of our young Colonials.

The barbarity of their behaviour was ruthless in the extreme; in fact, each time my dear nephew had the ball, one of the ungentlemanly fellows knocked him down and snatched it away from him, and the same thing occurred to his companions, all young men of good position, not once, but many times.

Is it sport? Is it even seemly? It would not have been considered so in my young day, or in the young day of my brothers and cousins, and it is to be hoped that such an exhibition will never again be witnessed on an English ground.

Believe me to remain, yours very truly,

(Miss) Martha Myttens.

◆ ❖ ◆

A member of the New Zealand team, in a private letter, says, 'We are having a great time, but the people are not too lavish with their hospitality. I suppose we have ourselves to blame in giving out that we did not wish to be entertained.'

In regard to this, I should like to say, in justice to the English, that

WOMEN AND CHILDREN among the 15,000 spectators for the Gloucester match.

their hospitality has been restrained precisely as my correspondence suggests, in deference to the wishes of the management of the New Zealand team.

The various towns would be delighted to fête and banquet the redoubtable visitors but it has been stated again and again in the papers that the New Zealanders are in strictest training and wish to live as simply as possible while on tour.

Gloucester furnishes this week a case in point. The Mayor and High Sheriff had expressed their desire to entertain the New Zealanders at a banquet at the Guildhall but the invitation, according to the *Chronicle*, has been courteously declined 'as the team are in strict training'.

Consequently, though the team were entertained after the Gloucester match, the hospitality was not on so lavish a scale as it would have been but for the New Zealanders' own plea for simplicity.

And so it is in other places. Everyone entertains the kindliest feelings towards the visitors and would be glad to show them hospitality but the general impression undoubtedly is that the New Zealanders are anxious to avoid banquets, in order to keep fit.

You see, an Englishman's idea of hospitality is to give his guests a huge repast. Probably it does not occur to him that the visitors might be entertained in other ways, which would not interfere with training, and allowance therefore should be made for the difference in his habit of thought as compared with the practice towards visiting teams in the colony.

BOB DEANS, IN A LETTER HOME

On Monday (16 October) we journeyed down to Gloucester where we stopped till Friday. In the meantime, we had a very good practice and one afternoon watched a game of 'soccer', which did not appeal to us like rugby, and seemed slow and poor in comparison.

There were large numbers of Welshmen to watch the Gloucester match and altogether there was a crowd of 15,000.

We expected a very close fight but eventually won by the very fair score of 44 points to nil. Gloucester were rather unfortunate in having two men knocked out. One retired in the first spell and almost as soon as he came on in the second, another had to go off.

We have been unfortunate in losing the services of some of our men for a day or two, seventeen having been disabled since the start, although most of them for only a short while.

The front rankers especially have been unfortunate, and in the last two matches we had to play one man who had only played there once before in his life, and consequently the ball was not heeled out quite so often as previously.

The grounds we have played on have been irregular. Some of them have been splendid, the ground like a lawn, and good accommodation for changing, but in some of the others there is no room to dress and the ground is all hills and hollows.

BILLY WALLACE'S RECOLLECTIONS

The weather was now beautiful and we were driven in state to The Ram Hotel amid a cheering throng. When we began to stroll around the city we at once realised how great was the interest in the forthcoming match. Businessmen would bail us up in the streets and have a yarn with us and so we made many friends.

In the afternoon we were taken for a drive round the city and surrounding countryside in motor cars which could travel at about ten miles an hour.

We had a private dining room to ourselves and we used to open our letters at the breakfast table while we were sitting there.

Massa Johnston called out 'Hullo boys, I've got a letter from a girl called Zoe asking for my hat-band.' 'So have I,' said another. 'And so have I,' chorused several members. About seven or eight of us had all received the same letter. Zoe was evidently a very clever little girl and was making sure of getting her

request answered one way or another .

Special trains were rushing into Gloucester, bringing crowds of people from Wales and all the surrounding country for miles around.

The Great Western Railways workshops were closed down for the afternoon — an event that had never happened before. Every shop and factory was closed at midday and the employees poured out in streams to the ground to see the match.

GLOUCESTER CHRONICLE

AFTER THE GREAT FOOTBALL MATCH at Kingsholm on Thursday, the members of the New Zealand and Gloucester teams, with other guests, were entertained to a high tea at the Guildhall by the Mayor and the City High Sheriff.

The Mayor (Councillor Langley-Smith), who presided, was supported by the High Commissioner of New Zealand (the Hon. W. Pember Reeves), Mr G.H. Dixon (manager of the New Zealand team), Mr A.W. Vears (chairman of the Gloucester Football and Athletic Ground Company) and Mr J.H. Tratt (president of the Gloucester County Rugby Union).

The Mayor extended a hearty welcome to the New Zealand team, assuring them that their excellent qualities were nowhere better appreciated than in the city of Gloucester.

His Worship alluded to the remarkable exposition of the rugby game which had been witnessed on the Kingsholm Ground and said that he, in common with others, had been trying to ascertain the secret of the New Zealanders' great success. He thought that a great deal of it was attributable to the fact that the Colonials were 'sons of the soil', having been brought up in enjoyment of the freedom and fresh air of their beautiful New Zealand.

The Mayor spoke of the interest which Gloucester had in New Zealand by reason of the fact that many of her sons had gone there and mentioned that their excellent assistant surveyor, Mr E.W.A. Carter, was born in the colony.

He concluded a much-applauded speech by wishing the hitherto invincible 'All Blacks' every success during the remainder of their tour. The City Member, Mr Russell Rea, said that while the New Zealanders were conquerors the people of this country declined to say that anybody was invincible.

The City Member recalled what England had done in the realm of cricket and how the 'ashes' had been brought back from Australia, and remarked it was extremely probable that the New Zealanders were teaching Englishmen a lesson in regard to football, which was a progressive game and one to be developed.

At the conclusion of formalities, the guests proceeded to the Theatre Royal where the Mayor and Sheriff had kindly booked 70 seats to enable them to witness the performance of *Hamlet* by the Benson Company.

Large crowds of people outside the Guildhall and in the vicinity of the theatre gave the New Zealanders a cordial greeting. There was a full house and the excellent performance, with Mr Henry Herbert as Hamlet and Miss Dorothy Green as Ophelia, was greatly enjoyed.

ATHLETIC NEWS

A GOOD DEAL OF NONSENSE is being talked in the correspondence columns of the *Daily Mail* about the alleged decadence of the national physique, apropos of the crushing defeats inflicted on English teams by the New Zealand footballers.

Because the New Zealanders have been uniformly successful in their first 10 matches, various Cassandras in trousers have hastened to proclaim the physical and mental deterioration of the Old Country.

To argue from the particular to the general is always dangerous, and generally, as in this case, absurd. Suppose England's best international association team toured New Zealand and defeated all the provincial and city 'socker' teams there, and wound up by defeating a team representing the whole colony.

That is what would probably happen, for New Zealand is not strong in 'socker', whereas England is; but would those defeats prove that the New Zealanders are a decadent race?

ERNEST BOOTH

Otago — fullback/wing
29, 5ft 7½in, 11st 10lb

Booth's provincial career began in 1896 with the Athletic Club in Dunedin. An intelligent and deep-thinking player who was a journalist by profession, he was always known by his nickname — General — after the founder of the Salvation Army. An early selection for the Originals' tour, his international career began with New Zealand's short tour of Australia in July 1905.

GAME 11 — SATURDAY 21 OCTOBER 1905 — at Jarvis' Field, Taunton

NEW ZEALAND
SOMERSET COUNTY

23

0

FOR NEW ZEALAND
Tries by Mynott 2, Seeling 2, Wallace;
dropped goal, 2 conversions by Wallace.

NEW ZEALAND
Gillett, Booth, Harper, Deans, Wallace,
Mynott, Stead, Gallaher (captain), Corbett,
Seeling, Nicholson, O'Sullivan, Glenn,
Tyler, Casey.

SOMERSET COUNTY
A. Mead (Bridgewater Albion),
W.M. Penny (Taunton), J.T. Timmins (Bath),
H. Shewring (Bristol), R. Meister (Bath),
C. Kingston (Bridgewater Albion),
H.C. Jackson (Bridgewater Albion),
A. Vickary (Aberavon), R. Dibble
(Bridgewater Albion), H. Winter (Taunton),
G.V. Kyrke (Marlborough Nomads),
W.H. Neads (Bristol), Norman Moore
(Bristol), A. Manning (Bristol), W. Archer
(Bridgewater Albion).

Weather: Fine, ground firm
Referee: A.J. Davies (Cardiff)
Crowd: 9000

KICK OFF
Backs and forwards combined for Mynott to score. Wallace converted: 5-0.
Tyler launched an attack from which Seeling scored. Wallace missed: 8-0.
Wallace drop-kicked a goal from broken play.

HALFTIME
New Zealand 12, Somerset County 0

From a lineout, O'Sullivan broke through, Seeling scoring. Wallace converted: 17-0.
Mynott and Gillett combined to put Wallace over. Gillett missed: 20-0.
Stead, playing halfback, put Mynott in for the final try. Gillett missed.

FULLTIME
New Zealand 23, Somerset County 0

FROM THE SIDELINES

DAILY MAIL

THE ABSENCE OF SMITH, Hunter and Roberts seemed to put the New Zealand machinery out of gear against Somerset. The absence of Roberts as scrumhalf was perhaps most severely felt. He has to receive all the hard knocks and do all the dirty work. He gets none of the credit if things go right and all the blame if they go wrong.

The little man, who forms the connecting link between two great pieces of machinery, is scarcely noticed, but if his work is not done expeditiously the machinery is liable to break down.

His work may not be so showy as that of Smith, Wallace and Hunter, but if the New Zealanders are to be beaten probably it will be when this quiet, unobtrusive player is absent.

If the backs in the Somerset match did not reach the usual standard of excellence, the forwards were as good as ever.

Somerset, always a famous forward team, did not disgrace their traditions. The Colonials had to deal with a pack almost as powerful as themselves. The tackling of both sides was strenuous but there were no casualties.

NEW ZEALAND TIMES

IT ALMOST GOES WITHOUT SAYING that great interest was aroused in the West by the match. Taunton was quite full of excursionists, and the town club's ground was filled by almost 10,000 people, the biggest crowd ever seen at a football match in Taunton.

The visitors had a splendid reception and were heartily cheered both before and after the match.

Spectators came from places as far distant as Birmingham while Bristol, Bath and Exeter were strongly represented.

Other spectators included a large number of boys from the Royal Naval College at Dartmouth, and from Blundell's School at Tiverton.

CENSOR, ATHLETIC NEWS

HAD THERE BEEN ANY CONCEPTION by the Somerset authorities of the phenomenal interest our Colonial conquerors would arouse by their triumphal procession around the country it is pretty certain Taunton would not have been selected as the venue, for the rugby enclosure in the assize town is cramped and confined, and Weston-super-Mare, Bath or Wellington would have been preferable.

When they realised what a concourse would be attracted they made overtures to the Somerset cricket authorities for the loan of their ground, but strange to relate it was not treated with the sympathy in which sports are supposed to hold each other, conditions being imposed which were impossible of acceptance, one being that all members, numbering 700 to 800, could claim free entry to the best seats.

Remembering that the principal officials of Somerset cricket are old rugby players, and the unhealthy condition of the club's finances, their attitude aroused much comment.

Thus repelled, the football committee had to make the best use possible of Jarvis's Field, and with temporary vantage places arranged accommodation was excellent and sufficient, and everybody who attended must have had a good view.

It was computed that over 9000 people were present, and the receipts will exceed £400. The Taunton officials are to be congratulated upon the provision they made, and the Great Western Railway for helping them by lending 200 railway sleepers.

BILLY WALLACE'S RECOLLECTIONS

It was late on Friday afternoon of 20 October when our train drew into the station and we received a warm welcome from the people of Cider County. The officials of the Somerset Union were there in force to greet us and a host of football enthusiasts. As we drove through the town to the hotel we saw the town placarded with posters advising the people to come and see 'the Wonderful All Blacks play'.

The Somerset officials told us of the difficulty they were having to accommodate the huge crowd because the ground was only a small one, with a very small stand, and of course, all tickets had been sold out long before.

The name 'All Blacks' had now stuck to us. It is the name with which we were christened by the *Daily Mail* and it caught with the general public, though quite a number were misled into thinking we were a team of black fellows. The small boys of the town flocked round the hotel in swarms and knew us from our photographs which were in the daily papers.

That night George Dixon called our management committee together and announced he had a special letter from the Citizens Committee of Newton Abbot, asking us if we would go to Newton Abbot for our next match, against Devonport-Albion at Plymouth. The team members were unanimous on this point so George sent a wire in reply 'We are coming home' and this was fully understood by our good friends there.

On the Friday afternoon excursion trains arrived from far and near, bringing thousands of enthusiasts for the match next day. It was impossible for the town to accommodate this huge crowd and sleeping quarters were at a premium. Hundreds could not find beds at night and so the railway company came to the rescue and placed a couple of hundred cars on the siding. You can imagine the scramble there was for breakfast the next morning!

The selected teams spent the morning quietly; but the 'breathers' were freer and were able to enjoy a stroll around the town.

While we were waiting for lunch who should walk in but the parson whose church we had attended on our first Sunday in England! Some of the boys were rather afraid he was coming to save their souls (which we reckoned was part of our manager's job) and made themselves scarce, but he turned out to be a fine old sport.

EVENING STANDARD

With the advance of the season our teams have had time to make special preparations to meet the all-conquering Colonials, and it is only reasonable to expect that some diminution of the phenomenal scoring will occur.

It will, indeed, be truly astounding if the visitors, when not quite at the top of their form, do not on some occasion suffer defeat.

No reason at present exists for supposing that any particular side will earn the distinction such an achievement would bring, but some of the New Zealanders have suffered slight injuries and others feel bad effects from the climate.

These little untoward incidents have so far only served to bring out all the more plainly New Zealand's wonderful strength, and Saturday furnished a case in point.

The extent to which illness bothered them would not seem serious from the way the men played and despite the absence of two of their most brilliant exponents of the game they gave a display in dash certainly quite equal to their usual high standard.

Few teams could afford to dispense with the services of men like Hunter and Smith, who always take such a prominent part in the combined work of the backs.

LYTTELTON TIMES

The success of the tour of New Zealand footballers has had its inevitable result, and the games are engaging now the attention of the greatest stylists of the public press.

By this time probably Mr Gilbert Chesterton, Mr Masterman, Mr Street and Mr A.B. Walker are detailed by their respective journals to 'do' the matches. One inspired genius, whose effusions reached Christchurch yesterday, compares the New Zealanders to seven different beasts or birds in as many lines.

'They butt like goats and charge like bulls,' he says. 'They leap up at the ball like trout at a fly. They fling themselves down on it like a cat on a mouse. They swerve like swallows and zig-zag like snipe. A zebra is running like a Devon stag before the hounds.'

The same picturesque pen has been gracious enough to explain to the unenlightened what a 'scrummage' is in rugby football:

'It is a living rat-trap writhing round a dead rat. Now it is a beehive, now a battered bowler, now a brand new bustle, now a squashed Gibus.

'It is a giant crab trying to walk forty thousand ways at the same time. It is a mariner's compass with all its points fighting for the needle. It is a wheel whose spokes are wrestling for the hub.

'It is a human whale eternally spewing out a dirty little egg-shaped leather Jonah.'

After stuff of that kind, intended seriously, it is a relief to turn to the kindly efforts of the humorists. One cartoonist depicts the New Zealand fullback wrapped in rugs and taking hot coffee, while the game rages under the opposing side's goalposts.

The fullback's chief grievance, we are told, is that he has to walk from one end of the field to the other at halftime.

P.A. VAILE, THE DAILY NEWS

There is something much more important involved in the New Zealanders' string of victories than the question of superiority on the football field. Of all games that are played, there is none which calls so emphatically for all those qualities that go to make the ideal Briton as does rugby football.

The successful rugby player must be fast, strong, unselfish,

GEORGE GILLETT

Canterbury — fullback
28, 6ft, 12st 8lb

Born in Leeston but educated in Hamilton, Gillett played for Thames and Auckland before leaving for Kalgoorlie where it was reported that he represented Western Australia at Australian Rules. He returned to New Zealand in 1905 and played for the Merivale club in Christchurch, winning selection for both the South Island and New Zealand before representing Canterbury. Gillett's tour with the Originals was very successful. He played in 25 of the games, mostly at fullback but also as a wing-forward and once in the back row.

GEORGE DIXON'S DIARIES

From the point of view of our own performances, this was the most unsatisfactory game we had played.

Numerous changes in the team, and particularly the loss of Roberts, affected the combination a good deal. But apart from that there was much faulty, ill-timed and ill-directed passing.

Stead, at half, although playing soundly, did not get the ball away with the smartness and accuracy of Roberts and Mynott, only just recovered from an attack of influenza, showed scarcely his own dashing self.

Neither was Harper a conspicuous success at centre. He received too many of his passes standing, and rarely ran close enough up to his men before transferring to the wing threequarter. Several tries were missed in this way.

The narrowness of the ground was a disturbing feature.

We were unlucky to lose Deans very early in the first spell. He sprained his hip and had to go to fullback, Gillett taking his place at five-eighth, and playing a sound game.

Tyler also received a kick during the first few minutes, which rendered him of little use during the remainder of the game.

The Somerset forwards played a hard, bustling game and it took our pack, weakened as it was by Tyler's injury, all its time to hold them.

New Zealand v Somerset.

THE ALL BLACKS do battle with Somerset at Taunton.

resolute, resourceful, courageous, good-humoured, and able to take his punishment like a man.

There are other games that call for greater physical effort and which, perhaps, cause the individual greater mental strain, but the national game of England ought to be rugby football, for it is the highest test of manhood of any game I know.

If that point is conceded it follows that we must regard these contests which are taking place between New Zealand's doughty sons and the chosen of England and her counties with more gravity than we would if the issue were merely a question of superiority at a game.

The importance of these contests lies in the fact, fully realised by few, that the manhood of the Englishman is now being 'tried out' and it remains to be seen if the parent stock is as good as the vigorous young sapling.

No man who has studied men could fail to be struck by the contrast between the teams which contested the New Zealand v Middlesex match. The Antipodeans, although clad in sombre black, looked much bigger, stronger men. They carried themselves with an air of vitality that was lacking in their opponents.

They had the true athlete's walk, shoulders above hips, and the easy, confident bearing that a life of change, and athletics, and open-air freedom gives. It was apparent to a very superficial observer that if brawn and bone went for anything they were the winners.

This was made more manifest directly play began, and it was soon plainly apparent that in strength, speed, resource, originality, individual brilliancy, and in combination the men of the silver fern leaf were superior to their adversaries.

This may sound vainglorious and were I speaking of nothing more serious than a game of football, it would be so, although it is no more than many critics have already said.

We are concerned to know why it is that the New Zealander is able to make such a poor show of our best men. There are many reasons, and I must try to give some of them in their order of importance:

1. The New Zealander lives a more natural life than the Englishman, spends much more of it in the open air and is therefore stronger.

2. The men of the Antipodean team almost certainly have much more outdoor physical exertion than do those they are called on to meet in this country.

3. They are full of originality and resource, and do what occurs to them on the spur of the moment, so that it is hard to anticipate their movements. They are therefore far more 'tricky' than their opponents. This is shown in their scrum work, their dodging and in other important points.

4. They are full of overflowing vitality and virility — an abounding mental and physical force — which gives the team a moral which it is delightful to see in these days when enthusiasm and virility are negligible quantities.

A number of the New Zealand team have no doubt had their muscles toned up by plenty of hard outdoor work, and their lungs at the same time invigorated by breathing air second to none in the world, for down there the gentleman sometimes 'turns to' and 'breaks in' the forest, because he has to; and oftentimes he does other hard work which here is left to paid servants.

That, in short, is why New Zealand is beating England. That is why the men of the colonies will beat her more and more as years go on, unless she wakes up to the fact than men, and women, and children are of more importance than partridges and pheasants and grouse and gives them the chance that every Maorilander has, of getting their fair share of fresh air and 'the smell of earth'.

GAME 12 — WEDNESDAY 25 OCTOBER 1905 — at Rectory Ground, Devonport

NEW ZEALAND
DEVONPORT ALBION

21
3

FOR NEW ZEALAND
Tries by Thomson 2, Roberts, Nicholson, Gallaher; conversions by Gillett 2, Cunningham.

NEW ZEALAND
Gillett, Thomson, Stead, Hunter, Smith, Mynott, Roberts, Gallaher (captain), Johnston, Seeling, O'Sullivan, Cunningham, Nicholson, Tyler, Glasgow.

FOR DEVONPORT ALBION
Penalty goal by Spiers.

DEVONPORT ALBION
F. Lillicrap, C. Hosking, S. Irvin, A. Moir, W. Bateman, W. Dean, R. Jago, W. Spiers, F. Cummings, S.G. Williams, W. Mills, C. Edwards, H. Harris, W. Rooks, A.C. Campbell.

Weather: Sunny, ground firm
Referee: F.W. Nicholls (Leicester)
Crowd: 19,000

KICK OFF
Roberts worked the blindside from a scrum, Thomson scoring. Gillett converted: 5-0.

HALFTIME
New Zealand 5, Devonport Albion 0

Roberts launched an attack and Stead put Thomson in again. Gillett missed: 8-0.
Roberts scored a superb individual try from a scrum. Gillett converted: 13-0.
Nicholson scored as the forwards surged through a lineout. Gillett missed: 16-0.
Gallaher scored after a spectacular 60-metre rush. Cunningham converted: 21-0.
Spiers kicked a penalty goal for Devonport Albion.

FULLTIME
New Zealand 21, Devonport Albion 3

FROM THE SIDELINES

PLYMOUTH HERALD

WHAT WEATHER! What a crowd! What excitement! It was indeed an historic occasion and right royally did the district rise to it. The vast crowd — what was it, 20,000 — exercised wonderful patience, though they were helped in this regard by the band of the 2nd Devon Regiment, whose selections were most appropriate.

There have been big Rectory crowds before, but this surely whacked all records. We shall anxiously await the official return. Meantime, where's that fellow who said rugby was decadent in the West?

The first minute contained as much excitement as many a full game.

Hurricane football it might be safely described as.

What a pace they went! It was the most remarkable cyclone that ever swept the Rectory ground.

The first try was an eye-opener. Thomson slipped through like an eel and made the defence look absolutely rotten. His swerving was phenomenal, and the pace of the whole move bewildered the locals. Pace!

The New Zealand forwards were a bit too good for Albion in the tight packs, and they were a hotter lot in the loose rushes in one sense, yet Albion were holding them with fine determination and grit.

The excitement grew every second. This was the real article, rugby, thrilling, ever-moving, plucky, strenuous, English football. And the fine show Albion were making made everybody glad.

The tackling was something to revel in; clean, wholehearted, devoid of vice, and as sure as anything human can be.

When the interval came and the tally showed only five points against the Rectorians, there was an infection of happiness all round the enclosure.

Down hill next half; what about the record! New Zealand re-started with splendid verve, and quickly showed they meant business.

Their outsides put in one amazing round of passing, in which the ball simply flew from hand to hand, and it appeared as if a miracle only could save the position.

The miracle was the solidity and cohesion of the home defence. Albion were certainly 'doing us proud'.

What happened then? It was a frequent query all round the enclosure, and those who saw the game will appreciate its meaning.

The second try was the outcome of lightning passing wedded to phenomenal pace, the visitors leaving the home defenders standing.

The third score was also a flash like its fellows, but now the Colonials were rushing Albion badly. They were putting in every ounce, and there could be no mistaking their earnestness.

What tackling there was, to be sure. Such a display has certainly never been seen here before. Perhaps it may not again.

On today's form Albion would whack the best team Wales have ever sent this way, and Albion were badly beaten at that.

We had a comic interlude — the referee was bowled over!

— and then came a dash on the left, which resulted indirectly in a score, and must have taught Albion a lesson. This was that time is precious, even to a tenth of a second.

The ball went to touch but before half the locals were up, it had been flung out, taken, and a try notched.

As the sheriff's officer in The Lady Slavey is wont to observe, 'You've got to be smart nowadays!'

In a very true sense this is so of teams playing these Colonials.

Gallaher's try was a gem. It was a tearing rush for about fifty yards with clockwork-like passing all the way. The final dash was brilliant in the extreme. Pace told towards the finish.

Albion made a great fight, and until the third try they were almost as good a side as the visitors in a general way, but then the score seemed to appal them, and thereafter they were a confessedly beaten side.

◆ ❖ ◆

The following items appeared on the Albion programme this afternoon:

The enthusiasm engendered by the visit of New Zealand has exceeded our highest anticipations. The demands for tickets have been coming in for a month past, and at the time of going to press there did not appear any cessation.

The interest has not only been on the spectators' side but has spread to the team, and every man playing today has spared neither time nor opportunity to get fit, and is eager to be included in the side.

Hence the prospect of a keen game is bright and rosy. Undoubtedly the (Devon) county side would like to have another match with the 'Redoubtables' as Devon had certainly caught a Tartar and suffered from lack of training.

It is a pity that the burly figure of Cooms is not in the side. Weight of his calibre would be most welcome and it was a great disappointment when he had positively to refuse.

Both teams will have numbers attached to the backs of the jerseys agreeing with their names inserted on this programme. For purpose of identification this will help considerably in many future discussions on the play.

GEORGE DIXON'S DIARIES

Very social evening, but dragged a good deal — all of us are very tired of these functions but impossible to refuse good people of Newton Abbot.

◆

Lots of callers including a gentleman who has come all the way from Paris in order to try and fix up match in their city — sorry couldn't give him any definite answer. Offers £80 guarantee, half gross gate. Suggest 2 January or failing that 6 January — extraordinary determined to get us at any cost.

After match two teams dined together at Royal Hotel. Usual speeches — and left for Newton Abbot 8 p.m. train. On arrival were met by big crowd and brass band, who as on previous occasion marched us up to hotel.

THE AUTOGRAPHS of the Originals, virtually all of them legible.

NEW ZEALAND TIMES' UK CORRESPONDENT

OVER 20,000 PERSONS saw the Devonport Albion game; to be quite exact, the ground, which was crowded to its utmost capacity, held 19,351 persons, while another small handful of 5000 had a birds-eye view of this match from a hill overlooking the field. There was a large sprinkling of soldiers and sailors in the crowd, and one stand was given up to the convalescents from the military hospitals.

The 'gate' is stated to exceed £637. The game was generally regarded as a more searching test of the merits of the visitors than any of the eleven which had previously been decided.

Moreover, the New Zealanders were particularly keen to beat the champion South-Western club, so that the interest was keen all round; the home club suffered its first defeat on its own ground for 18 months.

J.H. SMITH, ATHLETIC NEWS

THE PHENOMENAL SUCCESS of the New Zealand team now touring in this country has created a widespread interest in Northern Union circles, and it is much regretted that so few of their matches are to be played within reasonable distance of the area covered by the professional body, because the differences in rules played by the latter and the English Union is not sufficient to prevent any commendable feature in the style of play affected by our visitors being absorbed by the Northern Unionists.

It is, of course, a debatable point how far the huge scores which have been compiled have been influenced by the superior excellence of the men, and how much is due to their methods.

At first, the success was almost wholly attributed to the latter, but opinion has now veered round in the other direction and a lot of 'rot' has been written about the degeneracy of the race, etc.

Basing an opinion upon the published views of those I consider best capable of judging, it appears to me that the Colonials are a clever combination of trained athletes who apply brains to their tactics and who are not slaves to strict orthodoxy.

BILLY WALLACE'S RECOLLECTIONS

That evening we were entertained to a smoke concert. As we entered the hall we saw it was beautifully decorated with flags and with banners bearing the message 'Welcome back to our New Zealand team'.

There was a fine musical programme by local artists who were assisted by Billy Glenn and Bubs Tyler. Billy sang 'The Old Brigade' but Tyler roused the audience with 'Ain't that a Shame!' and in response to a vociferous encore he gave them 'Just Because She Made Them Goo-Goo Eyes'.

MAJOR PHILIP TREVOR ('DUX'), THE SPORTSMAN

Rugby union football certainly owes the New Zealanders a debt of gratitude.

Our visitors have given the game an advertisement which those who control it in England could never have afforded to purchase, even if they had been inclined to do so.

With great interest, I read all or most of what is written in a variety of newspapers on the inexhaustible topic of how to beat this all-conquering team.

But there is a most unfortunate feature about the whole business. None of our teams seems to be profiting much from the wealth of good advice which we are kind enough to give them.

So some of us are now adopting another tone. We conveniently forsake the present and take refuge in retrospect and prophecy.

We explain with plausible skill, whenever the win is one of 40 points, that it ought only to have been 20.

Also we say: 'Ha, ha! A time will come. Wait till they get to Wales.'

As that time is the furthest off that we can choose we show our good sense in choosing it.

To few does it occur to say: 'The New Zealanders are infinitely better players than their opponents, and that fact has probably something to do with their victories.'

Yet in mere academic discussion we should admit certain contentions which we refuse to accept directly the subject has a New Zealand label attached to it.

If 'A' is bigger, stronger, faster and fitter than 'B'; if he picks up the ball twice as often and catches it ten times as often, we should be inclined to call him a better player than 'B'.

And fifteen 'As' we should rather expect to beat fifteen 'Bs' without very much trouble.

It is perhaps a shade degrading to have to admit the extreme simplicity of a little matter which we have magnified into a problem.

E.J. VIVYAN, DAILY MIRROR

There was no doubt which was the better team. The Albion, good team that they are, were outclassed by their brothers from across the sea. The question asked by all sportsmen is, 'Why do they beat us?' In the first place, they are quite three yards faster per man, and they are all certainly splendid athletes.

Every man is trained to the hour and knows exactly what to do at the right moment and his exact place. In the first half, they seemed to be upset by the determined tackling of the Albion, and great praise is due to them for making such a splendid fight.

But when they started the second half there was no holding the 'All Blacks'. The forwards and outside men act together splendidly, and when they started passing, everyone was a threequarter, their speed and tactics carrying all before them.

Hunter is certainly their star artist, but Stead and Smith are also very clear. Every man is a trier, and this is the cause of their success.

FRED NEWTON

Canterbury — lock
23, 6ft, 15st

The heaviest man on tour, Newton, from the Linwood club in Christchurch, picked up the affectionate nickname of Fatty from his teammates. He travelled to Australia in 1905 with the New Zealand team but was not considered a candidate for the Originals main starting fifteen, being regarded as an understudy to Bill Cunningham. Newton missed the first eight matches due to injury but recovered to play in 16, including the tests against England, Wales and France.

BILLY WALLACE'S RECOLLECTIONS

We were invited out to different parties. The crowd with which I went consisted of Dave Gallaher, Freddy Roberts, George Nicholson, Frank Glasgow and George Tyler. Our host was a Mr Bond, who lived about four miles from Newton Abbot and he drove in for us with a wagonette. It was a fairly hefty load for a wagonette and the springs creaked under the weight.

No sooner were we inside his gates than he went across to a haystack, out of which he pulled a revolver and ammunition. He then invited us to throw pennies up in the air. We didn't have too many but we threw up all we could muster and he hit them every time. He was a crack revolver shot, quite the best I have ever

seen. The fun was greater when he invited us to have a try and a sorry mess we made of the shooting.

We suggested having a shot at some pheasants, but he put the acid on that and told us about some of the shooting parties organised by the gentry. He may have been pulling our legs, but he told us that the men had to hide behind the hedges and throw pheasants into the air when the shooting party came stalking along.

From the haystack we adjourned to the cellar, into which we descended by means of a rather rickety ladder. Here we found about thirty barrels of cider and he would have us taste a sample from each. The last one he came to was covered with dust

and cobwebs and was evidently very much older than the others and, in honour of the occasion, he broached that one too. It had plenty of kick in it and coming on top of the other samples it began to make the room go round. It was great fun trying to get up that ladder into fresh air again, but we managed it at last after a fair bit of assistance.

When we got out into the open air we could scarcely see our way, as the cider seemed to affect our eyes.

Somehow or other we stumbled up the steps into the house and took our seats at the table, but we had to guess where the plate of soup was and then try to steer a direct course from the plate to the mouth!

GAME 13 — SATURDAY 28 OCTOBER 1905 — at Welford Road, Leicester

NEW ZEALAND
MIDLAND COUNTIES

21
5

FOR NEW ZEALAND
Tries by Hunter, Mynott, Roberts, Smith, Stead; 3 conversions by Cunningham.

NEW ZEALAND
Gillett, McGregor, Stead, Hunter, Smith, Mynott, Roberts, Gallaher (captain), Johnston, Seeling, O'Sullivan, Cunningham, Newton, Tyler, Glenn.

FOR MIDLAND COUNTIES
Try by Russell; conversion by Cooper.

MIDLAND COUNTIES
G.H. Rose (Stratford-on-Avon), A.E. Hind (Leicester), A.G. Neilson (Nottingham), J.G. Cooper (Moseley), J.H. Miles (Northampton), J. Braithwaite (Leicester), L. Kirk (Nottingham), V.H. Cartwright (captain, Nottingham), S. Matthews (Leicester), R.F. Russell (Leicester), H.P. Atkins (Leicester), D. Atkins (Leicester), A. Goodrich (Leicester), C.H. Shaw (Moseley), W.L. Oldham (Coventry).

Weather: Fine, ground soft
Referee: Gil Evans (Birmingham)
Crowd: 19,000

KICK OFF
Hunter and Stead combined to put Smith over, Cunningham converting: 5-0.
Robert passed to Hunter from a scrum and he scored. Cunningham converted: 10-0.
Stead charged down the fullback's kick and secured a try. Gillett missed.

HALFTIME
New Zealand 13, Midland Counties 0

Gillett mishandled near his posts, allowing Russell to score. Cooper converted: 13-5.
Roberts doubled round behind Mynott to score. Cunningham missed: 16-5.
Roberts and Mynott combined again, Mynott scoring. Cunningham converted.

FULLTIME
New Zealand 21, Midland Counties 5

FROM THE SIDELINES

DAILY EXPRESS

UNTIL YOU ARE ONE OF A CROWD of 20,000 watching the hot encounter of the New Zealanders with one of our best sides, you do not quite realise why the Colonials have given rugger a new lease of vigorous life.

The dash, vim and go they put into their play have an inspiring effect upon their opponents, with the result that the game is faster, more robust, far more interesting and infinitely more thrilling than 'every-day' English rugby of the past six or seven years has been.

Every one of the near-20,000 persons that thronged the Leicester enclosure on Saturday left the field delighted with what he or she had seen.

The match was a strenuous struggle throughout and in the second half at least, though having rather the worse of the game from the territorial point of view, the Midlands fairly held their own, and with a little luck might have lost by a smaller margin of points than any side the Colonials have as yet encountered.

McGregor, who has been called 'the greatest trygetter in the world' played for the first time on the tour. He did not belie his reputation as a wing threequarter, though he was obviously short of practice.

DAILY MAIL

ALL ROADS, ALL RAILWAY LINES seemed to lead to Leicester where the 'All Blacks' met a team chosen from the Midlands.

The visitors may have felt the effects of the hard game on the hard ground at Devonport, for they scarcely tripped on the field with their usual jauntiness.

An epidemic of boils afflicting many of the team is attributed to the change of climate and diet.

Although the New Zealanders were not seen at their best, the game was an intensely exciting one. One well-known Association international said, 'If all rugby matches generally were more like this sort of thing, I should go to few soccer games.'

Gallaher's opinion of Braithwaite and Braithwaite's of Gallaher, if it could be obtained, ought to be worth reading.

The New Zealand captain came off the field looking as if he had gone through a severe ordeal. Braithwaite, whose nose was barked and his features suffused with a rosy flush, seemed as though he had been dragged through a pond feet foremost.

Braithwaite is the sturdy little halfback pet of all the Midlands. For once in a way Gallaher, whose mission in life is to spoil the tactics of such men as Braithwaite, scarcely seemed to know what to do with the artful dodger, who darted from one side of the scrum to the other with lightning rapidity.

This battle between the New Zealand wing forward and the Midland half was worth going many miles to see. It was a case of cat and mouse.

On the other side of the scrum there was a different tale to tell. This may have been due to the fact that the Englishmen had no Gallaher to pounce on Roberts as Gallaher pounced on Braithwaite.

In the Devonport Albion match one reason given for the defeat was that the Blacks were three yards faster in one hundred than the local men.

This could hardly be said at Leicester.

The New Zealanders have no one who can show a clean pair of heels to Hind, the old Cambridge 100 yards Blue. He was expected to do something brilliant.

He rose to the occasion. Those who knew McGregor's marvellous burst of speed settled themselves in their seats when they saw him in full career, ball under arm, with no one between him and a try but Hind, racing along a yard or so behind, both going like the wind.

Like a flash from a gun Hind, with a supreme effort, flung himself full speed at McGregor's figure, missed his head and shoulders and just caught his last foot and brought him safely to earth.

Hunter did not shine so brilliantly as usual, Mynott making most of the cuts. Smith filled the eye of the crowd, not only for speed, but for extreme cleverness and evasion.

Gillett seemed a trifle nervous, and made one bad mistake, through

THE ALL BLACKS have the Midland Counties defence at full stretch at Leicester.

which the Midlands scored, but he did some very fine work.

Once he had hard luck in not having a try added to his name. He charged one of Hind's kicks down. The ball rebounding, he dashed on, picked it up and threaded his way over the line.

The referee evidently thought that the scorer was some other player and whistled off-side, to everyone's astonishment.

CUNNINGHAM leads the All Blacks onto the Welford Road ground.

NEW ZEALAND TIMES' UK CORRESPONDENT

Undoubtedly the hardest match of the tour so far was that played at Leicester on Saturday when the New Zealanders encountered the pick of the clubs under the wing of the Midland Counties union under the eyes of fully 20,000 enthusiasts.

Had the ground been half as big again, it would have been equally well filled. As it was, the 'gate' was worth over £700, whereas the 'gate' at the soccer match, Leicester Posse versus Glossop, which would have been the centre of attraction under ordinary circumstances, yielded barely £80.

When the New Zealanders visited Leicester in September, I had occasion to comment on the unsportsmanlike attitude of the crowd towards the visiting team. I came away with the idea that the local followers of football were a poor lot of sportsmen, but I find it necessary to reverse that opinion.

Last Saturday the spectators were all that a visiting side could desire. They applauded unstintedly every piece of smart play, and only once during the match did I hear the admonition, 'Play the game' specifically addressed to the wearers of the black.

It was no 'drawing room game' but a hard, fast fight from beginning to end and though the New Zealanders won easily enough by reason of the individual superiority of their back division there were many occasions when they were hard-pressed to keep their line intact.

Visitors to Leicester — they were many for 'specials' were run from all parts in order to enable people to see the New Zealanders — were encountered on arrival by quite an army of small boys vending with raucous yells . . . 'Portraits of the Noo Zealan' team, a penny!'

They were of the picture postcard variety, and as works of art could not be highly commended. Those who knew the members of the team individually could no doubt identify the men as depicted, but to those who had to consult the names printed below, identification was rendered impossible through printers' errors.

'Cassey', of course, only lightly conceals Casey, and 'Gallaghar' is easily spotted as Gallaher, but who on earth, you will ask, is 'Simmetts'? None other than our old friend George Smith!

After the match the boys added to their stock of penny souvenirs of the New Zealanders' visit a gruesome specimen of printer's art, a black-edged card, surmounted by a vehicle which might be a post van, but which was meant to represent a hearse. Below was printed:

IN DOLEFUL MEMORY
OF
MIDLAND COUNTIES
FOOTBALL CLUB

and neath this the following fearsome doggerel:

Although with smiles they enter the field
Determined that they would not yield,
But, alas, their fate was sealed
For today.
Still, next time a better show,
They may make for all we know,
If their men will show more go,
Let us pray.

◆ ❖ ◆

All the members of the team who are resting on account of injured limbs, boils and other mishaps, are almost right again.

Mackrell, who has been on the sick list with influenza since the start of the tour, has resumed practice and hopes to be fit to play soon. He attributes his illness to the change of climate.

◆ ❖ ◆

The complimentary dinner given to the New Zealanders by the High Commissioner and a few other New Zealand friends, following their arrival in London from Leicester, was quite a success.

Apart from the members of the team there were very few guests, as the manager was averse to the idea of a big public banquet, but the smallness of the company made for sociability and informality, and the speeches were as brief as they were cordial and appropriate in sentiment.

MAJOR PHILIP TREVOR ('DUX'), THE SPORTSMAN

The success of the New Zealanders has caused rugby football to break out in print in weird and unexpected places.

A blameless lady, who had only read the contents bill of her favourite newspaper, asked me if I had seen the lately landed missionaries; and, when she saw that I was in difficulties about the question, she quoted the headline that had attracted her . . .

BILLY WALLACE'S RECOLLECTIONS

There is one incident in connection with the visit to Leicester and it concerns a joke that misfired. Bob Deans had slipped down to the bathroom one morning and left his door open. On the dressing table was a valuable gold watch and chain and a sovereign case belonging to him, and as Billy Stead passed he thought he would play a joke and expected Bob would raise a hue and cry.

But not a word was said. After keeping it quiet for a few days, Billy said to him, 'Didn't you lose something at Leicester, Bob?'

'Yes I did,' he replied. 'I lost my watch and chain and sovereign case.'

'Here it is, Bob,' said Billy. 'We were playing a joke on you. Why didn't you complain before?'

'Well,' said Bob, 'when I looked at the two housemaids I could see by their faces that they were honest girls and I knew no member of the team would take it so I just thought I would shut up and say nothing about it.'

Perhaps this shows the generous nature of the great-hearted Bob and why we all loved him so much.

'Triumphant career of the New Zealanders — Great Revival.'

I explained, and then finding that it was she herself who had been lately landed, she anathematised football and all its ways, and was indignantly astounded that such a paper as . . . I dare not give its name . . . should have spoken admiringly of so brutal a pastime.

Yet are the New Zealanders rather healthy missionaries, and they have preached their doctrines excellently well without words.

Their lessons are simplicity itself, and it is the too curious amongst us who have discovered deep and abstruse meanings.

We hardly yet lay sufficient stress on physical advantages. Strength, pace and (up to a point) condition, accuracy of fielding and catching, and dash, are of course acquitted. How these qualities have been acquired by our visitors it is not necessary to discuss . . . but on the subject of the result we are all agreed.

It seems, therefore, that we should be more profitably employed in gauging the true values of these admitted advantages than in drawing over-learned deductions from tactical formations. The wingers, the five-eighths and the two front men in the scrummage may be instances of clever disposition, but they depend for success mainly on the capacity of the men who fill these posts.

FRANK GLASGOW

Taranaki — loose forward
25, 5ft 10in, 13st 3lb

A bank employee who was transferred to Taranaki from where he won selection for the Originals, Glasgow was educated at Wellington College and played for the city's Athletic club. A clever and busy loose forward as well as a competent hooker, he was a major contributor to the tour, appearing in 27 of the 35 matches, including the five internationals. With eight tries, five conversions and a penalty goal, he was the leading point-scoring forward.

BRONCO SEELING secures lineout possession for New Zealand against Midland Counties.

GAME 14 — WEDNESDAY 1 NOVEMBER 1905 — at Athletic Ground, London

NEW ZEALAND   11
SURREY   0

FOR NEW ZEALAND
Tries by Roberts, Johnston, McGregor;
conversion by Gillett.

NEW ZEALAND
Booth, Harper, Smith, Stead (captain),
McGregor, Mynott, Roberts, Gillett, Johnston,
Corbett, O'Sullivan, Newton, Nicholson,
Tyler, Casey.

SURREY
D.G. Schulte (London Scottish),
C.H. Grenfell (United Service), J.E. Raphael
(Old Merchant Taylors, captain), J.G. Birkett
(Harlequins), W.C. Wilson (Richmond),
C.F. Malkin (Civil Service), S.P. Start
(United Service), J.F. Shaw (United Service),
A.L. Picton (United Service), J.G. Bussell
(Harlequins), G. Fraser (Richmond), J. Ross
(London Scottish), C. Bourns (Old Merchant
Taylors), S.N. Crowther (Lennox),
F.C. Pheysey (Richmond).

Weather: Wet and windy, ground slippery
Referee: Billy Williams (England)
Crowd: 11,000

KICK OFF
Roberts scored a slick, solo try from a scrum. Gillett converted: 5-0.

HALFTIME
New Zealand 5, Surrey 0

When the Surrey fullback lost the ball Johnstone fell on it for a try. Gillett missed: 8-0.
Mynott and Smith cleverly contrived to put McGregor over for a try. Gillett missed.

FULLTIME
New Zealand 11, Surrey 0

FROM THE SIDELINES

J.A. BUTTERY, DAILY MAIL

IN FACE OF LOWERING CLOUDS which threatened every minute to burst — and which, in fact, did eventually drench the great majority of the spectators — over 10,000 people, many of them ladies, made their way from various parts of the metropolis to see the 'All Blacks' that everybody is talking about.

They expected to see some wonderful football but they had reckoned without one factor, the referee. This gentleman, a Londoner and a member of the Rugby Union committee, was evidently under the impression that everybody had come to hear him perform on the whistle, and as he was in charge of the stage, so to speak, he was enabled to indulge his fancy to his heart's content.

The finest artists are said to shut their eyes when whistling their hardest, and judged on that hypothesis, the referee must have had his eyes closed on and off for the greater part of the game.

The fantastia commenced in the first minute and continued, with brief intervals for respiration, throughout the game.

As one of the rules of rugby is that you may not kick or handle the ball while the whistle is blowing, it is obvious that there was very little actual football. Directly someone got the ball and there was a prospect of a bit of play worth seeing the referee would recommence his fascinating solo.

A young Scottish lady, whose first football match this was, and evidently with literary recollections of the efficacy of the pibroch in clan warfare, asked her escort, after one particularly dangerous 'All Black' movement had been stopped at the referee's musical behest, 'Why aren't the New Zealanders allowed to have a man to whistle for them, too?'

The rain came down in torrents, and between the bars of the referee's interminable selection, the players flipped and flopped about the slippery ground like seals on an ice-floe.

A confused, entangled mass of legs and arms and black and red and white but there was no football.

'When are they going to begin?' inquired a soccer enthusiast who had come many miles because a rugby friend had assured him that he would see something in the way of football he would remember all his life.

It was then closely approaching halftime. Twenty-five minutes from the start, however, the referee showed signs of fatigue, whereupon the 'All Blacks', quickly seizing their opportunity and the ball, crossed the Surrey line and kicked a goal.

Several explanations were advanced for the referee's extraordinary lapse, but the two most generally accepted were that he had either dropped his whistle or that the pea in it had stuck.

Unabashed by his temporary eclipse, however, he blew harder than ever, and for the remainder of the first half football was again out of the question.

During the interval, the referee was the recipient of many congratulations from musical friends on his magnificently sustained effort, though fears were expressed that the severe exertions he had undergone would tell on him in the second half.

And this proved to be only too true. His whistle failed him on at least two other occasions. The line was crossed twice more.

To their credit be it said, the crowd had by this time realised the mistake they had made in supposing that the affair would be an athletic display.

Some, stung to emulation, whistled obligatoes to the shrill music that arose from the middle of the field. Others, with their sodden coats over their ears, and their dripping umbrellas in front of their faces, beat time to the pulsating notes that indicated the whereabouts of the referee's triumphant march.

'What an awful day for an open-air concert!' shivered a young lady in the grandstand, as she gathered up her skirts to depart.

As for the game, there was no game. It was an exposition of the power of music to tame even the New Zealand rugby footballer.

Though unnoticed by the crowd, there were some highly interesting interludes to some of the referee's most brilliant flights.

BILLY WALLACE'S RECOLLECTIONS

Our manager George Dixon had selected West Ealing as it was a quiet place some distance out of London. We trained in the morning but in the afternoon the team seemed to vanish mysteriously into London. West Ealing was much too quiet for us and we were making so many friends who wanted us to go out with them.

After an enjoyable evening with relatives I caught the last train, which left somewhere about midnight to Shepherd's Bush and I was joined at various places by several other members of the team who had also left their homecoming to the last train.

When we got to Shepherd's Bush we found the last tram had gone and there was a walk of several miles ahead of us.

Needless to say we were too tired to take this on and the first thing we did was raid the pie-cart outside the station. There were no pies left, but plenty of hard-boiled eggs and hot potatoes.

Then we set out to find diggings for the night. We knew we would be in for it in the morning, but that did not spoil our sleep. We rose early and caught the first tram out, getting there in time for breakfast. One of the 'stop-outs' had a brainy idea to escape being on the mat. He had arranged with his teammate to put out his boots for him and he hopped upstairs quickly, ruffled his bed as if he had had a restless night and came downstairs in his sweater with a broad smile on his face. 'My word! I had a great sleep last night!'

But it didn't go down. Our manager had done the rounds and made a note of the missing ones and he was called up-stairs with the rest of us to explain. His bluff didn't come off, for the manager said to him, 'On your word of honour as a man, is that true?'

'Well, if you put it that way,' he replied, 'then I must plead guilty with the others.' I had to explain that I had been out with relatives, but George gave me a queer little smile as he said: 'I'm getting a bit suspicious of this relatives stunt.'

The 'All Black' captain, who evidently has no ear for music, desired enlightenment on more than one, to him, discordant passage. He is still pondering over the answers.

At the end of these games there is usually a rush for the jersey of the man who has scored, so that it may be kept as a trophy. Yesterday, there was a wild scramble for the referee's whistle.

BILLY WALLACE and Fred Roberts feature on a postcard.

NEW ZEALAND TIMES' UK CORRESPONDENT

THE DAY OF THE SURREY MATCH will be remembered in the New Zealanders' football diaries as their 'Black Wednesday'.

It is true that they added a thirteenth victory to their unbeaten record, but the game was a poor affair, played under peculiarly depressing conditions.

The weather and the referee combined to rob the match of most of its interest. Rain fell in torrents from a leaden sky, soaking the ground and greasing the ball as effectively as a coating of Vaseline.

It gave the ten or twelve thousand spectators a rare drenching and it sadly marred the fast, open game for which the 'All Blacks' are famous.

But even more of a damper upon their play was the whisteman, Mr W. Williams, a Welsh member of the Rugby Union Committee.

One might almost have imagined he was tooting on his whistle to keep himself warm, so constant a performer was he. In the first spell he awarded fourteen free kicks, thirteen of these against the Blacks.

As for the scrums ordered for alleged breaches of the knock-on and throw-forward rules, they were innumerable. No doubt the referee did what he thought was right and fair, but some of his decisions were decidedly open to question.

The effect upon the New Zealanders was most dispiriting, and although they left the field victors they were as downcast as though the game had ended in an ignominious defeat.

They could do nothing right, in the referee's eyes. Time after time they were pulled up by the whistle without the remotest notion of what went wrong.

At the interval Stead, who was acting as captain in the absence of Gallaher, went to the referee and asked him if he would mind pointing out what features of the New Zealanders' play he took objection to. But the referee curtly declined to talk, and the Colonials could get no satisfaction.

When the ball came quickly out of the scrum the referee seemed to take it for granted that hands instead of feet had helped it through.

The wing forward was penalised time and again for alleged infringements, which no one but the referee could understand.

One of the team told me afterwards that the referee had accused them of playing 'a dirty game' and had said that he was determined to put a stop to it.

Anything better calculated to take the heart out of a team who felt themselves to be wholly innocent of the charge can hardly be imagined.

They set their teeth and played on grimly to the bitter end. But it was a melancholy experience.

The spectators had a bad time of it, too. The great reputation which the New Zealanders have made in England was sufficient to draw as large a crowd as usually attends an international match, and this, too, on a midweek day in weather of the vilest description.

Only a fraction of the crowd could benefit by the shelter of the covered stands; the rest had to sit on damp seats in the open, or stand in the slush at either end of the ground while the rain fell pitilessly upon them throughout.

The match began late which meant that, in the last ten or fifteen minutes, the teams played in semi-darkness.

Towards the end the crowd broke through the ropes and swarmed up to the touchlines, forming a solid wall along Surrey's goalline, just at the time when the New Zealanders were fighting hard to get across.

Had a Colonial forced his way through the Surrey defence in the last few minutes he would have found it impossible to score a try. The wall of spectators would have stopped a score. Strangely, the referee took no notice of the crowd's encroachment.

Some of the critics are saying that Surrey gave the New Zealanders the hardest game they have had so far. This, however, is not the opinion of the team themselves who agree that their strongest opponents so far have been Devonport Albion.

The superiority of the All Blacks was greater than the score indicates. Although only three tries were registered, they crossed the Surrey line on five or six other occasions.

It is to be noted that in this match the New Zealanders were without the services of a number of their 'star' performers, including Wallace, Hunter, Gallaher and Cunningham.

ATHLETIC NEWS

THE EXTRAORDINARY CONDUCT of the referee in last Wednesday's match against Surrey at Richmond has been the chief topic amongst the New Zealanders ever since.

They are as much at a loss as ever to understand the attitude of the gentleman with the whistle. They state that he accused them of playing various 'dirty tricks' of which they protest their innocence.

Seen after the match, the referee said he quickly came to the

BILLY WALLACE'S RECOLLECTIONS

None of us are likely to ever forget this match, not because of any particularly brilliant piece of play, but because of the grilling we got from the referee.

This gentleman was a member of the committee of the Rugby Football Union and he had apparently made up his mind to give it to us in the neck. He whistled from the start of the game to the finish. He must have allowed his mind to get carried away by many of the silly little rumours that went round about the 'tricks we carried up our sleeves'.

One would hardly credit that anyone outside a mental hospital would believe them, but they went around all the same.

For example, one was that we played with two balls and Cunningham was supposed to keep the other one under his jersey. When the ball was put in the scrum he heaved the extra one back to Freddy Roberts, who at once set off with it. It was never satisfactorily explained what he did with the first one!

As for football in this match there was none. If a scrum was ordered, a penalty against us was sure to follow, either for Dave Gallaher allegedly putting the ball in

unfairly or our hookers lifting it. It was impossible to do anything right.

I was a 'breather' and took three of my relatives along to see the match. They had never seen rugby before and so I had to do all the explaining. When the first scrum went down one of them exclaimed: 'Look at them, they're butting one another like billy goats!' The lineout was called and one of them said, 'They'll murder one another.' And when they saw the first tackle they thought rugby was a genuine killing game. I was very pleased when the game came to an end.

conclusion that the All Blacks 'were not playing the game' in the scrum. He is of the opinion that the two front row forwards, known as the hookers, were handling the ball out of the scrum, screened by their bent knees. This was the reason of the frequent penalty kicks he gave against the Colonials, which were so tedious.

The New Zealanders, in reply to this, not only deny the charge absolutely but declare it to be absurd, for the reason that a front ranker could not possibly hand the ball out, his inner arm having to be around his partner's neck in order to hold the pack together.

Many good judges, whose fairness and sense of honour is above all question, declare that the referee penalised the New Zealanders again and again without any real justification.

The most trifling infringements, moreover, elicited the inevitable whistle with the result that the game as a spectacle was completely spoiled. Some spectators, noting the frequency of the whistle, took the trouble to count the number of times it blew and the total for the match was over ninety.

During the fifteen minutes from the scoring of the first try to halftime the whistle blew thirty-three times! Could any game be popular under such conditions?

When the acting captain approached the referee at halftime and asked the nature of the infringements it is alleged that that official told him to mind his own business.

◆ DUNEDIN EVENING STAR

Mr S. WHITTA THORNTON, formerly of Nelson, who has just returned to Dunedin from a seven months trip to the Old Country, saw the New Zealanders play against Cornwall, Leicester and Middlesex. He lived with the New Zealanders at the Manchester Hotel, London.

He said that what struck him most about the team was the exceedingly pure amateur way in which they were conducting the whole tour. He instanced the case of the Middlesex match, when the New Zealanders walked two miles and travelled third class on the underground railway to the ground.

'No one,' added Mr Thornton, 'but workmen with their picks and shovels would think of travelling third class at home. They repeated the same performance after the match, when they were pretty well fagged out.

'The expenses are kept down to the lowest possible margin. No English team would dream of travelling third class on expenses. It is not as if the gate money at Home was not good. They seem simply to be making money for the New Zealand Rugby Union.'

The English crowds are very impartial in their praise for the colonials, said Mr Thornton. 'In fact, New Zealand is in very good odour at Home just now, more so than any other colony.'

BILLY STEAD

Southland — five-eighth
28, 5ft 8in, 10st 9lb

A second-generation stalwart of the Star club of Invercargill, Stead was one of the outstanding players of the era. He captained New Zealand in its first 'home soil' test, against Great Britain in 1904, and famously received a congratulatory telegram that was simply addressed 'Stead Wellington.' He was vice-captain of the Originals and with captain Dave Gallaher provided the strong leadership that greatly aided the team's phenomenal success. He was a sharp thinker, chief strategist and tactical mainstay, worshipped by all his teammates. He played a whopping 29 matches on tour. At the conclusion of the UK section Stead and Gallaher, at the request of a British publisher, collaborated on a book, The Complete Rugby Footballer, detailing the reasons for the All Blacks' success. It is reputed that Stead wrote a staggering 80,000 words in a week, meeting one of the toughest deadlines in history.

GAME 15 — SATURDAY 4 NOVEMBER 1905 — at Rectory Field, London

NEW ZEALAND
BLACKHEATH

32
0

FOR NEW ZEALAND
Tries by Wallace 3, McGregor 2, Glasgow, Stead; 4 conversions, penalty goal by Wallace.

NEW ZEALAND
Gillett, Wallace, Smith, Hunter, McGregor, Stead, Roberts, Gallaher (captain), Johnston, Seeling, O'Sullivan, Cunningham, Glasgow, Tyler, Casey.

BLACKHEATH
H. Lee, S.F. Cooper, H.J. Anderson, B. Maclear, W.H. Newton, J.C. Joughin, C.T. Robson, B.C. Hartley, B.A. Hill, C.J. Newbold, W.L. Rogers, W.T. Cave, C.G. Liddell, J.E.C. Partridge, W.S.D. Craven.

Weather: Cloudy, ground firm
Referee: Percy Coles (England)
Crowd: 15,000

KICK OFF
Wallace hauled in a perfect centring kick from Smith to score, and convert: 5-0.
Wallace landed a penalty goal: 8-0.
Hunter harried the fullback into error, setting up another Wallace try. Kick missed: 11-0.
Wallace completed his hat-trick from a scrum. Gillett missed: 14-0.
McGregor took Smith's pass to score from a scrum. Gillett missed.

HALFTIME
New Zealand 17, Blackheath 0

Hunter and Tyler combined to put Glasgow across. Wallace converted: 22-0.
Smith's incisive running created another try for McGregor. Wallace converted: 27-0.
Smith put Stead into a gap, he kicked ahead and won the race. Wallace converted.

FULLTIME
New Zealand 32, Blackheath 0

FROM THE SIDELINES

HAMISH STUART, ATHLETIC NEWS

IT WAS THE OLD, OLD STORY at Blackheath on Saturday, the story that has been so often told, since England fell into the bad habit of attempting to imitate, without being able to adopt, the methods of her competition. She began to fall before Wales through attempting to imitate Welsh methods; she is falling before New Zealand for the same reason.

Her own old game is still a playing asset that could restore her prestige, if vigorously employed, but, like Roderick Dhu, she throws her targe away and suffers the fate of that redoubtable chieftain at the hands of the Fitz-James of the footer field.

The reason why I have been tempted to this preface of mixed metaphor and pointed moral is simple: in the first half the Blackheath forwards played, or tried to play, the 'hold and heel' game against a scientific set of scrummagers whose system of play and skill in giving that system practical expression make them invincible at the 'hold and heel' game.

The result was that Blackheath never got the ball in a single scrum through the whole half.

That the New Zealanders did not score more than four tries in this half was matter for wonder.

Lee, I believe, carried off the individual honours of the match but he could not stop five or six opponents, for every movement of the New Zealand backs was supported by the forwards. 'Backing up' was indeed the feature of the New Zealanders' play.

New Zealand plays the game as it should be played; that is, with all their might, mental and muscular. Apart altogether from method in the technical sense, New Zealand's victory over England's senior club by 4 goals, a penalty goal and six tries to nil was a triumph of resolution. For with all their individual pace and skill the New Zealanders would not be the side they are if they were not animated by a determination that is almost desperate in its intensity, yet is as calmly opportune in its co-operative aspect and practical expression as if the scoring of a try were the inevitable result of carrying the ball.

NEW ZEALAND TIMES' UK CORRESPONDENT

GREAT IS THE 'MANA' of the New Zealander. Their reputation for invincibility on the football field has captured the imagination of the British public from Land's End to John O'Groats, from Dover to far Donegal; while as for London, by their triumph over Blackheath on Saturday, the Colonials have fairly taken the metropolis by storm.

It was a brilliant climax to a long and unbroken series of victories.

England's senior club, with its strongest fifteen on the field, was hopelessly outclassed, and the display given by the New Zealanders will long live in the memory as a wonderful exposition of the rugby game.

It is no exaggeration to say that they played magnificently.

The weather was bleak and dull, otherwise a larger crowd than 15,000 would have faced the uncomfortable journey out to Blackheath.

All the stands were filled up, for the tickets had been snapped up days and weeks ahead, and standing room at the back of the crowd was all that was left when the teams lined out.

Fifteen thousand may not seem a particularly large attendance to those who have seen as many as twenty thousand 'roll up' to a big match at Wellington or Auckland, but in reality it was a great compliment to the fame of the New Zealand team.

A rugby match between two English teams would scarcely have drawn fifteen hundred out to Blackheath on a day like Saturday was.

Until the arrival of the Colonials, rugby was quite overshadowed by the association game, so far as public interested was concerned. New Zealand, however, has changed all that. Besides, 'Heath could have been sold twice over.

For the first time in the tour, there was a stand especially set apart for New Zealanders, and had this been twice its present size, it would have been filled to overflowing. So it was with the rest of the seating-accommodation on the ground.

The New Zealand stand, by the way, was reserved for the occasion by the London New Zealanders' Association whose honorary secretary, Mr Bockmaster, did Trojan service in carrying out all the necessary arrangements.

Need I say that the welcome given to the team on their appearance, hearty though it was throughout the crowd, reached its height in the stand set apart for their fellow New Zealanders.

Even if the blue ensign with the Southern Cross had not marked them out, the roar of cheering, mingled with snatches of Maori war cries, would have proclaimed them as kinsmen of the 'All Blacks'.

For the first time, too, the team treated an English crowd to their Maori 'haka' by way of salutation to their opponents. Halting in front of the New Zealand stand, they welcomed the Blackheath men with the old chant which representative teams in New Zealand have long since made their own.

Blackheath had whipped up what was thought to be a very 'hot' side for the occasion. Three men were brought over from Ireland and half the team were internationals.

London crowds, being so largely cosmopolitan in their elements, are generally 'sporting' and quick to applaud good work on either side, and though sadly disappointed by the failure of their own team, they freely acknowledge the superiority of the victors, and thoroughly enjoyed the game.

Fortunately, too, the referee, Mr Percy Coles, enjoyed the confidence of all concerned. There was no 'whistling fantastia' about this match.

And what a match it was! Those privileged to watch it need never wish to see a better display of rugby football.

◆ ❖ ◆

THE CAPTAIN and vice-captain: Gallaher and Stead.

I have never seen a better centre threequarter's game than G.W. Smith's against Blackheath on Saturday.

The Auckland crack was in grand form, and in judgement and execution was practically flawless. Although he never scored, himself, Smith had a hand in every try that was gained, and more than once his great pace and ready wit covered up a New Zealand blunder which otherwise would probably have let the other side in.

When a Blackheath man got right away with the ball, with several yards start and nothing between him and the goal, Smith was the first to set out in pursuit, and he it was who brought the runaway to earth.

In attack he played with masterly judgement and splendid unselfishness, and while Wallace and McGregor deserve high praise for their wonderful pace and precision in putting on the finishing touches to each attack, and Hunter and Stead for their dashing work, and Roberts for the great game he played behind the scrum, I still think that the palm for all-round brilliance on Saturday should go to George Smith.

'Old Athlete', who represents the *Athletic News* at all the big rugby fixtures, tells me that in all his 25 years experience as a rugby critic he has never witnessed so grand a display of football as that given by the New Zealand team against Blackheath.

CAPT. THE HON. SOUTHWELL FITZGERALD ('JUDEX'), THE DAILY GRAPHIC

I DO NOT KNOW WHETHER the British rugby football player or spectator has ever taken the trouble to realise that a good many reforms in different branches of sport have sprung from sources otherwise than purely British ones.

I will give a few instances. Mr Blackham, the Australian wicketkeeper, was the first to introduce into this country the innovation of standing up to the wickets to every class of bowling.

Mr Spofforth was the pioneer of 'mixing up' one's bowling by varying pace and pitch.

Our present style of riding on the flat was brought over from America by Ted Sloan, and the starting gate was first in use in Australia long before it became part and parcel of our racing over here.

British sportsmen will thus see that reforms or innovations in English sport which have now been proved to be for the good of whatever pastime they have been introduced into, have not always sprung from a British source.

They have been the ideas of an English-speaking race, and of English people, for I count our Colonies to be of the English race.

At the present moment we have now amongst us a team from one of our Colonies who are showing us 'at home' — as Colonials always talk of England in their own Colony — not only a reformation but a revelation in our rugby football.

The New Zealanders commenced their tour in September and since then they have beaten us Britishers horse, foot and dragoons.

In rugby football we are very conservative; we hate reforms, and we detest nothing more than the innovation of being soundly beaten by a team which up to last September had never set foot in England, and was unknown to the general rugby public.

I have written, and I still hold the same view, that the New Zealanders are the finest team who have ever played rugby football.

BILLY WALLACE'S RECOLLECTIONS

Blackheath played in the old Poneke colours of red and black.

Many New Zealanders were present to see us; in fact, it was surprising how many New Zealanders were in London. They had all joined together and reserved a small stand to themselves.

The start of the match was quite sensational. Massa Johnston picked the ball up in the loose and sent out a long pass to George Smith. George at once set off at full speed ahead for the corner flag but found himself blocked about fifteen yards from the line. He had drawn up all the defence and I was following up and right in front of the posts.

I called out 'Smithy!' and he at once sized up the position. He sent out a beautiful centering kick and all I had to do was to pick it up and walk over under the posts. I converted and in less than two minutes we were five points up. This had a great moral effect.

Our team was in splendid form for this match and on our play that day I think we would have beaten any team in the world at that time. Unfortunately after this game injuries began to take their toll and prevented us ever putting in so fine a team again on the tour.

THE ORIGINALS in playing attire: Back row: Gillett, Casey, McGregor, McDonald, Roberts. Third row: Harper, O'Sullivan, Seeling, Deans, Johnston, Nicholson, Corbett, Cunningham, Newton, Duncan. Second row: Abbott, Wallace, Tyler, Gallaher (captain), Dixon (manager), Stead, Mackrell, Glasgow, Glenn. Front row: Hunter, Mynott, Smith, Booth, Thomson. *Hardie Shaw photo*

I know a certain friend of mine differs on this point, and would probably write that some Scottish international team of some year was certainly their equal, if not their superior.

As there can be no chance of my friend's Scottish XV meeting the present combination I fear we shall agree to differ.

Holding as I do this view of the excellence of the New Zealanders' prowess, I should have thought that when we Britishers had been beaten, as we have been up to now, we should have consoled ourselves with the thought that we had been defeated by the finest rugby combination we have as yet seen.

I know it is very hard on us, in this little island of ours, to be beaten by, metaphorically, our rugby football children.

We naturally do not like being beaten at essentially one of our most British games, but this is no reason why we should endeavour to bolster up our defeats by excuse.

One word in conclusion to all British rugby sportsmen. We owe much to our New Zealand friends.

They have brought our game into such prominence this season by their sterling displays as not even the most ardent rugby enthusiasts could have ever dreamt of.

In doing so, I admit they have beaten us soundly, but they have never swaggered about their successes; they are too good sportsmen for that.

Let us, in these islands of ours, be thorough sportsmen also; let us admit we have been beaten by a grand rugby side, and not keep shifting about, as we have up to now, from one excuse to another, to try and account for our defeats.

GEORGE TYLER

Auckland — hooker
26, 5ft 10in, 12st 12lb

Tyler achieved fame in New Zealand when he shook the hand of King Edward VII during the tour. He claimed he would never wash that hand again! His nickname of Bubs (short for Bubbles) stemmed from his swimming prowess. He held several Auckland titles in 100-yard and 200-yard events and was reputed to have set an unofficial world record for the 100-yard straight swim. On tour, Tyler formed an effective front-row partnership with Steve Casey, and was one of only three forwards to appear in all five internationals. He played in New Zealand's first test match in 1903, at Sydney, and a year later was in New Zealand's second winning test side, this time on home soil, against Britain.

GAME 16 — TUESDAY 7 NOVEMBER 1905 — at Iffley Road, Oxford

NEW ZEALAND
OXFORD UNIVERSITY

47
0

FOR NEW ZEALAND
Tries by Hunter 5, Booth 2, Wallace 2,
Glasgow, Johnston, McGregor, Roberts;
conversions by Wallace 3, Tyler.

NEW ZEALAND
Gillett, Booth, Wallace, Hunter,
McGregor, Mynott, Roberts, Gallaher
(captain), Corbett, Glasgow, Johnston,
Newton, Nicholson, Tyler, Casey.

OXFORD UNIVERSITY
D. Davies (Jesus), A.A. Lawrie (Trinity),
A.E. Wood (University), L. Parker (Christ
Church), A.M.P. Lyle (Trinity), P. Munro
(Christ Church, captain), H.C. Jackson
(Exeter), W.W. Hoskin (Trinity), R.S. Wix
(Brasenose), C.J. Gardner (Trinity),
H.V. Hodges (Trinity), N.F. Howe-Brown
(Oriel), N.T. White (Trinity), G.D. Roberts
(St John's), H.A. Hoadley (Keble).

Weather: Fine, ground soft
Referee: Lindsay Soper (London)
Crowd: 5000

KICK OFF
Hunter put Wallace across from a scrum, Wallace converted: 5-0.
Gallaher set up Hunter for a try from loose play. Wallace converted: 10-0.
From a lineout Glasgow burst through putting Johnston across. Wallace missed: 13-0.
Gallaher and Mynott handled before Hunter scored. Wallace missed: 16-0.
Five players handled in loose play before Hunter scored. Gillett missed: 19-0.
Gallaher and Mynott combined from a lineout for Hunter to score. Hunter missed.

HALFTIME
New Zealand 22, Oxford University 0

Roberts and Mynott worked to put Booth in for a try. Gillett missed: 25-0.
Backs and forwards combined for McGregor to score. Wallace converted: 30-0.
Roberts darted through from a scrum to score. Wallace missed: 33-0.
Roberts worked the blindside from a scrum, Glasgow scoring. Newton missed: 36-0.
Wallace joined in from fullback and Booth scored. Glasgow missed: 39-0.
Wallace came up from fullback again and scored. Wallace missed: 42-0.
Roberts' incisiveness put Hunter across for the final try. Tyler converted.

FULLTIME
New Zealand 47, Oxford University 0

FROM THE SIDELINES

DAILY EXPRESS

THIS IS NOT FOOTBALL,' gasped a spectator at Oxford yesterday, 'it's magic.'

And while the people, to the number of about 5000, stay positively entranced by the spectacle, the Oxford team were bewitched into a state of active futility.

Nothing like this was ever witnessed on the ground before. The University towns have been accustomed to high scoring — indeed, prior to this season, both Oxford and Cambridge were prone to defeat their opponents with almost the same consistent irresistibility that characterises the New Zealanders; but the best football ever played by a University fifteen would not have appreciably lessened the triumph of the Colonials on this occasion.

Oxford are not a formidable lot this season, but they cannot be so weak relatively to contemporary form as they were made to appear yesterday.

One could not fail to sympathise with the Oxford fifteen. Fine, lusty types of English manhood reduced to helpless incapacity make no pretty spectacle.

A great melancholy fell upon the assembly when the vast superiority of the New Zealanders was driven home with relentless force.

The eye feasted while the heart hungered. The sense of exultation produced by the brilliant intricacies of the New Zealand attack found no audible vent. The people sat numb with admiration. They could not even cheer.

Mere applause indeed had been an absurd anti-climax. As well might one clap hands at the rapidity of the flash of lightning or the power of the roll of thunder.

Both elements play about the football as cultivated by the New Zealanders, these electric atoms of humanity who tackle with the hug of the bear or slide out of holds with the sinuous elusiveness of the eel; these quick-witted feather-footed athletes who sweep along on a tornado or dodge and twist a tortuous course through the merest crevices left by packed humanity.

One of the remarks made by an Oxford player yesterday was, 'Why, their forwards are better threequarters than ours.' When you play against these New Zealanders you do not have to deal with so many threequarters, so many halves, and so many forwards. Every man is what the occasion requires.

Almost without exception, the Colonials are adaptable to any position, and their attack resolves itself into a stampede right across the field.

Once in the second half when Hunter, who was the centre stone in a cluster of brilliants, exercised a characteristic feint and swerve, three Oxonians flung themselves at him for a tackle, and were left prone on the ground clutching each other, astonished to find that there was nothing black except their own looks of astonishment.

This Hunter got four of the six tries in the first half, and though he added only one of the seven accruing during the later stage of the game, he was the best of a universal attack.

It would be impossible to give adequate expression to the all but superhuman resource of this player, who emerges from a grip as though his assailants are spiritual, who must seem to his opponent to be coming two ways at once, who, indeed, appears to be running straight for and right through the man hopefully preparing for the reception.

Every now and again the New Zealanders came surging up like a broad, black tide, the rapidity of the passing almost baffling detection.

One of the last tries was obtained by Wallace, who, in the sweat of a tremendous run, retained sufficient calmness to say to Booth, 'All right, General!' meaning that his right wing partner was not to trouble about a pass.

The confidence was well placed. Lyle left barely a yard of space between himself and the touchline, yet Wallace got through on that side, and Lyle in making the 'tackle' clutched at the air and described a somersault among the people.

DAILY CHRONICLE

IF ANY OF THOSE who are puzzled by the uninterrupted success of the New Zealand football team should have the idea that their stamina is due to a special system of training, it may as well be dismissed at once.

The remarkable athletes who have conquered all our rugby teams so far do not train at all in the strict sense of the term; that is to say, they pursue no hard and fast method.

BILLY WALLACE'S RECOLLECTIONS

When we woke up we got our first experience of a black London fog. Though their clocks ticked steadily on no daylight broke that day. We got up and dressed by electric light and had our breakfast. When we looked outside the thick, black fog had effectively blotted everything out.

We had to go up to Oxford for our match against the University. We caught the train, which crept out of London as if it were a funeral train and proceeded at a snail's pace along the rails. It was not until we were quite close to Oxford that we ran out of the fog into bright sunshine, but by this time we were running a couple of hours late. We went straight to a hotel for luncheon and we had no time to lose either, for the match was timed to commence at 2.30 at the Iffley Road ground.

Jimmy Hunter had a field day and scored no fewer than five tries, General Booth got a couple, and Duncan McGregor, Massa Johnston, Freddy Roberts and Frank Glasgow one each. The kicks at goal were distributed around amongst myself, George Gillett, Frank Glasgow, Fatty Newton, Bubs Tyler and Jimmy Hunter, but only four were converted.

MEMBERS of the New Zealand and Oxford University teams.

They keep fit by living what they deem to be a natural life, and that they are really fit under those conditions their record proves.

Our Colonial visitors were staying at the Drayton Court Hotel and practising on the recreation ground of the Great Western Railway Company at Ealing, a fine open space remote from the smoke of London, over which the crisp wind blew with delicious freshness.

A representative of the *Daily Chronicle* saw the exercises of some of the members of the team, and afterwards conversed with them as to their method of life.

When he asked how they kept themselves in such good trim they seemed rather surprised at the inquiry. It was natural to them to be strong, robust and fit, and they smiled at the suggestion that any special regimen should be necessary to attain to that state.

'Oh, the boys just live as they want to,' said one, 'and of course they all want to be fit; but they don't upset themselves trying fancy tricks in diet and that sort of thing. We live according to no special rules.

'No, we don't get up too early in the morning and we don't go in, as a rule, for dumbbells on an empty stomach.

'But we get a good night's rest, and after breakfast we may turn

out about ten o'clock. Those of us who want exercise and practice put in an hour or two as you have seen us today, running, passing, kicking and generally getting rid of superfluous accumulation.

'We enjoy this sort of thing, but if one of us does not feel very well, or is not in the mood for it, he does not turn out, and lets the exercise stand over till another day.

'We find playing two matches a week quite enough to keep us in trim for the game, and those who may not be played — there are twenty-seven players in the team, you know — do not let themselves get rusty with idleness.

'But there is no exhausting strain, no constant endeavour to be in the pink of perfection. With the exception of the periodical practice and the games we live much as other men do who go to business and still keep healthy and in good condition.'

Then the training is over for today, our representative asked, as the clock struck the hour of noon?

'Oh, yes, the practice is over. We're going to have lunch now, then perhaps a walk, then dinner and to bed at a reasonably early hour.

'There will be no practice tomorrow; the match will be enough for those who are playing.

'Smoke? Why, bless you, yes, nearly all of the boys smoke. You'll see them at the game tomorrow having a cigarette at halftime, I daresay. A 'whiff and a spit' they call it.

'Smoking affect the wind? Well, I've heard people say it does, but we never notice it. I'm a heavy smoker, but it hasn't affected my wind, and I've got a bit of speed yet.

'It can't be the climate that makes the difference because our climate in many parts of New Zealand is very like your own. We just smoke as much as we want to, and we don't find it hurts us.

'Beer forbidden? Why, no, of course not. The boys take it if they like, or anything else they may fancy. And they are not restricted as to quantity either. There is no attempt to make them teetotallers, or to limit them to so many glasses.

'Some may think they keep better this way, that constant self-denial leads them when training to get too fine, and really to exhaust themselves; but when one is living in the ordinary way the morning practice soon gets rid of superfluities, and we all feel the better for it, and seldom get stale. And any rate, that's the way we work, and it seems to be justified.

'It's just the same in eating. We eat plain food, but just what we fancy. There's one thing, however, we find over here, that there is a scarcity of nice fruit at reasonable prices.

'At home, we never sit down to a meal without plenty of fruit, but here somehow we don't get it. Apples are terribly dear and in some towns you can't get them fit to eat. I paid a shilling for three nice apples the other day; in New Zealand I could get half a case for that sum.

'Perhaps the lack of fruit and the change of diet is responsible for the plague of boils which has affected some of us. Very few have escaped. It began on the ship coming over and some of the boys are troubled with them now. Still, that is the worst that has happened to us, and we have had a great time over here.'

NEW ZEALAND TIMES' UK CORRESPONDENT

G.H. DIXON, THE MANAGER of the New Zealand team, told us on Saturday that so far the enterprise had exceeded all anticipations.

From a playing point of view it had been much as they thought, but financially it had been a huge and glorious success. The guarantors in New Zealand who had pledged themselves for the expenses of the trip would not be called upon to discharge any liabilities, and if the gates kept up to the level they had now attained, the tour would be more than self-supporting.

It was a venture which had been undertaken with much thought and care, but the promoters could not fail to be pleased with the splendid results.

Asked when the New Zealanders were coming again, Mr Dixon very sagely shook his head and said that all depended.

No doubt, he admitted, this tour would be the forerunner of many others, but before the New Zealand Union sent a second contingent over, the British Union would have to organise a team to tour in the Antipodes.

This was the first lot of players that had ever travelled under the aegis of the New Zealand Union, for the Maoris who came over in 1888 were men selected by a syndicate of private individuals;

as a matter of fact, there was no Rugby Union in New Zealand at the time.

With reference to arranging any more matches this tour, Mr Dixon declined to voice an opinion. He said as far as his programme was at present compiled the playing tour finished at the end of the year, and the team were due to sail from Plymouth on 13 January.

We pointed out that at any rate there would be time before sailing to give Manchester a match. But he wore a smile that was childlike and bland and an expression worthy of a Sphinx.

At present he would not commit himself, but we think if the King, as the Duke of Lancaster, went down on his bended knees to Mr Dixon he might relent and Lancashire could rejoice.

◆ ❖ ◆

It is satisfactory to note that the English Rugby Union has risen to the occasion and has realised that the Rectory Field, which has been the scene of so many historic struggles, is too small to accommodate the many thousands who will want to witness the England-New Zealand match on 2 December.

There were three enclosures available, those at Crystal Palace, Stamford Bridge and Fulham, respectively. Of the three grounds, that of the Chelsea FC would have been thought to be the most suitable, if only on account of its central position, but the notice to hand tells us that the insufficiency of stand accommodation (though 5000 spectators can be accommodated under cover) was an insurmountable objection.

It was finally decided that the match should be played at the Crystal Palace where, as has been already demonstrated at final ties, 100,000 people can witness the whole of the play.

BILLY MACKRELL

Auckland — hooker
23, 5ft 10in, 12st 8lb

Poor health prevented Mackrell from playing a major part in the tour, though his manner won him many friends among his fellow players, including Billy Wallace, who said, 'Billy was always anxious and willing to play, but realised that the good of the team was the first consideration and never showed the slightest resentment when left out so frequently. He was a very sociable chap and entered heartily into all the fun that was going on.' Born in Australia, Mackrell moved to New Zealand when he was young, coming to rugby prominence in Auckland during a time of great strength. A strong showing in the 1905 inter-island match led to his selection as an Original. George Dixon called him 'the unlucky man of the tour'. He appeared in only six matches.

GAME 17 — THURSDAY 9 NOVEMBER 1905 — at Grange Road, Cambridge

NEW ZEALAND   14
CAMBRIDGE UNIVERSITY   0

FOR NEW ZEALAND
Tries by Deans 2, McGregor 2; conversion by Cunningham.

NEW ZEALAND
Booth, Thomson, Smith, Deans, McGregor, Wallace, Roberts, Gallaher (captain), Glasgow, Glenn, O'Sullivan, Cunningham, Nicholson, Tyler, Casey.

CAMBRIDGE UNIVERSITY
J.G. Scoular (St John's), J. Burt-Marshall (Clare), K.G. Macleod (Pembroke), W.M. Penny (Jesus), L.M. Macleod (captain, Pembroke), H.F.P. Hearson (Kings), J.V. Young (Emmanuel), T.G. Pitt (Emmanuel), H.G. Monteith (Pembroke), B.G. Harris (Pembroke), F.J.V. Hopley (Pembroke), R. McCosh (Trinity), W.C. Currie (Trinity), J.W. Alexander (Clare), R.B. Gibbins (King's).

Weather: Fine, ground firm
Referee: J. Crauford Findlay (Scotland)
Crowd: 7000

KICK OFF
Roberts kicked high, Smith chased hard and Deans scored. Wallace missed: 3-0.
McGregor eluded the defence in a blindside dab to score. Wallace missed.

HALFTIME
New Zealand 6, Cambridge University 0

In loose play, Wallace and Smith handled, McGregor scoring. Glasgow missed: 9-0.
Deans confounded the defence with a weaving run. Cunningham converted.

FULLTIME
New Zealand 14, Cambridge University 0

FROM THE SIDELINES

DAILY MAIL

FOR ONCE IN A WAY the New Zealand backs ran up against a threequarter line almost as fast as themselves.

It was only two days ago that the younger McLeod won his hundred yards as the Freshmen's sports in 10⅗ and his fellow Fettesian J. Burt Marshall is quite as speedy while L.M. McLeod, Hearson and Penny are all runners above the average in point of pace.

The consequence was that even when the New Zealand fliers got fairly going they did not have matters all their own way, and on more than one occasion a man was actually overtaken and brought down after he had broken right through the threequarter line.

But it was in kicking that the 'Varsity backs excelled most. Rarely of late years has better touchfinding been witnessed than when either of the brothers McLeod obtained possession of the ball. Both in regard to length and accuracy it was well-nigh perfect.

Unless when in their opponents' twenty-five the Cambridge threequarters kicked instead of opening up the game, and the amount of ground and the work saved their forwards by these tactics were enormous.

These novel tactics appeared to bewilder the All Blacks and for the first half-hour they had, if anything, rather the worst of the game.

Had the Light Blues possessed sufficient confidence in their own powers they must have scored more than once during that period.

On one occasion L.M. McLeod was given a capital pass by his brother right in front of the New Zealand goal. The fullback was out of position, and McLeod apparently had nothing to do except waltz over the line in between the posts.

For some reason or other, however, probably because he had made up his mind beforehand how to act, he elected to drop at goal, and although he made a capital attempt, the ball just went wide and the opportunity was lost.

Cambridge's other great opportunity of scoring came late in the second half, when they were awarded a penalty kick in a most favourable position. Hearson judged the angle and the direction to a nicety, but he did not get sufficient elevation on the ball and one of the New Zealand forwards managed to jump and divert its course.

For some reason or other the All Blacks gave a display far below that which they showed, for instance, at Blackheath. The absence of Hunter, Stead, Seeling and Gillett may have had something to do with it, but there was a want of certainty about their attack, due in a great measure to the way in which they were marked by the Cantabs but, above all, to the unaccountable weakness of Smith in the centre.

Time and again this fine player would dash through, only to hesitate at the critical moment. Once a pass to Booth would have meant a certain try, but it was not given and Smith, while standing irresolute, was thrown relentlessly to the ground by three of the heaviest forwards in the Light Blue pack.

When it was known that Mr J. Crauford Findlay, the 'Penalty King' of rugby football, was going to take charge of the game, many people expected a repetition of the Surrey match with its farcical whistle blowing, but they were agreeably disappointed.

Mr Findlay found occasion to penalise the New Zealanders four times in the first half and five in the second, but in the majority of cases the breaches of the rules were so obvious that the decisions were received without a murmur.

NEW ZEALAND TIMES' UK CORRESPONDENT

THINGS HAVE COME TO a remarkable pass when a defeat by 14 points to nil is looked upon as quite a 'moral victory'.

Yet such is the outcome of the match between the New Zealand footballers and the University of Cambridge.

The Cantabs are insufferably conceited because they prevented New Zealand scoring more than 14 points, the lowest score but one of their whole tour, so far.

They pass lightly over the fact that the Cantab score was . . . nil!

Nor is undue stress laid upon the astounding fact that at the time of writing the New Zealanders' total score is 554 points against England's miserable total of 15.

Very great surprise was felt and expressed when the result became known in London. It was quite expected that Cambridge would have suffered a defeat equal to that experienced by Oxford two days previously.

The Cantabs, however, played such a splendid game that they have received as much congratulation and praise as if they had won the match, or at any rate, as if they had scored any point, which they came near doing once or twice.

The University had quite two-thirds of the game, thanks to

ERNEST BOOTH writing home.

BILLY WALLACE'S RECOLLECTIONS

We left London just after breakfast and arrived at Cambridge just before lunch. We were driven to an old-fashioned pub and sat down at once to a midday meal. Immediately afterwards we undressed and got into our togs ready for the game.

The students were out in force to greet us in their characteristic and exuberant fashion.

In view of the approaching international match against Scotland it was thought advisable to give some of the best men a spell and several of us were chosen in new positions, which did not improve our combination.

Moreover, we found the opposition unexpectedly strong, both forwards and backs.

We returned to our hotel far from satisfied with our display, but full of admiration. It had been the hardest game so far and the Cambridge fellows deserved every credit for the great game they put up.

We then went back to the hotel where we found a dozen small baths put out for us in the commercial room. There were baths of all descriptions, such as washerwomen use, but one was a baby's bath with a high back and prettily enamelled in white.

Bill Cunningham, our burly lock who weighed 16 stone, promptly claimed that as his own. Bill sat down in his bath and we all roared with laughter. But the laughter increased when Bill tried to get out again. He had a fair-sized posterior and this had become jammed in the bath and he could not get out of it. The more worried he looked the more we laughed. The chaps tugged at it but it would not budge. Then he stood up with it still sticking to him and of course the water streamed all over the floor increasing the hilarity, but when the water was all out, the bath came off easily, much to Cunny's relief.

---

the splendid work of the forwards and the brilliant defence and kicking of the backs, and if luck had inclined at all their way the surprise of the season might have been effected.

A better or more exciting game has never been witnessed in the University town and the home side were, it is held, certainly deserving of a better fate.

The Cambridge supporters must have marvelled at the wonderful form of the Light Blues who had previously had a most disastrous season. They were without three of their best forwards, J. Horsfall, E.C. Hodges and A. Forman, and yet their exposition was about as fine as could be.

By a good many the visitors were expected to obtain a victory by a larger margin than they did against Oxford but instead they found the Light Blues a great side, their captain, L.M. Macleod, playing an extraordinarily brilliant game, and half an hour elapsed before New Zealand crossed their rivals' line.

PUNCH

MR PUNCH LEARNS FROM THE USUAL journalistic sources: 1. That the Antipodes can produce a dozen better teams than the stalwarts now touring in this country; 2. That the team at present engrossing attention was sent over for rest and change, and is under orders to 'go steady'; 3. That the chilblain on ——'s little toe is progressing favourably; 4. That one of the most striking points in the behaviour of the Colonials is their extraordinary good humour at the close of play; 5. That amongst other things the Maorilanders are teaching us moderation in language, Mr Dixon, their manager, stating that so far he is satisfied with the financial aspect of the tour, and is inclined to think it will be self-supporting on an average gate of £600; 6. That the Silverleaves are sensitive to our climatic conditions, and England may win in a fog; 7. That history repeats itself, and 'Scots wha hae wi' Wallace bled' are not unlikely, when again brought in contact with him, to renew this painful experience. 8. In the craze for international football, it is expected that in the year 1912 Great Britain will play Russia at Blackheath before a crowd estimated at 250,000 with their strongest possible combination composed of fourteen New Zealanders and one Welshman.

ATHLETIC NEWS

UPON THEIR RETURN TO LONDON following the Cambridge University match, the members of the New Zealand team were entertained at dinner at the Trocadero by a few Anglo-New Zealanders in London and were afterwards taken to the Palace Theatre. Mr Pember Reeves presided at the dinner, on his right hand being Mr Dixon and on his left Mr Gallaher.

Among those present in addition to the team were Sir Montague Nelson, Mr Moss Davies, Mr E.D. O'Rorke, Mr Logan (chairman of the National Bank of New Zealand), Mr C.V. Teschmaker, Mr W. Robison, Mr H.K. Bethune, Mr Percy Harris, Mr Wray Palliser, Mr W.H.S. Moorhouse, Mr J.A. Mason and Mr P.A. Vaile.

The toast of 'The King' having been duly honoured, the chairman said it had been agreed that there should not be a single speech. But they could not part with their friends, the footballers, without just one word or two of a friendly nature.

The public of England, Scotland, Ireland and Wales were very much interested in the team. Since he had been in England, nearly 10 years, he had never seen anything connected with a British colony as was the case at the present time with the New Zealand visitors.

Some of the interest had been of an amusing nature. A couple of days ago he had met an English gentleman, a man of great ability, who took great interest in the national history.

This gentleman said, 'I have been to the Zoo looking at your New Zealand birds. Extraordinary birds — they have no wings. But I was looking at your footballers at Leicester recently. But, by Heaven, they have got wings!' (laughter).

The chairman told the team that they must not think the friendly little gathering at all represented, as far as numbers went, the enthusiasm and delight which were felt by all New Zealanders in England.

If they had wanted to give a banquet to express New Zealand feeling, the room would not have been large enough to hold those who would have come.

But that strict disciplinarian, Mr Dixon, had asked that there should be no banquet. Therefore that small and homely assembly had been for the team's benefit.

DUNEDIN EVENING STAR

It was definitely known in town on Saturday that the relations between certain sections of the New Zealand football team are very much strained. From inquiries which the *Star* has made, there seems to be little doubt that the team are anything but a happy family. This can be easily gathered from the contents of numbers of the letters which have been received in the last mail by friends of the Otago members of the team.

Trouble has apparently arisen out of the old sore feeling over the appointment of (Jimmy) Duncan as coach. The letters received indicate that, from the first, the Auckland members set themselves in sharp opposition to Duncan, and then to the Otago members in general. A number of the others, including Stead of Southland, sided with the Auckland contingent and the general result has been that every attempt by Duncan to assert his authority as coach has been met with open hostility at meetings of the team, and on the field it has been simply ignored.

'He is just nobody,' is the way one writer sums up the position. Unfortunately, it has not been possible to confine the trouble in question to between Duncan and certain others. The Otago members have been drawn into it, and so bitterly that it is rumoured a well-known Otago player applied the *argumentum ad nominem* to one of the Aucklanders, and gave him a thrashing.

Rightly or wrongly, the Otago members also believe that, owing to the influence of the northern opposition, they are being kept out of matches to which their claims as players entitle them. Says one: 'None of us, except Steve Casey, are getting a hearing and they would leave Steve out too, only they can't do without him because he's the best hooker they've got. Duncan is sick of the whole business and will have something to say on his return.' Before Duncan left Dunedin to go Home with the team,

JIMMY DUNCAN

Otago — coach
35

Duncan captained New Zealand in its first ever test against Australia at the Sydney Cricket Ground in August 1903, a match New Zealand won 22-3. An astute tactician, Duncan, a saddler by trade, was credited with creating New Zealand's unique five-eighths alignment for back play, arguing that it was logical to name them so with 'half, threequarters and full, the two between the halfback and threequarters being the first and second five-eighths'. By 1905, Duncan was retired from active play but was co-opted onto the tour as coach — despite protests from several provinces, headed by Auckland. He helped weld the Originals into a powerful attacking combination.

he expressed to the *Star* his strong disapproval of Mynott's style of cross-cutting and running in, and hinted that he would use his best endeavours to make both that player and his colleague, Hunter, 'run out'. This meant simply that the bulk of whatever scoring was done would be done by the wing and centre three-quarters, and not by the five-eighths. The cables show that something like the reverse has been the case.

However unfortunate the position now may be, there can be no doubt that Duncan was quite wrong on the five-eighth business, whatever he was on the other parts of the game. As a player, he generally ran out himself, but evidently forgot that the game which suits one man doesn't suit another, and to try to materially alter the styles of play, which men like Mynott had acquired by long habit and experience, was practically attempting to throw the whole machine out of order.

CHRISTCHURCH PRESS EDITORIAL

No one who remembers the opposition that was raised by several of the unions to Jimmy Duncan's appointment as coach to the New Zealand football team will be greatly surprised that his counsels have been ignored by at least a majority of our representatives, or that his presence with the team has been the cause of some ill-feeling.

The announcement of his intended appointment met with such a hostile reception, especially in Auckland, that the NZRU practically had to make the question one of no confidence before they secured the support of the objecting unions.

It is doubtful whether this would have been accorded had it not been that a crisis in the government of rugby football would have been awkward just at that juncture. The members of the team who went to Australia before leaving for Home protested against the appointment of a coach, and before the team sailed it was predicted that if Duncan accompanied them it would cause ill-feeling among the members. Duncan has admittedly a great knowledge of the game, and has been a fine player, but he has been so long an active figure in Otago football that he apparently thinks no other style than his can be correct.

This is no place in which to enter into a disquisition on the respective merits of 'running out' or 'cross-cutting'; it is enough to say that the one, which is practised by Duncan, is the stereotyped style, while the other is a comparatively recent development, which adds variety to the attack and, given a first-class exponent, extremely effective. For Duncan to assert before leaving Dunedin, as he is reported to have done, that he meant to make experienced men like Hunter and Mynott change their style of play because he strongly disapproved of it, explains, to a great extent, why he is not a *persona grata* among the footballers, and confirms the unwisdom of sending him as coach.

The team did not need a coach at all, for a large proportion of them have been playing for a number of years, and if they do not now know enough about the game to tell the younger members all that was necessary they had no right to be in the team. Further proof that no coach was required is afforded by the fact that although Duncan's advice appears to have been ignored the team has achieved unprecedented success.

GAME 18 — SATURDAY 11 NOVEMBER 1905 — at Athletic Ground, London

NEW ZEALAND
RICHMOND

17
0

FOR NEW ZEALAND
Tries by Wallace 2, Deans, Hunter, Stead;
conversion by Wallace.

NEW ZEALAND
Booth, Wallace, Deans, Stead, Harper,
Mynott, Hunter, Gallaher (captain), Johnston,
Glenn, McDonald, Newton, Corbett, Tyler,
Glasgow.

RICHMOND
G.H. Glover, B.B. Bennetts, R.E. Godfray,
H.M. Lawson, W.C. Wilson, N.G. Aveling,
L.C. Smith, H.A. Alexander (captain),
G. Fraser, C.B. Smith, R.C. Grellett,
F.T. Turner, F.C. Pheysey, W. Blake-Odgers,
E.C. Chase.

Weather: Fine, ground greasy
Referee: E.T. Andrews (London)
Crowd: 8000

KICK OFF

From a scrum, Hunter wriggled his way through to score, failing to convert: 3-0.
From the re-start, Wallace was in again, Stead giving the final pass. Harper missed.

HALFTIME
New Zealand 6, Richmond 0

Stead chased a Wallace kick through and scored. Wallace missed: 9-0.
Glenn dribbled, footpassed to Gallaher and Deans scored. Wallace converted: 14-0.
From a lineout, Tyler and Deans handled and Wallace scored. Harper missed.

FULLTIME
New Zealand 17, Richmond 0

FROM THE SIDELINES

ATHLETIC NEWS

NEW ZEALAND'S LATEST HARVEST was not an opulent one. They only beat Richmond by 17 points to nil, but it would be wrong, unfair and unwise to assume that the narrowness of the victory makes up for the staleness of clever, all-conquering hustlers from the colonies.

Their propensity for prodigious work is still wonderfully, strangely great. Their stamina is colossal; and yet we are amazed they spurn hard and fast unbreakable training rules. They set their own fashion, and it is assuredly this originality, this thinking and acting for themselves that has produced their invincibility.

I saw them play Oxford as they would do with mere schoolboys; I was present at the great punishing game at Cambridge; and yet at Richmond, in their third match within a week, and on a day when the elements conspired to bring depression to the frank enthusiast, they were fifteen sprightly men, terrific workers to the last.

It may be, indeed it is true, that they fell below the lofty standard they set up on the previous Saturday at Blackheath and that their latest contest did not fire the imagination or take hold of one as completely as some of their previous encounters, but it was a game that was good to watch if it were only that it showed the remarkable keenness of the black-garbed tourists.

The New Zealanders are razor edged. The surest, easiest opening is magnified into one of almost insurmountable difficulty. Nothing is taken for granted until it is gained and as in every single engagement though they must have been conscious of their ability to beat Richmond they were just as watchful, just as keen, just as tenacious in their tackling and general methods in the last minute as when the game kicked off.

◆ ❖ ◆

Hunter is a distinct personality; he is the type of man who worms his way through the opposition. He will bounce forward with the ball in his hands, pretend to lose it, or kick, and all the time he is rushing in and out for the goalline.

He is a human will-o'-the-wisp.

DAILY EXPRESS

BRILLIANT INDIVIDUALISM enabled the New Zealanders to score two tries in the opening half when otherwise Richmond had as much of the game, and on two occasions flattered considerably.

First, Wilson, upon receiving the ball from Godfrey, kicked across the line and was not the first to touch down while again, but for a miraculous relief kick by Booth, the Colonial fullback, it would have been 'all agley' with New Zealand.

Then Hunter, who was playing in Roberts' position at half-back, got one of his famous 'wriggling through' tries. His effort was nothing short of astounding, and the effects of it had not worn off when Wallace failed at goal.

The last-named was responsible for the other try, and it was the result of brain over club football! He hesitated (in a position when it looked as if it would be either 'touch' or 'tackle') and quite deceived Wilson who, evidently believing that Wallace was about to pass out, failed for once to go for his man. Before Wilson could retrieve his error Wallace had realised the intention.

The home line was crossed again three more times, by Stead, Deans and Wallace. Stead's try was a triumph of speed. Following a neat kick over the Richmond line, he beat the defence by seconds and touched down in comfort.

MORNING LEADER

NEW ZEALAND'S TRIES in the Richmond match were the outcome of characteristic play, mostly individual, and Stead's magnificent follow-up of a punt by Hunter, in which he outpaced three Richmond backs for possession of the ball, was a splendid lesson in the art of accepting opportunities.

Deans, who played at centre threequarter, is a giant standing well over 6ft, heavy in proportion, and his run round from the near side of the scrum and straight through to the posts was perfectly irresistible.

It was merely a question of how long the Richmond forwards could prevent the opposing pack from heeling-out properly, and when at length the New Zealand front rank got the better of the struggle, the issue was not long in doubt.

New Zealand rested six of her best men — Smith, McGregor, Roberts and Gillett behind the scrummage and the forwards Cunningham and Seeling.

HAMISH STUART, ATHLETIC NEWS

NO SIDE HAS MADE HISTORY, or ensured a permanent place in the annals of the game, with the same dramatic suddenness as the New Zealand team now delighting the whole footballing community of the Mother Country with their splendidly vigorous yet highly scientific methods of play.

The team has leaped into fame not solely through its long sequence of successes and its wonderful record of points scored, but also because the New Zealanders' style of play has shown the public that the rugby game can be made as fast, interesting and attractive to, and almost as simple to understand by, the average spectator as the other code.

Rugby can truly be called the national pastime of New Zealand, where it is played with the same exclusive persistence and enthusiasm as soccer was in the Scottish villages before the days of professionalism.

In each case, New Zealand and Scotland, the cultivation of a national pastime produced a collective and individual skill and aptitude for the game which in process of time would become a racial and hereditary characteristic.

ACTION from the Richmond game in London — a lineout, left, and a scrum, right.

The secret of the All Blacks' success lay in the policy of 'backing up' in its fullest sense. That was the secret of the success of the Scottish team in 1901 and of the Merchiston School team of the same year, a side who were just as good in their own small way as the New Zealanders, for they won all their matches without a single point of any kind being scored against them.

To play this sort of game well, a side must, of course, have speed and stamina. The New Zealanders are so richly endowed with both that they would play any game well.

Little wonder then that they play their own game to perfection, and with such telling effect against sides of mongrel methods, inferior pace and less individual excellence.

MAJOR PHILIP TREVOR ('DUX'), THE SPORTSMAN

ONE MUST CONFESS that one has seen the New Zealanders play rather better. The ground of course was heavy and the ball was greasy, but even so, such is their reputation, one expected rather more.

They had not, however, their best side in the field. Certainly greater care to avoid irregularities would pay them better.

Mr Andrews, the referee, was compelled in the first few minutes to penalise them several times; and there is no doubt that the opponents of our visitors, match after match, are often saved from danger, if not from disaster, in this way.

The New Zealand play is so clever, both in design and execution, that one is forced to the conclusion that they one and all know the game excellently well.

They have now played nearly twenty matches in this country and however our administration of the game may differ from what they are used to in their own land, they have had time to get accustomed to our interpretation of the rules.

On Saturday one ludicrous case occurred. A New Zealander at least twenty yards in front of his comrade who kicked the ball picked it up and ran across the Richmond line. Of course the try was disallowed, but the incident caused one to wonder how so clever a player could possibly make so inexplicable a mistake.

With a more scrupulous endeavour to avoid illegalities their margins of victory would, I believe, be even greater. Fortunately for themselves they are in their opponents' territory when free kicks are awarded against them.

Still, they are a great side, easily and incomparably the greatest side now playing rugby union football; in fact, the greatest side that has ever played it.

NEW ZEALAND TIMES' UK CORRESPONDENT

LAST SUNDAY SOME OF THE NEW ZEALANDERS paid a visit to Mr Tom Sullivan's riverside hostelry, the Spencer Arms, Putney, where the famous ex-Auckland oarsman entertained them to lunch.

Several members of the team are amateur oarsmen, and an impromptu four-oared race against an English crew was suggested but, unfortunately, there was not time to get an English crew together that day.

It is still hoped, however, to have a race on some future date before the Colonials leave for home.

The previous evening G.W. Smith, E.E. Booth and J. Duncan were present at the London Press Club's monthly 'smoker' where some of the best talent from the concert and music halls supplied the programme.

The whole team took a 'busman's holiday' on Monday afternoon and journeyed in the rain to Queen's Club, Kensington, to watch the rugby football match between Swansea and London Welsh.

The conditions were about as bad for football as they well could be. Rain fell steadily all through the match, and with ground and ball both thoroughly sodden the game degenerated into a mere scramble, in which weight and strength were more important qualities to possess than speed and cleverness.

If the New Zealanders went to Queen's Club with the notion of gaining some idea of Welsh methods and tactics, their visit was fruitless, for neither set of backs was able to field the ball properly and, it being soon proved that passing was so much wasted energy, very few attempts at it were made by either side.

On Tuesday the team accepted an invitation from Mr Bernard Bletsoe, of the Elms, Denton, near Northampton, to pay a visit to his stables.

Mr Bletsoe is the owner of Grudon, the winner of the Grand National of 1901, and an evening paper here is responsible for the statement that 'the horse of all others that the New Zealand footballers have expressed a wish to see is Grudon.'

DAILY MAIL

THE CROWD WAS TREATED to several characteristic touches of All Black brilliancy against Richmond, the tries by Hunter and Deans being magnificent individual efforts.

Hunter, playing in Roberts' normal position at scrumhalf, went through nearly every member of the Richmond team from the 'twenty-five' line and was greeted by a perfect tornado of cheers when he safely grounded the ball behind the posts, scarcely a hand having been laid upon him.

It was one of the few flashes that redeemed the game from mediocrity.

WILLIAM JOHNSTON

Otago — loose forward
23, 6ft, 13st 6lb

A colourful character, Johnston was a side row forward who played for the Alhambra club in Dunedin. He relished the game's robust, physical aspects and impressed selectors when he appeared for the South Island in 1905 after playing only six times for Otago. He won selection for the tour of Australia prior to touring Britain. Unfortunately, illness, including a debilitating throat infection, hampered his tour and he made only 13 appearances. The illness caused him to remain behind in England when the team sailed for North America. Known by his nickname of Massa.

THE ORIGINALS AT EALING. Top row: Glasgow, Wallace, Newton, Mynott. Fourth row: Deans, Hunter, Nicholson, Johnston. Third row: Duncan, Booth, Corbett, Tyler, McGregor, Seeling, Roberts. Second row: Gillett, Abbott, Dixon, Cunningham (standing), Gallaher, Stead, Glenn, Mackrell. Front row: Casey, McDonald, Smith, Thomson, O'Sullivan. Absent: Harper.

GAME 19 — WEDNESDAY 15 NOVEMBER 1905 — at Goldington Road, Bedford

NEW ZEALAND
BEDFORD

41
0

FOR NEW ZEALAND
Tries by Hunter 4, Deans, McDonald,
McGregor, Mynott, Roberts, Seeling;
conversions by Gillett 2, Tyler 2; goal from a
mark by Gillett.

NEW ZEALAND
Gillett, Harper, Deans, Hunter, McGregor,
Mynott, Roberts, Gallaher (captain),
McDonald, Seeling, Corbett, Nicholson, Tyler,
Casey.

BEDFORD
G. Romans, E.R. Mobbs, B. Maclear,
M.E. Finlinson, H.J. Anderson, A. Hudson,
H.C. Palmer, T.H. Preston, A.L. Rogers,
R.B. Campbell, H.B. Follitt, W. Johns,
J. Mason, A.V. Manton, R. Maclear (captain).

Weather: Showery, ground slippery
Referee: F.W. Nicholls (Leicester)
Crowd: 8000

KICK OFF
Roberts kicked high for McGregor who put Hunter across. Harper missed: 3-0.
Mynott put Hunter across for another try, Harper missed: 6-0.
Roberts weaved through the defence from broken play. McGregor missed: 9-0.
Gallaher broke from a scrum and put Seeling in. Gillett converted.

HALFTIME
New Zealand 14, Bedford 0

Hunter ran hard from a scrum and put Deans in for a try. Gillett missed: 17-0.
McDonald scored at the conclusion of a dribbling rush. Gillett missed: 20-0.
From a mark called by Seeling, Gillett landed the goal: 23-0.
Nicholson burst through a lineout, creating a try for McGregor. Gillett converted: 28-0.
Hunter handled twice from a scrum before scoring. Tyler converted: 33-0.
The backline swung into action and Hunter scored again. Gillett missed: 36-0.
Mynott handled twice from a scrum before scoring. Tyler converted.

FULLTIME
New Zealand 41, Bedford 0

FROM THE SIDELINES

BEDFORD CHRONICLE

EVER SINCE IT WAS KNOWN that the Bedford RU had secured a fixture with the visitors from New Zealand great interest was taken in it, and since the Colonials have become so famous, their career has been followed with the keenest interest, not only in Bedford but all over the country.

This enthusiasm in no way abated as time went on, but rather increased until it culminated in their appearance on the Goldington Road ground on Wednesday afternoon.

Never before has any team created such a sensation in the rugby football world, proof of which is shown by the tens of thousands who flock to witness their matches, and many are now willing to admit that they are far and away the best rugby combination seen for many a long year.

They have carried everything before them; no matter what the team, they are all treated alike, in that all have had to lower their colours to our visitors from 'down under'.

Their style of play, which is somewhat different to that in vogue in this country, has certainly had something to do with their marvellous run of successes, but this is not the only reason and principal reason lies in the fact that they are in real earnest, are a magnificent set of athletes and always keep in the pink of condition.

Before they left New Zealand each man had to pass a medical examination, and no one was chosen unless the doctor certified him as sound in wind and limb.

When the English international team, under the captaincy of Mr J. Bedell-Sievright, visited Australia a couple of seasons back, they had a similar run of success, until they met these same New Zealanders in the very last match of the tour when they had to chronicle their first and only defeat.

This was very significant, and the game was a foreshadowing of what might be expected when they visited England.

> ## BILLY WALLACE'S RECOLLECTIONS
>
> On Tuesday we paid a visit to the Duke of Portland's famous place Welbeck Abbey. It was a beautiful place, but a peculiar feature was the numerous underground passages leading from the castle to the stables, where the Duke kept his racehorses. The secretary took us into one very luxurious stable where we found the old New Zealand racehorse Carbine, who was then too old for racing but was kept for stud purposes.
>
> When we entered his stable, the secretary said, 'Hullo Carbine, I've brought some of your New Zealand friends to see you.'
>
> And you would have thought the old horse understood us, for he turned his head and looked us all over as if we were old friends. We all admired and patted him and, as a souvenir, the secretary pulled a number of hairs out of his tail and gave them to us.

The town officials and more especially the secretary (Mr Willett) and treasurer (Mr Flook) have had an anxious and busy time in doing their best to cope with the difficulties in providing extra accommodation; that they succeeded in making the most of the space at their disposal no one will deny.

The Duke and Duchess of Manchester motored over from Kimbolton Castle, with a couple of friends, and from their chairs in front of the grandstand seemed to thoroughly enjoy the progress of the game.

And now that it is all over, and we are beaten, we are still well content. It was a grand game and played with a dash and determination on both sides that speedily infected and at the last almost carried away the amazed spectators.

Truly, it is not possible in ordinary newspaper jargon to describe the keenness, the alertness, the smartness, the trickiness, the eeliness of these 'black' fellows. The ball could not go wrong for them, whether it went to their hands, or body, or back, or head, it was all the same; they were ready to receive it and they held it. Only once was it dropped all through the hundreds of passings it made.

They are simply invincible on the form they showed against Bedford. It is evident that, at all events for the duration of this tour, they live for football; they take care of themselves and each other; they are in perfect condition; they know one another's play absolutely.

J.B. MINAHAN, DAILY EXPRESS

SO MUCH HAS BEEN SAID about the abilities of the All Blacks that the only remark I can make is they should be styled 'the Slaughterers'.

Bedford make a bold effort to stem their victorious career by soliciting the aid of many well-known players, and their chagrin was great to be beaten by so many points.

One fact was made manifest at the start — combination was absent from their ranks, and it was that that beat them.

The ground was slippery owing to a heavy hailstorm a few minutes before the start and initially neither team could handle the ball.

As the ground dried, we were treated to some fine football. Greasy as the ball was the Colonials could handle with more accuracy than Bedford and time after time great efforts by the visiting threequarters were made.

The second half proved most exhilarating. Bent on teaching the scholastic town a lesson, the visitors played beautiful football.

Every time the ball came to Roberts things became lively. The passing was simply bewildering and altogether greater speed and better football was shown than I have seen before by them.

Hunter was great and so were Roberts and Gallaher; in fact, everyone fore and after played superbly.

I cannot but think more spirit and determination were shown by the All Blacks because of Bedford daring to play 'outsiders'.

BEDFORD PLAYER GEORGE ROMANS, IN THE DAILY EXPRESS

BEDFORD HAD SOME OUTSIDE HELP yesterday but all the same the 'Blacks' got a nice lot of points.

This is the first time I have had the pleasure of playing against them, and I must say that, without any exception, they are the finest team I have ever seen. What they do not know about rugby football is not worth knowing. Let us hope here in England we shall study the game as they do, to a man.

Hunter was a perfect marvel and fairly electrified our defence. The secret of their success is their pace, and every man in the team knowing what to do with the ball when he gets it — that is, going straight for the goalline.

Some of the tries in the second half were simply splendid, as quite eight or nine men handled the ball, and then they had men to spare when the final transfer was given.

◆

DAILY EXPRESS

BEDFORD PEOPLE ARE VERY KEEN on rugby football but after seeing the New Zealanders defeat their fifteen by 41 points to nil there is still a misgiving as to whether it really was rugby they so often applauded previously in their own townsfolk.

Rarely has such a fine exhibition of open play been seen as that given by the Colonials. Their advertised backs did most of it but it is by now nothing new to state that every man in the side fills the role of a back once the ball is set rolling from hand to hand.

There was so many superb bits of accurate understanding in the lightning-like passing runs that they cannot be all dealt with.

However, it is improbable whether any football spectator has ever seen such a movement as that which led up to McGregor's score in the second half.

The fullback did not handle the ball, and perhaps two or three other members of the team did not either, but so many did that a torrent of enthusiasm distracted all attention from mere detail for the meantime. It was a marvellous try.

There was one grain of comfort for Bedford folk left at the conclusion of the game of their lifetime. They had produced Basil Maclear.

Without underestimating the way his companions stuck to solid tackling, there can be little doubt that but for him New Zealand would have exceeded the half-century.

He downed the Colonials incessantly; in fact, he once tackled three opponents in the space of a few seconds. He was responsible, too, for bringing Bedford to as near as they got to scoring, but the ball was kicked dead just in time.

◆

NEW ZEALAND TIMES' UK CORRESPONDENT

THE MAN WHO COMPLETELY BAFFLED and bewildered the Bedfordians was 'Jimmy' Hunter, whose eel-like zig-zags reduced the home defence to a state of mute helplessness and despair.

A well-known rugby critic declares that there has never been a player of such marvellous individual scoring capacity before.

He was certainly in scoring mood on Wednesday, scoring four tries and gifting another to Mynott. The ease with which he deluded the home team upon occasion was ludicrous, and set the whole crowd laughing.

Once he drew the defence over to the left by heading diagonally towards the left-hand corner and then, stopping dead in his stride, was off like a flash in the other direction, cutting past the threequarters and fullback before they could check their pace.

Needless to say, the manoeuvre ended in a ridiculously easy try. On another occasion Hunter got through so unexpectedly that the locals were too astonished to give chase and the unusual sight was witnessed of the man with the ball slowing down to a walk before crossing the line and touching down.

The quiet humour shown in the scoring of this try was greatly appreciated by the crowd who will long remember the wonderful doings of the little Taranaki marvel.

His fifth 'try' as already related was calmly presented as a gift to Mynott who received the ball from Hunter after the latter had eluded all opposition and the Blacks had the enemy's goalline to themselves.

I notice that the *Daily Telegraph* critic compares him favourably with two well-known giants of the past, A.E. Stoddart who 'in his prime made splendid zig-zag runs through his antagonists' and A.L. Brooke of the Leysians who 'possessed a remarkable swerve'.

'But neither,' says the *Telegraph* critic, 'was more difficult to tackle than the famous five-eighths who is such a tower of strength to the New Zealanders.'

JIMMY HUNTER

Taranaki — second-five
26, 5ft 6in, 11st 8lb

Born in Hawera and educated at Wanganui Collegiate, Hunter made his international debut by captaining New Zealand on its short tour of Australia prior to the Originals' great venture. He was a versatile player, having previously represented his province at halfback, wing and fullback. He was one of the superstars of the 1905 tour, being described as 'one of the most sinuous runners ever seen' and scoring an astonishing 44 tries in his 24 tour matches, including all five tests. Coming from a wealthy background, Hunter was one of the three members of the originals (Deans and Harper were the others, with O'Sullivan also involved) who each Monday put £2 into a fund for the less fortunate members of the team.

MONA THOMSON, Billy Wallace and Fred Roberts resplendent in bowler hats.

GAME 20 — SATURDAY 18 NOVEMBER 1905 — at Inverleith, Edinburgh

NEW ZEALAND
SCOTLAND

12
7

FOR NEW ZEALAND
Tries by Smith 2, Cunningham, Glasgow.

NEW ZEALAND
Gillett, Smith, Deans, Hunter, Wallace,
Stead, Roberts, Gallaher (captain), Seeling,
McDonald, Glasgow, Cunningham,
O'Sullivan, Casey, Tyler.

FOR SCOTLAND
Try by MacCallum; dropped goal by Simson.

SCOTLAND
J.G. Scoular (Cambridge University),
L.M. MacLeod (Cambridge University),
K.G. MacLeod (Cambridge University),
T. Sloan (Glasgow Academicals),
J.T. Simson (Watsonians), L.L. Greig (Glasgow
Academicals), E.D. Simson (Edinburgh
University), P. Munro (Oxford University),
L. West (Carlisle), W.P. Scott (West
of Scotland), W.L. Russell (Glasgow
Academicals), J.C. McKenzie (Edinburgh
University), J.C. MacCallum (Watsonians),
W.E. Kyle (Hawick), D.R. Bedell-Sivright
(captain, Edinburgh University).

Weather: Fine and cold, ground icy
Referee: W. Kennedy (Ireland)
Crowd: 21,000

KICK OFF
Simson drop-kicked a goal for Scotland: 0-4.
Seeling dribbled and caught the fullback, Glasgow scoring. Wallace missed: 3-4.
The All Black backs attacked from a scrum, Smith scoring. Wallace missed: 6-4.
Scotland surged 50 metres from a lineout, MacCallum scoring. K. MacLeod missed.

HALFTIME
Scotland 7, New Zealand 6

Four minutes from time Smith, in a great run, eluded the fullback and scored. Gillett missed: 9-7.
Stead kicked deep and in a frantic chase Cunningham scored. Wallace missed.

FULLTIME
New Zealand 12, Scotland 7

FROM THE SIDELINES

ILLUSTRATED AND SPORTING NEWS

THE NEW ZEALAND TEAM reached the zenith of their fame on Saturday when after one of the most exciting contests ever seen in the history of rugby football they won the first of their international matches, with Scotland as their opponents, by 12 points to 7.

The match was played at the Scottish union's headquarters at Inverleith, Edinburgh, and its many exciting incidents which had a very sensational finale will be talked of in rugby circles for many years to come.

It is no exaggeration to say that since international football was inaugurated nearly 35 years ago no match under the handling code in Scotland has evoked such widespread interest as this game.

There are no official figures by which a comparison of the attendance can be made, but so far as general appearances went the 'gate' on Saturday was the largest ever seen at a rugby match in Scotland.

Certain it is that there was never such a terrific scramble for seats or conveyances from Princes Street to the ground, and such a wild rush to secure positions from which the best view of the match could be obtained.

The eagerness thus shown before the match furnished on the one hand a striking indication of the interest which the performances of the 'All Blacks' have aroused in the United Kingdom, and on the other demonstrated how little was known a few months ago of the great prowess of the New Zealand exponents of the handling game.

In arranging their tour the New Zealand Rugby Union had to form a guarantee fund of £4000, and for the international matches, it is understood a sum of £500 was asked to be guaranteed by each national union.

Apparently the Scotsmen could not see their way clear to give a guarantee of this kind. What they did was to promise the New Zealanders the whole of the takings of their match as their contribution towards the expenses of the tour.

This was an effort which in its results enabled the Scottish Union to take credit to themselves for magnificent generosity.

One does not know what the sum actually taken at Inverleith on Saturday was, but as 2500 reserved seats were paid for long before the match took place, and over 20,000 persons paid for admission to the enclosure, it is not an extravagant estimate to place the receipts at more than £1000.

THE NEW ZEALAND TEAM en route to Inverleith.

BILLY WALLACE'S RECOLLECTIONS

When New Zealand decided to send a team Home in 1905, it had to undertake the finances of the tour itself and consequently it asked the various counties and Home Unions for guarantees for games.

These were forthcoming readily enough but the Scottish Rugby Union refused to give a guarantee, though it also said New Zealand could take the whole of the gate, less match expenses.

The year before, a Canadian team had toured the Home Countries and had asked for guarantees, which were given. The team proved very much a 'frost' and the guarantors were, in most cases, heavy losers.

Naturally the Scots did not want to be caught twice. Then, too, they were told the New Zealand team was not really a strong combination. It would probably beat the counties but stand no chance in the international games. Acting on this information they made the offer which New Zealand accepted.

Of course it was not long before the All Blacks were the drawcard of the year and the crowds flocked in their thousands to see us play. The clubs and counties that had given guarantees were in clover and some of the papers began to poke fun at Scotland over the bad bargain that had been made.

The Scottish Union began to get the huff and before the match they announced that it would not be regarded as an International match and the players would not get their caps for playing in it.

Of course this was quite ridiculous and we were about as popular as a plague of the smallpox in the eyes of the Scottish Union. Yet we ourselves had done nothing to warrant this treatment. The fault really lay with the English papers for rubbing it in so hard.

Consequently Edinburgh was the only place on tour where we did not receive a warm official welcome as we stepped off the train. Several of us (myself included)

were of Scottish descent and were proud of it. We were in no way responsible for the bad advice on which they had acted.

Yet during our stay in Edinburgh the Scotch officials did not come near us or recognise us in any way. Indeed, they did everything to make the match a 'wash out'. They refused to protect the ground from frost, as is always done by covering it with straw the night before, and so when we stepped out for the match the ground was positively dangerous. It was as hard as concrete and we slipped around as if we were running on ice, as indeed we were.

The selection committee decided to leave the final selection of the team until we reached Edinburgh. We had quite a number of players on the injured list including three of our wing threequarters — Mona Thomson, Duncan McGregor and Bunny Abbott — and some of our best forwards.

BOB DEANS,
IN A LETTER HOME

On our arrival in Edinburgh we were received with cheers and war cries from a large number of Australasian students, a large proportion of whom were from New Zealand.

We had two or three days' hard frost, and in the morning it was thought the ground would be too hard to play on, but on inspection we decided not to postpone the match.

Generally straw is put on the field of play in cold weather, so as to counteract the effects of frost, but the committee evidently thought it was too early in the season for a hard one and they neglected this precaution.

The result was a ground as hard as a board, and almost as slippery as ice. The ball, which was very light, bounced anywhere and the men slipped whenever they made a sharp turn.

This was all against back play, and Scotland played a spoiling game, using their forwards as much as possible and playing on to our backs.

The referee, Mr Kennedy from Ireland, was not of the best. He stopped two scores of ours on the plea of a forward pass, he himself being about twenty yards behind, from which position he could not possibly see.

Scotland drew first blood with Ernest Simson potting a goal but we responded with two scores, one by Glasgow from a fine forward rush and the other by Smith from a bout of passing amongst the backs.

Scotland then scored a try through John MacCallum, thus leading by a point, a position they kept all though the first spell and most of the second.

New Zealand were having the better of the game and only the referee's whistle and a few minor infringements kept us from scoring. Wallace hit the post once from a free kick.

With six minutes to go and Scotland in our twenty-five, it looked as if we were in for our first reverse, but the forwards worked gradually down the field and the ball came out amongst the backs, Smith scoring his second try after a beautiful run.

Soon after this Cunningham scored from a dribbling rush, time being called with New Zealand 12 points, Scotland 7.

The crowd (which numbered 21,000) were not very fair. They hooted our players for hard tackling and took no notice when one of their men charged Wallace and knocked him out after he had kicked the ball.

The Scottish forwards were the best we have yet met, being big and active and playing a dashing, hard game. They kept the ball tight as much as possible, their backs preferring to find touch instead of making the game open.

Their potted goal was a smart bit of work but their try should have been disallowed for a most palpable knock-on.

Our team hardly played with as much dash as usual but they were hampered by the ground to a large extent and the referee's allowing their backs to play offside.

In the evening we were entertained at a smoke concert by the members of the Australasian Club.

Whether the Scottish Union will pass over a cheque of these dimensions without thinking that their judgement has been somewhat at fault is not a matter that need be here discussed.

It was very freely commented upon in football circles at Edinburgh on Saturday, but, of course, a bargain is a bargain and a Scotsman's word is as good as his bond. Financially, as in a football sense, and really one follows the other, the New Zealanders' tour has been extraordinarily successful.

It must, however, be borne in mind that the estimate of the expenses of the tour fixed a sum of £7000 as necessary for defraying its total cost, and the football community may be assured of this, that if there is any surplus when the accounts are squared, it is the game at large, and not its Colonial personalities, that will in any way benefit.

Saturday's match came desperately near being wrecked by the first grip of winter. There was a very sharp frost in Edinburgh on Friday night and when the Inverleith ground was inspected its surface was found to contain an unpleasant quantity of 'bone'.

The rumour went round that the match might after all not take place, but fortunately this was not well founded. At the same time it is doubtful if the state of the turf was quite safe for the playing of rugby football with that abandon which is usually seen in international matches.

The players had to contemplate the barking of shins, and this was one reason why so many of them were found to have their knees swathed in bandages, lint having been freely used as a precautionary measure.

It was known that Dr Fell would persist in his refusal to play for Scotland against his native New Zealanders, but not until just before the match did it become public property that Greig, of the Glasgow Academicals, would take his place.

SCOTLAND desperately close to scoring.

SCOTTISH EVENING DESPATCH

PERHAPS WE EXPECTED TOO MUCH of the visitors. They had been lauded to the clouds in every one of their previous matches, and a team of almost superhuman strength and skill were looked for.

They won, and the greatest credit is certainly due to them for the never-say-die spirit which they showed at the finish, and for the manner in which, when all seemed up, they pulled off the match.

But even allowing for their magnificent finish, they were a trifle disappointing. They were speedy; there is no doubt about that, and they were physically fine types of men, but when passing they did not give or take the ball in the clean way we had been led to expect they would, and they were often faulty in their fielding.

It is no exaggeration to say that but for their blundering they would have given the Scotsmen a much sounder thrashing than they did, and on the whole Scotland had good reason to be thankful, though it was in a sense rough on the Scots, both the players and spectators, to see the glories of what would have been a great victory elude them in the last minutes.

The New Zealanders recovered themselves in time to keep their record spotless, and their joy was unrestrained when ultimately they put the issue out of doubt.

The scorer, G.W. Smith, one of the famous men of the side, was embraced, and literally wept over by his fellows, and if they did not kiss him, well, they came very near to it. Their delight was natural, for it meant that they had won their first international, even though by the narrowest margin yet recorded against them.

YORKSHIRE POST

That the scotsmen were much disappointed at the prize of victory being wrested from their grasp at almost the last moment was but natural. The result, however, was a just reflex of the play.

New Zealand won because they proved themselves to be the better exponents of football. To Scotsmen remains the credit of a great fight worthily fought against a superior combination. There is no sting in a defeat thus endured.

It may be argued that the Scotsmen were unfortunate in losing the match after being ahead until a few minutes of its close. Such a contention, however, is wrong.

A victory for Scotland would have been a triumph of dash, pluck and endurance, but it would not have been in keeping either with the run of the play or the comparative skill of the combatants.

New Zealand would, in short, have been unlucky to lose, for the simple reason that they were the better team, and on the play, were entitled to victory.

At least four times during the match, the superior speed and combination of the Colonials' backs broke the defence down completely, but the referee adjudged the pass to have been forward.

BILLY WALLACE'S RECOLLECTIONS

One amusing little incident reminded us that we were in the land of canny Scots. When we retired for the night we put our boots out to be cleaned but neglected to put in anything by way of a tip. When we went out the next morning we found them filled with hard, mouldy breadcrusts!

◆

On the morning of the match Bedell-Sivwright (the Scotland captain) and the secretary of the Scottish Union came to inform us that the match couldn't be played as the ground was too dangerous. This was about the last straw. You can well imagine what we were thinking among ourselves about the Scotch idea of 'playing the game'.

By this time we were stubborn too. Our committee which consisted of George Dixon, Jimmy Hunter, Billy Stead and myself, went with Bedell-Sivwright and Aickman-Smith in cabs to have a look for ourselves. When we got there the ground was already packed with spectators. The ground was absolutely iron and slippery, being almost impossible for players to keep their feet.

The crowd guessed our object as we came out to inspect the ground and called out to us to play. We were there for about half an hour and finally decided we would play, much to the disgust of the Scotchmen. Then we went back to the hotel and told the team — we were pretty wild at the treatment that was being meted out to us.

When we were in our togs and ready to go on the field there was an argument about the lengths of the spells. Finally we compromised. Then there was an argument about the ball. The Scots reckoned we should have supplied the ball, but we had not brought one with us. At last they brought out an old thing shaped like a torpedo and all out of shape. Where they dug it up from I don't know, but it was well past its prime.

We all had our studs on our boots, but when the Scotsmen came out we noticed they had bars on their boots which gave them a much better grip on the ground. As for us it was almost agony to run after we had been playing some little time; we all had blood blisters on the soles of our feet.

Shortly after Scotland scored I was laid out by a foul charge. I was in midfield at the time and had made one of my long kicks for touch near the corner flag. The ball was travelling nicely and I was watching it bounce into touch when all of a sudden I felt a bump. My feet flew up from under me and I landed with a crack on the back of my head. I was, of course, rendered unconscious.

Then as I began to come to I heard voices, faint and far away, but gradually coming nearer while dark shapes hovered over me. 'Are you all right, Bill?' and I started to sit up a little but I felt very groggy. Naturally our fellows were very wild and I am afraid this particular player came off very badly later in the game in a merry mix-up.

Then in the second half, just as things were looking

black for us the winning try came. A scrum was formed near halfway and about fifteen yards in from touch. Our forwards hooked the ball, and the opposing halves bore down with a rush on Freddy Roberts and Billy Stead. Freddy summed up the situation quickly and threw a beautiful dummy which sent the opposing halves past him. Then in a flash he was racing diagonally across the field, and at the right moment he sent out a perfect pass to Bob Deans, who drew the wing threequarter and sent the ball on to George Smith.

By this time we were on our toes. George was already well into his stride and sailing like a bird for the goalline. The fullback came at him, but George left him standing with a swerve and raced ahead with an open paddock. We were cheering wildly. They had no chance of catching George and he grounded the ball in the corner.

We chaired him back into the field of play and shook his hand until it must have been nearly wrenched off.

There were still most unpleasant incidents to come. After the match no jerseys were exchanged, and they filed off to their dressing rooms and we to ours. We dined at our hotel, very pleased with ourselves, but the Scotch Union put on a dinner to which we were not invited. The Australasian Club, however, determined that we would not be left in the cold and they put on a fine smoke concert for us. They gave us a royal time and Dr Leighton, who proposed our health, extended to us the heartiest of welcomes. The toast was drunk with great enthusiasm.

That he may have been accurate in his decisions is possible. As a matter of opinion, however, the writer must state that two of these attacks were accurately carried out, and should not have been nullified by Mr Kennedy's whistle.

We do not think the New Zealanders will have to face such splendid forwards as fought for Scotland during the remainder of their tour.

FLANEUR, ATHLETIC NEWS

AT THE PRECISE MOMENT, the centre (Deans) handed it on to Smith who was rushing down the left wing at top speed, and the famous hurdler gathered it magnificently and, dashing past Scoular, the Scottish fullback, planted it over the line in the corner.

This was the winning point and Smith was the hero of the day and the object of boisterous congratulations from his delighted comrades who had almost given up the game as lost. It did not matter that the goal missed. The match was won.

It was a match that kept the excitement at fever heat throughout, and that try of Smith's, that brought such a well-merited victory to the New Zealanders, was worth going a long way to see. The greatness of the try was in the brilliant seizing of a bare opportunity. Had the pass been missed, had Smith wavered when he met Scoular, probably all would have been over and Scotland victorious.

But the brilliant sprinter is nothing if not an opportunist, and this try was a fitting wind-up to an afternoon's sparkling display. Smith was always doing something smart and he was the bright star of the side.

The New Zealanders played a fair and sportsmanlike game. They took and gave little quarter in tackling, but there were no unfair tactics, and the only unpleasant incident in the match was the charging over of Wallace by one of the Scotsmen after the New Zealander had kicked the ball.

It was a magnificent match from start to finish. Quarter was neither given nor asked for, play being of a most resolute character throughout. For reasons best known to themselves the Scottish Committee refused to recognise this fixture in the light of an International and in consequence no caps were awarded.

BILLY WALLACE lines up a conversion attempt.

GEORGE DIXON'S DIARIES

On arriving at the ground found a big crowd assembled, estimated to be the biggest ever seen at Inverleith and the teams were welcomed onto the ground, at different ends, by a brass band and a pipers band respectively. The same bands continued to march round the ground at the interval.

The ball provided was of the very long, torpedo variety, and being too tightly blown, and consequently very light, the already great difficulty of playing good football was largely increased. I never saw a ball cut such extraordinary antics in my life, and having regard to the slippery foothold, it is wonderful that the players on both sides caught and fielded it as they did.

The committee of the Scottish Rugby Union decided not to award 'caps' for the match, but nevertheless the great public interest in the fixture and the immense attendance caused it to be regarded as 'an international'.

G.A.W. LAMOND, SCOTTISH REVIEW

OUGHT THE ALL BLACK methods to be copied?
The New Zealand wing forward Gallaher's habit of wearing shin-guards was unusual. And part of the team's unpopularity was because he was pitted against some of the most diminutive halfbacks on record and the sympathy of the crowd always goes forth to the little one.

The wing-forward game as we have seen it played here during the last three months has not been an edifying spectacle, nor one of instruction either, and one shivers to think what would be the outcome of all these new-fangled ideas if all our clubs and counties were to adopt, say, three wing-forwards. There have been many fine wing-forwards playing footer, but till the New Zealanders arrived here one has never seen any with such presumption and certainly never one who wilfully obstructed the opposing halfbacks.

Bar giving a fillip to the rugby-football-going public, I don't honestly see that much good has been done to the playing community by this tour.

SCOTLAND prepare to throw to a lineout.

THE ALL BLACKS complete their haka prior to the kick-off against Scotland.

C.B. FRY'S MAGAZINE

THE TREATMENT OF THE NEW ZEALAND footballers in Scotland is forever a blot upon the fair fame of Scottish hospitality.

That this treatment is no imagination may be clearly shown by narrating the series of things which happened which should not have happened:

(1)   Refusal to give dates.

(2)   Refusal to award caps to the Scottish team, which at once brought the game down to the level of an exhibition, a decision that was in itself a slur on the New Zealanders.

(3)   Non-protection of the ground from frost or snow.

(4)   Colonials given no option over the choice of ball.

(5)   Chilling reception by the crowd of a great victory won in the last few minutes, but a feat of scoring on such a pitch that was probably quite beyond the powers of any other team that has ever played!

(6)   Wrongful accusations of rough and foul play by writers to the Press. In this matter no blame can be attached to the players or officials.

(7)   Ignoring of their guests by the Scottish players.

YORKSHIRE POST

THAT THE SCOTSMEN were much disappointed at the prize of victory being wrested from their grasp at almost the last moment was but natural. The result, however, was a just reflex of the play.

New Zealand won because they proved themselves to be better exponents of football. To Scotland remains the credit of a great fight worthily fought against a superior combination, a fight that was very nearly won. There is no sting in a defeat thus endured. It may be argued the Scotsmen were unfortunate in losing the match after being ahead until a few minutes of its close. Such a contention is, however, wrong.

A victory for Scotland would have been a triumph of dash, pluck and endurance, but it would not have been in keeping either with the run of the play or the comparative skill of the combatants.

There was this great contrast between the two teams, and whereas Scotsmen played for dear life as it were, fearing to risk nothing on the hard ground — and the turf was frozen really dangerously — the New Zealanders trusted to the more skilful methods which mark the modern game.

It was a triumph of brains over brawn, of mind over matter. The New Zealanders captured the Scotch citadel by brainy, flank movements; the Scotsmen fell in a dauntless frontal attack. Of individual skill as well as courage, there was no lack on the Scotsmen's side; it was in the art of combined application that the team were found wanting. Daredevil individuality has ever been a prized possession of the fighting Scot, but this is not the first time that slimness has prevailed against it.

BOB DEANS

Canterbury — centre
21, 6ft, 13st 4lb

From an old Canterbury family, Deans came on the scene as a 19-year-old for High School Old Boys in 1903, scored Canterbury's only try against the British team in 1904 and was an early selection for the 1905 New Zealand team. A naturally gifted footballer, he was described by Canterbury contemporary Leo Fanning thus: 'He's 13st of fleetness, 13st of courage and 13st of deadly tackling. On the field he was a castle in defence, with wall and moat, and a mountain battery in attack. Off it, he was a man for all to respect and esteem.' His death in 1908 at the age of 24, of complications from appendicitis, plunged the rugby fraternity of New Zealand into grief.

GAME 21 — WEDNESDAY 22 NOVEMBER 1905 — at Hampden Park, Glasgow

NEW ZEALAND
WEST OF SCOTLAND

22
0

FOR NEW ZEALAND
Tries by McGregor 2, Mynott, Roberts,
Seeling, Smith;
2 conversions by Wallace.

NEW ZEALAND
Wallace, Harper, Smith, Stead (captain),
McGregor, Mynott, Roberts, Gillett, Glasgow,
Seeling, McDonald, Newton, Glenn, Tyler,
Johnston.

WEST OF SCOTLAND
H.N. Tennant (West of Scotland),
W. Church (Glasgow Academicals), T. Sloan
(Glasgow Academicals), C.W. Stewart (West
of Scotland), C.C. Fitzgerald (Glasgow
University), J.A. Findlay (Kelvinside
Academicals), L.L. Greig (Glasgow
Academicals), A.C. Frame (Glasgow
Academicals), W.L. Russell (Glasgow
Academicals), W.P. Scott (captain, West
of Scotland), R.B. Waddell (Glasgow
Academicals), H. Wilson (Glasgow
University), G.M. Fred (Glasgow High
School), W. Kaw (Kelvinside Academicals),
E.G. Copestake (Clydesdale).

Weather: Showery and windy, ground heavy
Referee: J.T. Gillespie (Edinburgh Academicals)
Crowd: 8000

KICK OFF
Harper secured the ball in the loose and put McGregor across. Wallace missed: 3-0.
Seeling broke from a lineout and Mynott put Smith over. Wallace converted.

HALFTIME
New Zealand 8, West of Scotland 0

Roberts broke from an attacking scrum, scoring a solo try. Wallace missed: 11-0.
Stead and Smith combined to put McGregor across. Wallace missed: 14-0.
Mynott scored from good play by Roberts and McGregor. Wallace converted: 19-0.
Seeling scored following a loose rush from a scrum. Wallace missed.

FULLTIME
New Zealand 22, West of Scotland 0

FROM THE SIDELINES

ILLUSTRATED SPORTING AND DRAMATIC NEWS

WHEN THE WESTMINSTER GAZETTE, referring to Mr Seddon's cable message to the *Daily Mail* rejoicing in the prowess of the New Zealand footballers, reproachfully asks, 'Is this really quite the sort of thing for a premier to cable?' it is evident that it does not yet appreciate what a very unconventional premier New Zealand possesses.

It is precisely because Mr Seddon is not cast in the stereotyped mould of other premiers that he has managed to attract so much notice in the English press. That enterprising paper, the *Daily Mail*, far from holding up its hands in shocked surprise at Mr Seddon's lack of reticence, simply makes use of him.

LONDON, 12 OCTOBER

Seddon, Premier of New Zealand — British public amazed brilliancy New Zealand footballers. Could you kindly let us know what New Zealand thinks of their remarkable success? Sincere thanks,

(signed) Editor, *Daily Mail.*

WELLINGTON, 18 OCTOBER

Editor, *Daily Mail*, London —

Not surprised British public amazed brilliance of New Zealand footballers. British team visiting the colonies in 1904 beaten by New Zealand and in two other matches gave an index of the standard of rugby football in England, and augured success for our pioneer team's visit to Mother Country.

Confidently anticipated present team prove equal to strongest team in England, demonstrating advancement scientific rugby football in this colony.

As indicating public interest here, information respecting contests taking place Great Britain awaited almost as eagerly as news late war South Africa and results received with great enthusiasm.

The natural and healthy conditions of colonial life produce stalwart and athletic sons of whom New Zealand and the Empire are justly proud.

(signed) Seddon.

Where a less up-to-date journalist falls back upon the big gooseberry, or a discussion on 'thriftless wives', this up-to-date editor proceeds to 'draw' Mr Seddon. That is what happened in the present case. Parliament being 'up' and finding things, no doubt, a little dull, this designing journalist — we blush for our profession! — telegraphed to Mr Seddon, 'British public amazed brilliancy New Zealand footballers. Could you kindly let us know what New Zealand thinks of their remarkable success?'

And then, with that species of gratitude which looks for favours to come, he confidently added, 'Sincere thanks'.

Nor was his confidence misplaced. There was that wonderful man, Mr Seddon, in the thick of parliamentary business, turning a blind eye, we are afraid, to the trust business about which we hear nothing, but finding time to make speeches to marine engineers and even to keep a fatherly eye on the editor of *The Press* and his Public Works statistics.

Yet in the midst of all those distractions Mr Seddon found time to send to the editor of the *Daily Mail* a flamboyant cable message which must have delighted that designing person's heart, and which, we may be quite sure, was honoured in very large type on the *Daily Mail*'s contents bill.

It was not a merely polite and conventional reply to the inquiry sent; if it had been, it would not have been worth its wire charges to the *Daily Mail*.

Mr Seddon let himself go in the most approved halfpenny paper fashion. So far from being surprised at the New Zealanders' success, it was only what he expected from the first, and the editor of the *Mail* must please understand that it is quite hopeless for Englishmen to think they have any chance of retrieving their position in the future — the New Zealanders will simply walk over them.

We shall not go into the question raised by the *Westminster Gazette* as to whether this is the sort of cable message a Prime Minister ought to send.

One thing we are quite certain of, namely that no other Prime Minister in the British dominions could have written it. And we have no doubt there was much joy in the *Daily Mail* office when it came to hand.

◆

GLASGOW NEWS

IT DID ONE GOOD, TO SEE THE burly fellows coming down the stairs, hear them passing the time of day quietly with their clubmates and asking, 'Where is that smell coming from?'

The interviewer tackled the first man he saw coming out of the scrum.

'Really,' he said, 'I would rather not say anything and, as a matter of fact, I have nothing at all to say that would interest anybody. But if you wait here a minute I'll send out Johnston; he can talk.'

Johnston duly emerged from the chamber of ham and eggs.

'Talk!,' he said, 'I can't talk. The man you want is Smithy. He'll keep you going.'

But Smithy had accepted a long pass and was far beyond the interviewer's reach.

The manager was in the smoking room, and so was captain Gallaher. Mr Dixon was settling some arrangements for tomorrow's match, evidently very busy, so the interviewer approached the captain. The captain shook his head and said not a word, and pointed to Mr Dixon.

Mr Dixon spoke — not much, it is true, but he spoke.

'It is very kind of you to call and inquire after us,' he said, 'but we have really nothing to tell you. We may have impressions and ideas but they are our own. We play our games as well as we can, and leave the spectators and the reporters to form their own impressions of us.'

'There is an impression,' said the interviewer, 'that you were lucky to win at Inverleith. Do you share that impression?'

'Certainly not. The score speaks for itself.'

'But if Scoular hadn't — '

'Quite so. But don't you think that there are as many "ifs" that could be advanced in our favour?'

'Were you surprised at the strength of the Scots?'

'No, we are never surprised at anything because we never form an opinion of any team till after we have played them.'

'Having played them, then, what do you think of them?'

'They were a very good team.'

'Were you particularly impressed with the forwards?'

'The whole team was good.'

Beyond this, however, Mr Dixon would not go. In answer to other questions, he said that the attendance was 'large' and the ground 'hard'. Matters of management called for his attention and, with a courteous 'Good morning' he ran out of touch.

◆
SCOTTISH EVENING DESPATCH

In 1896, the Hampden Park vacated by Queen's Park FC two seasons ago, and now occupied by the Third Lanark Club, was the scene of the rugby international between the representatives of Scotland and England, and a monster crowd saw the Scots triumph by a goal and two tries to nil.

Since then, no representative rugby event has been held on an association play ground, so that Queen's Park FC should feel flattered that their magnificent new enclosure at Mount Florida was selected from among the several fine grounds in the city for the match between the doughty New Zealanders and a picked Glasgow fifteen.

Had it been possible to devote a Saturday to the fixture, Hampden Park would, in all likelihood, have been set to accommodate a record crowd, but even in midweek there was the certainty of a considerable gathering. To allow the boys, and possibly the masters also, the opportunity of seeing the famous Colonials at play, most of the secondary schools were given a half holiday.

Since the New Zealanders arrived in the city on Monday they have had no special training, which, indeed, is to them superfluous, their frequent appearances in serious engagements being preparation enough.

Last night the majority of the party spent some time at the billiards match between Rae and Mitchell in the Renfield Rooms, and later witnessed the second performance at the Empire. Coming after the frost, the rain had a bad effect on the playing pitch which was rendered soft and slippery. This, of course, was just the condition calculated to give the city players a chance of playing the heavy, plodding game most suited to them, besides being inimical to the methods of the Colonials who like a fast-going surface.

When the New Zealanders drove up in their covered coaches, they were virtually overwhelmed with the flattering attention of some ladies, evidently Colonials, who shouted 'Miora', evidently a term of well wishing.

◆
JOHN J. RYCE, IRISH INDEPENDENT

FOOTBALL MARVELS

No event in recent times has excited such general and intense interest in sporting circles in these countries as the tour of the New Zealand rugby football team.

Theirs has been a remarkable record. What the Australians have been in cricket the New Zealanders are in football.

There was no agent in advance to 'puff' and herald the coming of the footballers. When, about ten weeks ago, they landed at Southampton to play a series of matches in England, Scotland, Ireland and Wales they were an unknown quality in football in these countries. Their fixtures were looked forward to with more curiosity than interest.

Already the Colonials, who in August last came into England

BILLY WALLACE'S RECOLLECTIONS

We saw little — or rather nothing — of the Glasgow officials or players until we met them on the field of play but we found many warm-hearted people in the city of Glasgow.

Perhaps our greatest admirers were the ladies, but here we were often at a disadvantage for we couldn't understand what they were saying! It was a bit hard on us when we were talking to a rosy-cheeked Scotch lassie with whom we were anxious to make a hit and we couldn't make out half of what she was saying.

The ladies would often come to us with their autograph books and ask us to write something in them. Then they would ask us to write something in Maori. We would scratch our heads, think out something nice and write down "Hurunui Waipiro Rotorua Taihape Ruapehu" or something like that.

It looked all right but then the girls would insist on us writing the translation! That made us scratch our heads a little harder but we would make up a very nice message and they were happy and so were we.

Sometimes, too, after a match a girl would come up and ask if she could see 'the man who played No 12 in the match'. If she was very nice looking the first man she happened to speak to was sure to have been No 12. But if she had a homely face she was quickly passed on to someone else. No one would claim the honour of having played No 12!

quietly, unostentatiously, and unknown, have created a revolution in the game of rugby football. They are feared, admired, marvelled.

The New Zealanders have defeated, one after another, the very best football combinations in England, Oxford and Cambridge Universities amongst the number. When clubs and counties failed, it was hoped that international teams would succeed in checking the onward triumphal march of the visitors from Maoriland.

Scotland was looked to to administer the first setback and last Saturday at Inverleith, in one of the most thrilling and most sensational football encounters ever witnessed in these countries, the Scotsmen, specially picked and obviously trained, had to admit defeat.

They could not maintain the awful pace set them by the New Zealanders, who scored a dramatic victory in the last two minutes.

To date, the Colonial footballers have won all 19 games played and scored 646 with only 22 points being scored against them.

For the next few days these wonderful missionaries of football will be in our midst, and it will be interesting to turn to a discussion as to how these New Zealanders came to be so proficient at this game which they, in common with Scotchmen, Welshmen and Irishmen, learned from John Bull.

What is the reason for the visitors' extraordinary success? It is simply this. In New Zealand, rugby football is the national game. The interest it excites and the followers it claims eclipse any other sport in the colony.

The configuration of the country, clear atmosphere and immediate access to grounds are conducive to a vigorous study of the game. Each leading club has its own gymnasium where, on wet half-holidays and evenings, the art of scrumming, hooking and defeating an opponent in the lineout are reduced to a science.

Spectators at football games in Maoriland are of all ages, from the youngster of ten to the old veteran of fifty.

Matrons don't take kindly to the sport, but numbers of young girls attend regularly and are quite as interested in the scores and almost as excited as are their brothers, fathers and lovers.

Girls down in that interesting colony will discuss football by the hour. What they don't know of the points of the game is not worth knowing. They rarely go to football matches without sporting proudly the colours of the club they follow.

The Government of the Colony, quite as much as the people, help to sustain the intense interest in the game. Footballers generally vote Mr Seddon, of frozen meat fame, a perfect president.

His Government openly sympathises with the national game. All official telegrams sent from England to New Zealand conveying the results of this tour's matches are at the expense of the Colonial Government. A correspondent tells us that when the news of the first New Zealand victories in England were made public through the Colony, men, women and children thronged the streets singing, cheering and enthusing. It was a time of general rejoicing.

One important matter that may largely explain the splendid success of the Colonial team is this. When the tour through Great Britain was decided on, the Maoriland Rugby Union made no class distinction in the selection of the footballers who were to invade England. No candidate was asked who he was or what he was or what his trade or profession was. The man is quite as good as his master in Colonial sport.

Of the fifty-three men nominated, six were navvies, four were carpenters with boilermakers and blacksmiths making up another six. There were ten farmers and farm hands, four frozen mutton specialists, three storemen, five miners, four bricklayers and one doctor (Fookes, who formerly represented England). One schoolmaster and one clerk completed the nomination from which the 27 footballers who have staggered the Britishers were selected.

Only four of the team had a real good English accent.

This tour is really the outcome of a tour made by British footballers to New Zealand not long ago. In that visit the British team was beaten by the All New Zealand team by 3 tries (9 points) to 1 try (3 points).

The total receipts were £5636 with the travelling expenses of the British team through the Colony amounting to £669.

The New Zealand union arranged this through Great Britain on a decidedly sound business basis. They got a guarantee from the English union of 70 per cent of the profits, besides a guarantee of a minimum of £500. They got a similar guarantee from Wales but Scotland said, 'We can't give you anything like that English or Welsh guarantee but you can take the entire profits of the match at Inverleith.' The New Zealand union, with commendable foresight, agreed and have pocketed £1100 as a result. The Scots weren't so canny after all!

Ireland is in a somewhat happier and luckier position. The Irish union, like the Scotch, never for a moment conceived that the New Zealanders would be surrounded by such a golden glamour.

The Irish proffer to the Colonials was the entire profit with a minimum of £100. The Colonials wanted £100 and half the profits and the Irish Union, with over £4000 to credit balance, agreed. It is safe to say the New Zealanders will make at least £500 from their visit to Dublin.

BILL CUNNINGHAM

Auckland — lock
31, 5ft 11in, 14st 6lb

A day before the S.S. *Rimutaka* sailed for Britain, Cunningham was added to the New Zealand team, as an extra lock, following the match against Wellington. It was a fortuitous decision, for Cunningham was a great hit on tour, both on and off the field. Full of humour and witty repartee, which left his team mates in fits of laughter, he was highly popular. The efficiency of the scrum was largely due to Cunningham's influence, dating back to the ship voyage where, with captain Gallaher's blessing, he taught two sets of forwards how to pack down against each other at lightning speed. 'Before our opponents realise what's happening, we'll have the ball in Freddy Roberts' hands and our backs galloping down the field . . .'

GAME 22 — SATURDAY, 25 NOVEMBER 1905 — at Lansdowne Road, Dublin

NEW ZEALAND
IRELAND

15
0

FOR NEW ZEALAND
Tries by Deans 2, McDonald;
3 conversions by Wallace.

NEW ZEALAND
Wallace, Smith, Deans, Hunter, Mynott,
Stead (captain), Roberts, Gillett, Glasgow,
Seeling, McDonald, Cunningham, O'Sullivan,
Casey, Tyler.

IRELAND
M.F. Landers (Cork), H. Thrift (Dublin
University), B. Maclear (Blackheath),
J.C. Parke (Dublin University), C.G. Robb
(Queen's College, Belfast), E.D. Caddell
(Dublin University), T.H. Robinson (Dublin
University), J. Wallace (Wanderers),
H.G. Wilson (Malone), A.D. Tedford
(Malone), H.S. Sugars (Dublin University),
H.J. Knox (Dublin University), G.T. Hamlet
(Old Wesley), J.J. Coffey (Lansdowne),
C.E. Allen (captain, Liverpool).

Weather: Drizzly, ground firm
Referee: J. Crauford Findlay (Scotland)
Crowd: 12,000

KICK OFF
Several players handled from a lineout before Deans scored, Wallace converted.

HALFTIME
New Zealand 5, Ireland 0

Roberts, Stead and Hunter handled before Deans scored. Wallace converted: 10-0.
McDonald picked up from a scrum on the Irish line and scored. Wallace converted.

FULLTIME
New Zealand 15, Ireland 0

FROM THE SIDELINES

DUBLIN EVENING HERALD

ONCE AGAIN THE NEW ZEALAND team has proved its superiority, and the great event of the football season is over, with Ireland as the latest of the Colonials' victims.

It was a magnificent struggle, worthy of the occasion, and few of those who were present at Lansdowne Road are likely to soon forget the scene.

Many famous battles have been fought in the same arena, but never was witnessed such a struggle as this.

From the start until the game had ended, it was one terrific combat for supremacy, in which the better team came out triumphant, for Ireland was fairly and squarely beaten.

But she has the satisfaction of knowing that no disgrace attaches to her failure, and can flatter herself with the knowledge that on Saturday her powerful opponents were kept at bay for 32 minutes, the longest time since the tour commenced.

Till close on the end of the first period the hopes of Ireland's supporters rose high, as up to this the Colonials were being hotly pressed, but the unfortunate want of scoring powers, which has often spoiled an Irish victory, made all these efforts valueless.

Then followed the first real opening to the visitors, which resulted in a score, and from this point on New Zealand had the match almost won.

Long before the match was timed to commence people began to take up their positions round the ground and by two o'clock, half an hour before the game started, there must have been at least 10,000 present.

Shortly afterwards the Chief Secretary for Ireland, accompanied by Lord Grenfell, Commander of the Forces, and a party arrived and was conducted to a specially erected dais on the Wanderers' touchline.

Ireland played as selected while the Colonials had to suffer the loss of their captain and famous wing forward Gallaher, who is at present on the injured list. This entailed a slight rearrangement of the team, Gillett going up to the scrummage, Wallace occupying the fullback position while Mynott was brought in as a wing threequarter.

INDEPENDENT

THEY'RE HERE AT LAST, these wonderful footballers from New Zealand, who have vanquished the very best players that could be pitted against them in England and Scotland.

They won their last match at Glasgow on Wednesday, drove back from the ground to the hotel, dined, took the train to Ardrossan, crossed over that night to Belfast and walked on to the platform at Amiens Street Station yesterday morning looking none the worse for their night Channel passage.

A nice warm bath and a hearty breakfast at the Imperial Hotel, Lower O'Connell Street, their headquarters in Dublin, and the Invincibles looked quite ready for further glorious athletic achievements.

Such a splendid lot of fellows are these Colonials. Any one of them might pose as an artist's model in physical development.

BILLY WALLACE'S RECOLLECTIONS

After our treatment at the hands of the Scottish Union how different it was in Ireland! As our train drew in to the station at Dublin thousands of people who had been waiting outside the gates surged forward, with the results that the gates were broken down as they surged onto the station.

When we stepped out of our carriages we were at once surrounded by a cheering throng and it was with the greatest difficulty that we eventually collected ourselves together again to drive to the hotel. The Irish people took us right into their hearts and hundreds of them came into our hotel to have a yarn. Among them were many representatives of firms doing business with New Zealand.

After lunch we were taken to see Guinness' famous brewery. When we arrived we found a miniature train drawn up for us. It had a little engine and baby carriages, each of which held one player. We got aboard with much fun and banter and off we went, the engine puffing bravely in front of us and trailing the long string of carriages. We waved and cracked jokes as we wound round the corners and bends or crossed the bridges.

We had a great afternoon and arrived back at our hotel very hungry — but not very thirsty!

When we got back to the hotel we found a magnificent supper all set out for us by the manager. We were on a great fuss and we all thought Ireland was the place for us.

On the Friday night before the game the weather changed for the worse and rain poured down. Picking our team was a very anxious job, for Gallaher had hurt his leg in Scotland and had to lay up. He was so bad he could not even attend the game. So George Gillett had to take his place at wing-forward and I had to go to fullback. We had not another sound wing-threequarter left.

Indeed it was with great difficulty that we could scrape together enough men to make up the backs. Eventually we decided to try Simon Mynott on the wing as an experiment and, though he had never played there before in his life, he made a great fist of it.

The referee was Mr Crauford Findlay of Scotland and he made a very good job of it.

There was the keenest interest in the game. All tickets had been sold days before and tickets which cost five shillings found ready buyers at forty-five shillings.

Ireland's best man was Basil Maclear, a big tall chap about 6ft 4in, powerfully built and able to do the hundred yards in a fraction over 10 seconds. He had a very strong run and was a most difficult man to stop when in his stride. He made several determined dashes but we did not let him go too far.

The Irish fellows played the game in the very finest spirit and tested our defence to the utmost. Their forwards were the finest pack we had struck and they never let up from start to the final whistle. The fact that they did not score was a wonderful tribute to our defence.

Broad-shouldered most of them, strong-limbed all of them, they show the clear eye and the resolute square jaw that bespeak the spirit of men who glory in achievement of the seemingly impossible.

And while they know their strength and their powers, and cannot but be cognisant of the golden glamour that surrounds them, they do not put on 'side'. They don't swagger.

In conversation they are easy and interesting. They won't talk about themselves. Those of them with whom the *Independent* representative chatted were anxious to learn as much as possible about Ireland, its industries and its people.

'Where's the dry dock about here?' asked one, anxious to see shipwrights at work, and another was very keen on seeing the inside of an Irish carpenter's shop during business hours.

When two of their number visited the *Independent* office last evening they were interested to see the manner in which we print off *Evening Herald* editions. The Goss machines were not new to them; they had seen one already at work in Auckland but said 'these were beauties'.

Generally speaking, our visitors will talk freely on any subject but themselves and football. However, one of them was found not so diffident as his colleagues. To give point to his denial of the statement that the players don't smoke or drink, he disposed of two cigarettes and did not pass over our best brand of Irish beverage.

At the suggestion that their food differed from the diet of ordinary mortals, he produced the menu of the dinner they enjoyed last evening at the Imperial Hotel. Each dish was introduced in Maori:

MENU

Ika (hors d'Oeuvres)
Ma a Ho Opi (creme Palestine)
Ta Muri (fillets of whiting)
Pi iwhi, Pu Ha a, Ri wai (roast ribs of beef,
green vegetables, potatoes)
Hei Hei, Ka Puti (roast chicken, salad)
Puku Nui (orange pudding)
Kati po (dessert)

'You ask me how we train. 'Twould take too long to tell you. Besides, you wouldn't print it all if I did tell you.

'But just to show you what we've done every day since we started playing matches in England, I'll tell you what we'll do between now and Saturday.

'Tonight we'll be at the Theatre Royal and we'll go to bed reasonably early. Tomorrow morning we'll get up about nine o'clock, have a breakfast and a smoke and saunter off to your football grounds here for an hour's run around.

'We'll do as we jolly well like for the rest of the day. Lunch some time after one, dine about half past six and after that I believe we're going to a performance at the Empire Palace Theatre.

'Do we go for dumbbells? Yes, and most of us can do a bit in the way of boxing. All useful out there, you know.' A comprehensive wave of the hand was meant to convey that he spoke of New Zealand.

MENU FOR THE All Blacks' post-test banquet in Dublin.

Is it true the New Zealanders left many broken hearts behind in England?

'That little joke is going the rounds of the papers. But don't you believe it. None of us are much of ladies' men. Though we have had letters.

'How many Irishmen on our team? None of us are Irish born, but some of us are of Irish descent. Personally, I should like to take back a sod of grass from Tipperary.

'I know one of our crowd who longs to have a peep at a place called Enniskillen. This is our first time in Ireland and I must say we like it. As we drove here to the hotel we felt we were amongst a good-hearted people. There is a warm, cheery feel about the place. I am sure we shall bring away with us many kindly memories.'

And then finally, 'You want me to tell you briefly the reasons of our success?

'Well, this is how it is. We have rapidity of attack, we use the science we have learned, each man exercises individual dash and discretion.

'We have beaten teams possessing weight, pace and fitness, but they have not what we have — science. The Scotchmen were the only ones who hustled us.

'Any one of us can play in any division of the team. For instance, I'm quite as happy back as I'm forward.'

IRISH TIMES

MANY GREAT BATTLES HAVE been fought on the football pitch at Lansdowne Road, but none has aroused curiosity or expectation in an equal degree with today's New Zealand international.

We say 'curiosity' advisedly, for there has been strangely little of the fiercer local sentiment that pertains to our yearly struggle for championship with England, Scotland and Wales.

Propinquity, doubtless, has its ardours, and next door neighbours make the fiercest rivals. Colonials we are apt to regard with commiseration as unfortunate relations whose business takes them from home, videlicet, Great Britain and Ireland.

Gentlemen from the Antipodes, it is said, take a different view, but that is a matter of detail. For the Colonial as such we have a kindly feeling that makes us want to pat him on the back when he offers to put himself against us, until he has beaten us, and knocked us about a bit, and then, indeed, we want to 'go' for him badly.

Not having suffered, or at all events having pretty well forgotten that we had suffered at Maori hands some seventeen years ago, our fiercer zeal was absent.

But the doings of the New Zealanders since their arrival a couple of months ago had certainly been such as to arouse a very legitimate curiosity to see them.

Such a triumphal procession from victory to victory never, surely, fell to any football team before, culminating in their defeat of Scotland a week ago. The visitors' method of play, too, or rather their formation on the field, was new.

Football is a progressive game. From twenty the number of players in a team was reduced to fifteen. Then the arrangement of the backs was altered: first from one threequarter to two, with two fullbacks; then to three threequarters with one fullback; and finally to four threequarters, as at present, with two halves, a fullback and eight men in the pack.

Now come the New Zealanders with a new arrangement of the fifteen men — seven in the pack, one wing forward, one halfback, three threequarters and two five-eighths and a fullback.

Whether it is the superiority of this re-arrangement, or whether the superiority lies in the men and their training, the results have been highly satisfactory to the visitors.

Irish Rugby Football Union

IRELAND v. NEW ZEALAND.

DINNER

IN HONOUR OF THE

New Zealand Team

AT

THE GRESHAM HOTEL,

DUBLIN,

On Saturday, the 25th November, 1905,

AT SEVEN O'CLOCK. P.M.

ADMIT BEARER.

Waller & Co., Printers, Dublin

THE INVITATION TO the Irish test dinner.

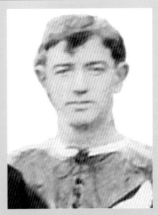

DUNCAN McGREGOR

Wellington — wing threequarter
23, 5ft 9in, 11st 3 lb

Dubbed 'the Flying Scotsman' for his phenomenal try-scoring feats on the field, McGregor originally came to Christchurch from Kaiapoi. In 1902 in just ten matches he scored 17 tries for Canterbury, a New Zealand record. He was an outstanding member of New Zealand's 1903 team to Australia, with 10 appearances including the inaugural test match. He was transferred with the railways to Wellington in 1904, where it was reported that McGregor's defence was sometimes less than perfect, but on attack he was tremendously fast and could sidestep off either foot. He scored both of New Zealand's tries in the country's 9-3 win over the 1904 touring Great Britain side. On the 1905 tour he achieved his greatest feat, scoring a record four tries in the 15-0 win against England.

DAILY MAIL

THE GAME WAS STRENUOUS almost to the point of ruthlessness, but there was not the faintest suggestion of unpleasantness or any suspicion of foulness.

The 'All Blacks' were evidently captivated by the frank charm of their opponents, and it was refreshing to see during the little pauses in the game how pleasantly the teams fraternised, or the concern which each side displayed when one of their opponents was temporarily disabled.

There has never been a game played in a better sporting spirit in Ireland, and it is doubtful if there ever will be one.

The Irish players are unanimous in their tribute to the cleverness and sportsmanship of the New Zealanders.

Mr Landers, who, by the bye, opened an old wound in his finger which may keep him out of the Munster match on Tuesday, was very emphatic on the fairness of the 'All Blacks'.

'I never wish to play against a finer set of sportsmen,' he said on Saturday night, and that was the verdict of every Irishman at the match.

HAMISH STUART, ATHLETIC NEWS

AS AT INVERLEITH, so at Dublin, New Zealand won by their ability to turn openings to profitable account, but there the resemblance between the two games ends.

At Inverleith, Scotland played for the most part a defensive game, and the Scottish forwards rarely got the ball; at Dublin, after the first ten minutes (during which New Zealand were all over Ireland, yet failed to score) the Colonial forwards could boast no superiority at all, and for the first time in the tour met their masters in the tight.

This was the surprise of the match. One was quite prepared to see the Irish forwards make many of the furious rushes associated with their name, but no one could have foreseen that they would hold their own in the scrummages and beat the New Zealand seven for the ball during a period of about fifteen minutes' duration.

Yet this was the strange sight we saw at Dublin and at once explains the conditional statement that Ireland would not have lost if the backs had been as good as the forwards.

Ireland obtained a sufficiently complete control over the game for fifteen minutes or so in the first half to have scored two or three tries if the backs had been able to turn their chances to account.

At other periods of the game, the backs were given opportunities to score but they were again unequal to their chances, their failure being chiefly due to the lack of head shown by the centre threes, Maclear and Parke, though the poor passing out of Caddell and Robinson was a contributory cause.

One has emphasised this aspect of a fast and exciting game simply because it points to the possibility of a Welsh victory at Cardiff on 1 December.

Hitherto, I have been of the opinion that the scientific scrummage work of the Colonials, and their ability to get the ball, precluded hope of a Welsh success.

After Saturday's experience, however, one can no longer describe the New Zealand seven as invincible in the tight.

GEORGE DIXON'S DIARIES

Found Dublin a nice city with wide streets. Jaunting cars in common use here (up to date cars with rubber tyres). I have not yet seen a Hansom cab on the streets.

◆

DUBLIN MAIL

THERE WAS NO DOUBT the better team won. Not that the New Zealanders had such a preponderance of the play. Indeed, the run of the game was as much in our men's favour as in that of the 'All Blacks'.

The gallant wearers of the silver fern did not get more than four or five real chances of scoring, and when it is remembered that three of the opportunities were accepted, the marvellous scoring powers of the Colonial team are realised.

Ireland got quite as many chances, but we had not the nippiness to accept any of them; indeed, a couple of rare openings were simply thrown away, while an unlucky bounce of the leather into touch lost us a tray at the end.

It was admitted that Ireland's hope lay in her forwards, and although we have been unable to check the victorious career of the New Zealanders and have succumbed to their prowess by three scores to nothing, there must be naught but praise for the scrummagers, who did duty for the Shamrock.

Our team of last spring was a good one, and as we had seven of the eight who represented us in the past season's match at Lansdowne Road, we anticipated great things of them. And they did not belie our faith.

In fact, they exceeded our anticipations, and no one who saw the great struggle can ever forget the thrilling rushes of the Irish front rank.

The struggle between the teams was, in the first half especially, one of the grandest and most exciting ever witnessed in Ireland. The fierce dash of the home lot was checkmated by the daring tactics and deadly tackling of the Colonials.

Contrary to all expectations the New Zealanders were not so successful in getting the ball in the scrum as they have been in previous matches. This fact alone speaks volumes for the Irish pack, who got possession repeatedly.

The agility of Gillett, however, neutralised several rare openings, and this player's spoiling was very effective, but when we did get the leather out, and our threequarters showed us some of the best passing of the afternoon, the resource of the Colonials' defence was only too apparent.

In a twinkling the forwards had broken away from the scrum and were tearing across the ground to back up their 'threes', so that by the time the leader reached Thrift or Robb there were at least three or four Maoris to bottle up the Irishman.

When the New Zealand backs got going, the reverse seemed to be the case, and Deans was only one of a trio who had only Landers to beat for the opening score.

We only put seven men in the pack; we fairly held the burly Colonials. There was a time in the second half when it looked as if the tremendous strain would be too much for our men, but they rallied magnificently and were going stronger than the New Zealanders when the final whistle went.

We have heard a lot about the visitors' great staying power, and they certainly got rarely tested. The forwards, at any rate, got more than they bargained for, and the majority of them were 'pumped' at the finish.

Coming to the backs, there was no doubt about the Colonial supremacy in the rare division, taking the men as a whole, and our men were practically at the top of their form. There was nothing, so far as we could see, of unfair tactics practised by the visitors.

◆

THE SPORTING LIFE

THE MORNING WAS USHERED IN with typical November weather, dark, damp and giving every indication of proving anything but pleasant before the day closed.

Not a glimpse of sunshine came through the thick bank of leaden-hued clouds, but happily noon arrived without the dreaded rain making an appearance. It cannot be said to have come on, but all through there was a nasty drizzle and about the interval the light became bad.

It is perfectly safe to say that the generally staid capital of the Emerald Isle had for a couple of days past put on an air of excitement, only known to it at the periods when Punchestown and the Horse Show are in progress, and all through this forenoon enthusiasm in the trial of strength between New Zealand and Old Country fairly bubbled over.

AN ADVERTISEMENT PLACED in several tour programmes that extolled the virtues of New Zealand as a great destination for tourists and settlers.

GAME 23 — TUESDAY 28 NOVEMBER 1905 — at Market's Field, Limerick

NEW ZEALAND
MUNSTER

33
0

FOR NEW ZEALAND
Tries by Abbott 3, Booth, Glasgow, McGregor, Roberts, Stead; 3 conversions, penalty goal by Glasgow.

NEW ZEALAND
Booth, Abbott, Smith, Stead (captain), McGregor, Mynott, Roberts, Gillett, Glasgow, Corbett, Nicholson, Cunningham, McDonald, Mackrell, Newton.

MUNSTER
A. Quillinan (Garryown), A. Newton (Cork), B. Maclear (captain, Cork), W.O. Stokes (Gayyowen), R. McGrath (Cork), J. O'Connor (Garryowen), F. McQueen (Queen's College), J. Wallace (Garryowen), J. Lane (Landsdowne), A. Acheson (Landsdowne), J. Reeves (Cork), W. Churchward (Cork), M. White (Queen's College), R. Welply (Queen's College), S. Hosford (Cork).

Weather: Fine, ground uneven
Referee: J.M. Magee (Bective Rangers)
Crowd: 3000

KICK OFF
Gillett secured from a lineout and put Abbott across. Glasgow missed: 3-0.
Glasgow landed a penalty goal: 6-0.
Cunningham and Mackrell created a try for Roberts. Glasgow converted: 11-0.
A McGregor centring kick produced a try for Glasgow. His conversion missed: 14-0.
Roberts probed the blindside and McGregor scored. Glasgow missed: 17-0.
Six players handled before Abbott scored. Glasgow missed.

HALFTIME
New Zealand 20, Munster 0

Seven players handled before Booth went across. Glasgow missed: 23-0.
Roberts attacked off a lineout and Abbott scored. Glasgow converted: 28-0.
The forwards attacked the Munster scrum and Stead scored. Glasgow converted.

FULLTIME
New Zealand 33, Munster 0

FROM THE SIDELINES

CORK EXAMINER

IT WAS A BIG UNDERTAKING ON the part of the Limerick syndicate to secure a local venue for the match between the invincible New Zealand team and a selection representing Munster.

They deserve the utmost credit for their plucky enterprise, and the big gate receipts from all parts of the Markets Field enclosure was only a fitting reward, for the treat they afforded to rugby players in the south of Ireland.

It must be admitted that 'high hopes' were not entertained as to even the probability of Munster showing up in anything like even moderate form before the All Blacks; but there was expectancy in all minds, and not a few devoutly wished that the crushing defeat administered on Saturday to the all-Ireland team would not be repeated in more marked form in Limerick, and that Munster would not be wiped out with a clean slate.

The representatives of Munster, though a sturdy lot, were not as wisely picked as the opportunities for selection offered.

It was originally entirely a one-county team, no less than eleven footballers being picked from Cork alone. It was not the best team that could be picked from the Munster clubs.

Magill, of Garryowen, and the Ryans and Thade O'Connor of Rockwell were passed for footballers of indifferent records.

Pace was wanted to make the Munster forwards effective today, and Magill's speed, evidenced in not a few hundred and 120-yard races, would have made him 'the right man in the right place'.

It must be borne in mind that North Munster defeated South Munster by a double score recently, and in face of the fact South Munster got a representation of eleven in this match while North Munster only got four; no justification for such disproportion can be maintained.

HECTOR THOMSON

Wanganui — wing
24, 5ft 8in, 10st 12lb

A small, pacy winger, Thomson had dreadful luck in 1905, missing the preliminary tour to Australia through illness, then on the Originals tour suffering a leg injury that kept him sidelined for much of the tour. He featured in only six of the first 29 matches, making 11 appearances altogether. In this brief foray he still managed to score 14 tries, three against Cheshire and six in a scoring spree against British Columbia in San Francisco. Thomson was known to all his teammates as Mona because of his passion for the popular song of that name.

GEORGE DIXON'S DIARIES

The home team were overmatched from the first in every department of the game. Eight tries were scored and the final score was 33 to nil.

Smith had the misfortune to bruise his shoulder during the first half and retired altogether in the early part of the second.

For the rest of the game, the wing forward was dispensed with and Gillett went to fullback, McGregor to centre and Booth to wing threequarter.

There were some very fine bouts of passing, notably the play leading to the sixth try, the ball going through seven hands.

BUNNY ABBOTT poses for the camera.

THE SPORTING LIFE

WHY DO THE NEW ZEALANDERS WIN? Probably no question has of late occupied the attention of the athletic world to so complete an extent as the above.

Briefly, the position is this: New Zealand as one of the flourishing offshoots of the British Empire has sent a representative rugby team to try its fortunes in these isles.

The team has not only come up to the expectations of the Colonists, but has completely quashed our best teams — individual and international — they have yet met. Nothing seems able to stay its victorious career, and the scores piled up against them have been prodigious. To date, the Invincibles have played 22 matches, all of which they have won. They have scored 661 points to 22, or 85 goals, 1 penalty goal, 1 marked goal and 80 tries to 1 goal, 1 penalty goal, 2 dropped goals and a try.

Their line has been crossed only twice, once by Durham and once by the Scotchmen.

Athletes have been stirred by questions as to the reason for the Colonists' phenomenal success, and rugby men have spent much time in comparing them in the hope of discovering the secret of

BILLY WALLACE'S RECOLLECTIONS

We got to Londonderry about 1 a.m. on the Sunday and the only people on the station were our relations. My old grandfather was there and as he was 92 years old I had no difficulty in picking him out.

We took a jaunting car to my grandfather's place and there I met my grandmother, who was 88 years of age. They had supper ready for me and then I was very pleased to get to bed.

The next thing I knew it was 2 p.m. Sunday afternoon when they woke me up to have lunch. I gave my grandfather all the news of my father in New Zealand. In the evening along came an uncle and a couple of aunts.

While we were yarning round the fireside the old chap brought out an ancient family Bible showing our genealogy. Actually, we trace our family history back to Sir William Wallace. The family had not seen my father since he was about 18 years old and so they were very anxious to hear all the news about him.

Billy Glenn was also visiting relatives in Londonderry and we returned to Dublin to rejoin the team, who had been down to Limerick to play Munster. They had a great time there and again the crowd at the station had broken down the gates in their excitement.

They stayed at Cruise's Hotel and were wonderfully treated. Several of the Munster team had played against us for Ireland and their captain was Basil Maclear.

The Munster team was welcomed on to the field by a band playing 'Garryowen'. The match was not a very interesting one, but in it we lost George Smith, who injured his shoulder. This was a very serious loss because our next match was against England and we were shortly to go to Wales where we were to meet the strongest opposition. It was hard enough to field a sound team against Ireland and George was a wonderful scoring man.

A BRITISH–BASED MAORI artist's idea of Scotland after the All Blacks' first test.

those constant uninterrupted defeats.

Perhaps the matter which most attracted the attention of the average onlooker at the matches of the last couple of weeks was the wonderful fitness of the men. Their dash and vitality was amazing, even marvellous, and indeed too marvellous for our home players. The reason for this is not far to seek. The men comprising the New Zealand team have been accustomed to an active and out-of-door life, have had plenty of practice and have been trained with the greatest care and discretion.

Comparing them with the English teams, the inferiority of the latter becomes apparent. Most of these players are young professional or business men, healthy specimens enough, but seldom trained athletes in the sense that the Colonists are.

As a rule, our men have been accustomed to play a match once or twice a week, and dispense with practice almost entirely. Of systematic coaching or training there has been little or none, and hence our men — as was particularly the case at Dublin on Saturday — though willing to work to the last ounce, are from an athletic standpoint more or less unfit.

How this was clearly shown in the scrums. Here the New Zealanders usually made their presence felt at once, and moved the scrum before the opposition had scarcely time to settle down.

In connection with the question of physical fitness, it is well to consider the physique of the men themselves. Anyone glancing over the names and weights of the men cannot fail to be struck by the heaviness of the Colonials team.

They are nearly all big men and practically all heavy. The plan of training in Ireland has, as a rule, been to sweat down a man as soon as he shows signs of becoming weighty. The idea was, of course, that weight was nearly always accompanied by slowness of pace.

How fallacious is this idea is shown by the tremendous speed of this heavy New Zealanders' team. Unquestionably, they are an exceptionally fast lot. The impression of tremendous dash and go appeals to all who have seem them play.

Thomson, of course, is one of the fastest men who has ever turned out, having sprinted his 100 yards in 9¼ seconds. Yet he appears nothing out of the way in proportion to the team. The great point is that they have weight and yet are absolutely fit, while their opponents have weight for weight proved considerably slower.

GEORGE DIXON'S DIARIES

No brakes in town so a local resident drove both teams to the ground in his 4-N-Hand. A great crowd of people accompanied us to the ground, cheering, but apparently did not possess the small amount necessary to gain admittance. They waited outside and escorted us back to town again!

Found the ground uneven but the turf in good condition. The home team were over matched in every department.

Abbott had his first game since Hartlepool and put up a really good game. Mackrell played his first game on tour and shaped up well indeed, being prominent in the loose.

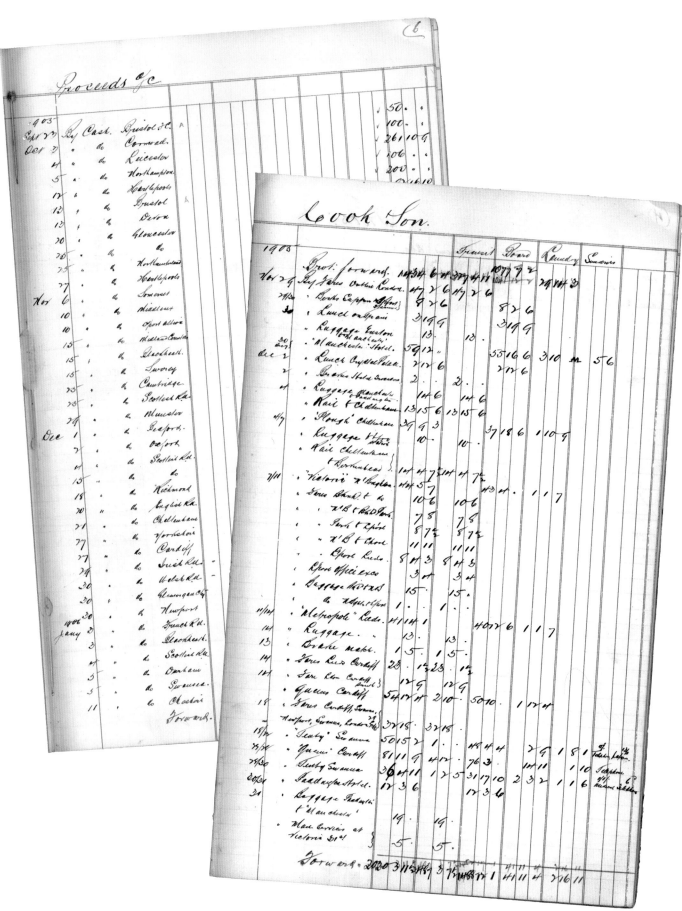

GEORGE DIXON KEPT meticulous records, as seen in these two accounts for Thos. Cook & Sons, the team's travel agent.

GAME 24 — SATURDAY 2 DECEMBER 1905 — at Crystal Palace, London

NEW ZEALAND 15
ENGLAND 0

FOR NEW ZEALAND
Tries by McGregor 4, Newton.

NEW ZEALAND
Gillett, Wallace, Deans, Hunter, McGregor, Stead, Roberts, Gallaher (captain), Seeling, McDonald, Glasgow, Newton, O'Sullivan, Tyler, Casey.

ENGLAND
E.J. Jackett (Cornwall), H.M. Imrie (Durham), R.E. Godfray (Middlesex), H.E. Shewring (Somerset), A.E. Hind (Leicester), D.R. Gent (Gloucestershire), J. Braithwaite (Midlands), J.E. Raphael (Surrey), G.E. Summerscales (Durham), R.F. Russell (Midlands), E.W. Roberts (Devon), J.L. Mathias (Gloucestershire), B.A. Hill (Kent), V.H. Cartwright (captain, Midlands), C.E.L. Hammond (Middlesex).

Weather: Dull and cold, ground wet
Referee: Gil Evans (Midland Counties)
Crowd: 70,000

KICK OFF
Roberts worked the blindside, putting McGregor across. Wallace missed: 3-0.
Gallaher, Stead and Hunter handled before McGregor scored. Wallace missed: 6-0.
Roberts and Stead probed the blindside and McGregor scored. Wallace missed.

HALFTIME
New Zealand 9, England 0

Newton scored from scrambly play near the goalline. Wallace missed: 12-0.
McGregor bagged try number four from loose play. Wallace missed.

FULLTIME
New Zealand 15, England 0

FROM THE SIDELINES

NEW ZEALAND TIMES' UK CORRESPONDENT

PROBABLY NEVER BEFORE HAS a football match received such bold advertisement. The newspapers took it up as a great popular attraction and 'England v New Zealand' was served up day by day in columns of anticipation for a week or more before the great event. The fixture attained all the importance of a first or a final test match in Anglo-Australian cricket.

Very wisely, the Rugby Union authorities had recognised in good time that Blackheath, the ground originally chosen for the match, was quite inadequate to the demand for seats and standing room. The changing of the venue to Crystal Palace was amply justified.

The 15,000 seats were bought up a fortnight before the match and speculators who retailed their tickets on Saturday demanded and received the most extravagant prices. Half-crown seats were selling at from 7s 6d to 17s 6d while five-shilling seats realised as much as 30s. The price of standing room, however, was one shilling and the public took full advantage of the fact.

By half-past two the waiting multitude numbered something like 45,000 people. (This is considered a very conservative estimate. 60,000 seems nearer the mark.)

C.B. FRY

MOST NOTICEABLE WAS THE UNIFORM corporate instinct of the New Zealand pack of what was happening in the thick. They played like eight men with one eye, and that an all-seeing eye.

BERNARD ESPINASSE, THE BRITISH AUSTRALASIAN

I KNOW A MAN WHO LEFT his home in Islington a few minutes after eight in the morning to take the train to Ludgate Hill for the Palace. Unsympathetic friends reminded him that the gates did not open till ten. He is an old man and dogged.

He said, as he took his hat and stick, 'I was born, bred and made my money in Otago. It's three and twenty years since I've seen any of the folks I grew up with. I'm going today to see what the new generation is like, and give 'em hullo for their fathers' sake. I can't afford £1 for a seat; standing room's good enough for me; but I'm going to be the first on that ground!'

THE TIMES

NEVER IN THE HISTORY OF rugby football has such a multitude assembled to watch a game. The vast attendance was a wonderful tribute to the fame of the New Zealand football team. People came to the Palace to see the New Zealanders play and not to see England win.

BILLY WALLACE'S RECOLLECTIONS

The English team had been assembled in London four days before the match to undergo special training and the English selectors had decided on a new formation to stop our scoring machine. They played five threequarters. Inasmuch as this was a purely defensive measure, it was really an admission of weakness on their part, for after all, the match is won by the points you score yourselves.

We had an early breakfast on the day of the match as we had to leave for the Crystal Palace at 10 a.m. This was necessary because of the tremendously heavy traffic going to the Palace and there was a risk if we left our departure later we might not arrive at the ground in time.

DAILY MAIL

IT WAS WORTH GOING TO the Palace to see the crowd alone. The slopes above the field of play were black with humanity, in serried ranks so closely packed that the faces formed one long, broad band of flesh colour against the black background. Every tree that commanded a view was laden with spectators and one daring spirit climbed the tall central pole of Maxim's captive flying machine.

But the height of ingenuity was reached by an elderly enthusiast who made no attempt to raise himself above his fellows. Instead, he stood at the back of the crowd with a long pole on which were fixed two mirrors, the upper one tilted so as to reflect a view of the game upon the lower glass. There he stood, holding his pole aloft and gazing serenely into his looking glass, oblivious of the gibes of his neighbours.

A more cosmopolitan crowd has never gathered at a football match. On Saturday people flocked to the Palace from all parts of the Kingdom. Excursions were run from as far north as Dundee in Scotland, from Ireland, Wales, the West Country and the Midlands. Every Colonial within a day's journey of London had set his heart on going to the Crystal Palace match, and five

EVERY CONCEIVABLE vantage point at Crystal Palace was taken.

hundred fortunate New Zealanders secured seats in one of the covered stands.

The pavilion was crowded with notable figures in the social world — dukes and duchesses, earls and countesses, and any number of lesser lights. Everybody who was anybody in the great world of sport was present as a matter of course.

Football matches all over London and in other parts of the country were cancelled or postponed, in order that followers of the game might come and learn 'the lesson of the All Blacks'.

People who had never seen a football match in their lives were drawn to the Palace by the same magnetic influence, the fame of the New Zealanders, with their astonishing record of twenty-three victories off the reel, and 694 points to 22.

A quiet, orderly well-dressed crowd it was. The rough element so much in evidence at a Soccer Cup tie at the Crystal Palace seemed to be entirely absent. There was no pushing and scrambling for places, no 'drunks', no fights, no hooting or groaning.

The 'All Blacks' had a fine reception as they filed on the ground, looking very workmanlike in their sombre uniform. The English team wore white jerseys and knickers, and where the New Zealanders sported the silver fern their opponents displayed the red rose of Old England.

England rather welcomed the muddy ground, believing it would help their own safety tactics while hampering the Colonials' attack; but in practice this theory was not fulfilled.

DAILY EXPRESS

PROBABLY MOST OF THE 50,000 spectators at the rugby football match between England and New Zealand at the Crystal Park on Saturday were conscious, as they departed from the ground, of a feeling of disappointment.

It did not arise from the simple circumstance of being beaten.

Ninety-nine people out of a hundred expected her to lose. It was the fact that England had never looked in the smallest degree like making a close fight of it that gave rise to a sense of dissatisfaction.

Scotland had only been beaten in the last few minutes of the game; Ireland had done more attacking than any other side in the kingdom.

The England team were never anything but losers.

GEORGE DIXON

Wellington — manager
46

The right man in the right place, Dixon was described by Billy Wallace thus: 'His first thought was always for his "boys" and there were no thoughts of self. He had a very arduous task, for in addition to looking after us, he also had to look after the finances. Thanks to George's careful and prudent managership we brought back a profit of almost £10,000. Sometimes he was so overburdened with work that some of the members of the team had to help, but he was so loved and respected that it was a pleasure to assist him. He's a keen observer of the game, very tactful in handling difficult situations, but not afraid to act with decisions should that become necessary.' According to the British press, Dixon was 'genial, but as sharp as a tack – the hardest worked man on the tour.'

There was no suspicion of a soft heart but there was all too clear evidence of an absence of skill . . . in the scrums the New Zealanders generally had the better of matters.

Their wedge-like formation and concentration of power on a certain point made them invincible.

It was most noticeable, too, how their 'lock' F. Newton, a fine specimen of the colonial, standing some 6ft. 2in. in height, kept the pack compact. One solid body, not seven individuals did the pushing . . .

For England J.E. Raphael, the 'roving' threequarter and E.J. Jackett at fullback played splendidly. Would that we had more men of their calibre!

There was quite an aristocratic assembly on the grandstands and of course there was a large attendance of ladies, who seemed to take the most absorbing interest in the play and asked all manner of confusing questions, the dear things.

THE NEW ZEALANDERS line up for the official team photograph prior to kick-off against England.

BILLY WALLACE (4) kicks to relieve pressure against England.

ENGLAND throws to a lineout.

NEW ZEALAND TIMES' UK CORRESPONDENT

AFTER THE INTERNATIONAL MATCH with England the New Zealanders were entertained at dinner at the Trocadero Restaurant by the English Rugby Football Union. Mr Rowland Hill, president of the RFU, was in the chair and among those present were Lord Ranfurly and the Hon. W. Pember Reeves.

The usual loyal toasts having been given, the chairman said he had the honour of proposing the health of the first Colonial team that had ever come to the Mother Country under the auspices of the Rugby Football Union. 'It was due to New Zealand and their far-reaching affection for the game that is loved so well, that we in England, who have perhaps become a little slack, were receiving a lesson for which we should be grateful . . .' He had never wished Britishers to give too much attention to the game and neglect the higher duties of life, but at the same time it was right that they should take their great games seriously.

(The chairman continued.) He was willing to say that night that the present visit would probably never have been possible but for the firm stand taken against professionalism, in which they had received the loyal support of that colony. Their game had passed through strange and troublous times, and certain sections of public opinion had been against them, but the Rugby Football Union had made up their minds, and having done so, had set their backs to the wall to protect, for the benefit of this and future generations, the good game they had themselves played. This Colonial support had been of great service to them and they also had the support of the sister unions of Scotland, Ireland and Wales . . .

Mr D. Gallaher, captain of the team, acknowledged the toast.

He said that they had in England met with clean sport and sportsmen and as cousins from across the sea and chips off the old block, had a reception which exceeded all expectations. They had come Home to wake up the Old Country which, it was quite right, had, in its conservative spirit, gone to sleep. They wanted to stir up John Bull a little, though when they had stirred him up, he might want a lot of stopping. (Laughter and applause.)

Mr G.H. Dixon also replied in an able speech. He said that the success of his side, of which one and all naturally were proud, had exceeded their most sanguine hopes though they thought they had got together a fairly good team and might win a few matches. They had, through the long controversy on professionalism — watched with the keenest interest — been absolutely loyal to the Mother Union as they were still. (Applause.) He did not think this team would be the last that would visit the Mother Country from New Zealand. (An English voice: 'We will beat you next time!') Before he sat down Mr Dixon wanted to nail Mr Rowland Hill to the statement he had made as to the probability of a British team being sent to New Zealand. The colonists wanted to see that. New Zealand dated its improvement in football from 1888 when a British team visited the colony.

England captain Mr H.V. Cartwright, heartily received, said he was afraid they had been rather badly beaten, and would rather see in print 'fifteen points' than 'five tries'. It looked rather better (loud laughter). Perhaps England had been asleep. In a brief, but pithy and manly speech, he placed the Colonial team as 'amongst the best set of sportsmen' he had ever met.

Mr C.A. Crane (vice-president RFU) proposed 'The Colonies' with 'Imperial Unity', as his text.

Lord Ranfurly, who rose amid cries of 'Kia Ora!', said he was quite sure an English team would be warmly welcomed in the

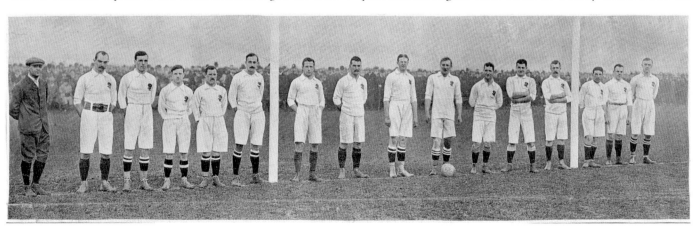

THE ENGLAND PLAYERS pose for their official team photograph.

AN ARTIST'S IMPRESSION of Crystal Palace game. The passer depicted is George Gillett.

colonies. No one knew better than he what a colonial welcome was, he added. The New Zealanders at this stage arose, and drank the health of the ex-Governor of New Zealand, shouting 'Kia Ora'.

The High Commissioner for New Zealand, W.P. Reeves, was also warmly received, the chairman thanking him for the services he had rendered the Rugby Football Union in connection with the visit. Mr Reeves said combination was the essence of the rugby game and football, after all, was a type of the British Empire. Combination was the soul of the Empire. They had that afternoon heard the cry of the New Zealanders as they greeted their friends, the enemy. The first two lines of that greeting ran:

'In death, in death,
In life, in life, we are one together.'

That spoke the spirit of New Zealanders and Britons all through the Empire. (Applause.)

During the course of the evening a number of musical items were contributed, and the New Zealanders were induced to give one of their 'cries'. The 'Rugby Song' was given with great heartiness and the National Anthem and 'Auld Lang Syne' brought to a close a pleasant evening's entertainment shortly before midnight.

◆

TATLER

I WAS SORRY TO READ Rover's epigram in *The Morning Leader* on the England and New Zealand match. 'One side played the game, the other side played the fool.'

◆ ❖ ◆

About an incident in the England-New Zealand match a correspondent writes: 'When Jackett, the Englishman, was "laid out" three New Zealanders sprang at once to his side. An English friend tapped me on the arm. "We are an insular folk," he said. "I have heard these men referred to lately as 'farmers' and 'blacksmiths' as if that was any disparagement." He pointed to the little knot of New Zealanders helping Jackett to his feet. "They are gentlemen!" said my friend.'

◆ ❖ ◆

Wallace had just got into his stride when Shewring made a dive at his legs, caught him by the ankle and brought him down on his left shoulder. It was a 'purler' and his shoulder joint was displaced. Happily it went back and he was able to keep playing.

After the match it began to pain the New Zealander, but hot fomentations and massage brought him speedy relief and he was able to go to the Rugby Football Union banquet at the Trocadero that night with his arm in a sling.

BOB DEANS, IN A LETTER HOME

A few of us went to the Islington Show (Agricultural) and while there were presented to the King, who shook hands with Tyler, his Majesty congratulating us on our victories, and hoping we would enjoy our stay in England. Those of the team who were presented were: Glenn, Tyler, Hunter, Thomson, Deans, O'Sullivan, McGregor and Glasgow.

On Saturday we played our third international (v. England) and won rather easily by 15 points (five tries) to nil. The ball and ground were the worst we had yet contended with, being so greasy that it was very awkward either to pass with accuracy or keep our feet when dodging. This spoiled the game from a spectator's point of view, and there were none of those fine passing rushes for which our team has become famous. If we had had a dry ground I think we would have put up a much larger score.

There was a huge crowd, officially numbered at about 45,000 but much nearer 75,000 in reality.

BILLY WALLACE'S RECOLLECTIONS

The night of the dinner was a pretty heavy one and it was late when we arrived back at the hotel. We all slept in late but about 11 o'clock I was invited into Steve Casey's room to meet 'a real live count'.

When I got there I saw a gentleman in full evening dress lying on the floor in a state of great insobriety and the boys were all writing their autographs on his immaculate shirt-front. His name was Count Peter Bastogi of Florence, Italy . . . or that's what he told us. He had been to the dinner and taken a great fancy to Steve so they went back to the hotel and Steve let him sleep on the floor of his room.

Some brainy one suggested 'pinching' his clothes as souvenirs and the idea was taken up with enthusiasm. The first one got his top hat, another got his dress coat, and, in turn, we 'souvenired' his waistcoat, his pants, his socks, his suspenders, braces, singlet and boots. Then to cover his nakedness we dressed him up into an All Black uniform. He entered enthusiastically into the exchange and insisted on being rigged out complete with jersey, shorts, stockings and boots. We had a great day with him and he invited Steve to go to his castle in Florence any time he liked.

The last we saw of him was late in the afternoon when we bundled him into a hansom cab and saw him off to his flat. He was beaming all over with smiles as he proudly strutted out in his new togs with his autographed shirt crumpled under his arm. 'Won't the Countess be jealous?' he yelled after us as the car drove away.

EVENING STANDARD

Macaulay's fabulous New Zealander was to sit on the broken arches of London Bridge and survey the ruins of St Paul's. The 'All Black' sits on the broken arches of our reputation and surveys the ruins of British football.

C.B. FRY

The New Zealanders won by 15 points to nil; and they deserved to win by this margin. Had the ground been firm instead of a quagmire, and had the ball been dry, instead of more than wet, they would have won by double this number of points — these New Zealanders.

The notion that these men beat us because of our physical degeneracy is nonsense. They beat us by organisation and tactics.

(At the interval.) Where are the Zeiss binoculars? Let us look at the men closely. My word, what a hard lot the New Zealanders are. You can see it in their shape, in the colour of their skins, in the cut of their hips. Hard sorts, as one says of the right kind of hunter; temperate, sound, and keen, with a genuine competitiveness about 'em. Not one of them has turned a hair, except that young great forward, Tyler, is over ruddy with the face-scraping of the scrum, and that tall Seeling has a warmer tint on his long jaws. Gillett, the back, is spotless. Gallaher is waiting for nothing better than to start again, and McGregor — confound his slippery pace — is standing like a runner who even at rest is on his toes. Unfold your arms young man, and don't look so much like another three tries. Even all this mud does not take the surface off their fitness. The English team are right enough, of course. Not quite so hard looking, but fit, except a couple of rather pale faces, and pink . . .

Those tight black scrummagers got the ball. Every time they answered 'yes' with their feet to Gallaher's war-cry of 'Heel!' which boomed out like a melodious fog-horn or the night cry of some deep-throated wild beast.

NEW ZEALAND TIMES' UK CORRESPONDENT

There was an interesting meeting at the Royal Agricultural Hall (London) between the King and the New Zealand footballers. It was the opening day of the Smithfield Cattle Show and a number of the 'All Blacks' were being shown around the hall when his Majesty arrived. On hearing that the New Zealanders were present, the King asked that they should be presented to him.

Shaking hands with George Tyler, who was standing nearest, his Majesty said he had read with great interest how they had beaten All England the other day. He also expressed the hope that they were enjoying their stay in the Old Country. The footballers acknowledged his Majesty's kindly greetings with a rousing cheer. Brief as the incident was, they will remember it with pleasure as one of the most interesting experiences on tour.

DAILY NEWS

The New Zealand football team has been invited by the Rev. W. Carlile, head of the Church Army, to have tea with him next Sunday at his rectory adjoining St Mary-at-Hill, Monument and to attend the evening service afterwards. One of the team will read the lessons and Mr Carlile will preach on the 'All Blacks'.

THE ENGLAND TEST BANQUET at the Trocadero Restaurant.

GAME 25 — WEDNESDAY 6 DECEMBER 1905 — at Recreation Ground, Cheltenham

NEW ZEALAND
CHELTENHAM

18
0

FOR NEW ZEALAND
Tries by Abbott 3, Roberts;
3 conversions by Harper.

NEW ZEALAND
Booth, Abbott, McGregor, Deans,
Harper, Mynott, Roberts, Gallaher (captain),
Mackrell, Glenn, Nicholson, Newton,
Corbett, Glasgow, Casey.

CHELTENHAM
B. Davey, L.W. Hayward, F.H.B. Champain,
G.T. Cottrell, C. Clifford, R.P. Burn,
A. Goddard, G.T. Unwin (captain),
W.N. Unwin, F. Jacob, F. Goulding,
C. Cossens, L. Cook, H. Pike,
J.V. Bedell-Sivright.

Weather: Fine, ground firm
Referee: Percy Coles (England)
Crowd: 7500

KICK OFF
Roberts charged down the halfback's kick and scored. Harper converted: 5-0.
Roberts and Mynott worked the blindside and Abbott scored. Harper converted: 10-0.
Roberts and Mynott combined again for another Abbott try. Harper converted.

HALFTIME
New Zealand 15, Cheltenham 0

Deans and McGregor worked well to put Abbott across again. Harper missed.

FULLTIME
New Zealand 18, Cheltenham 0

FROM THE SIDELINES

DAILY EXPRESS

THIS WAS THE TWENTY-FIFTH match of the tour and it produced the twenty-fifth victory for the 'All Blacks'. But, though plainly outclassed, Cheltenham provided a very bright and interesting game. Like the Irishmen in the Dublin match they decided to play to win and it was not for want of trying that they failed to score against their opponents. Where England, Scotland, Cambridge and so many other sides had been content with safety tactics Cheltenham strained every nerve to score. Until the match Cheltenham had not been beaten this season.

Wednesday's match attracted 7000 — a record for the ground, which could have been filled twice over, so great was the demand for admission tickets.

◆

ILLUSTRATED SPORTING AND DRAMATIC NEWS

IT IS EXPECTED that 150 people will sit down to the 'high tea' which Mr J.T. Agg-Gardner, MP is providing for the benefit of the New Zealanders when they visit Cheltenham. Afterwards the party are invited to witness 'My Lady Molly' at the Opera House.

SIMON MYNOTT

**Taranaki — first-five
29, 5ft 7in, 11st 9lb**
Mynott came from Taranaki where he and Jimmy Hunter made the Taranaki team one to be feared. One of the most brilliant five-eighths New Zealand has produced, he and Hunter were said to lead their opponents a merry dance. On the Originals tour there was a dilemma as to which of the team's three outstanding five-eighths, Mynott, Hunter or Stead, should be left out of the team. Against Ireland, the difficulty was resolved by playing Mynott as a wing, where he handled his new position with competence. He played in 22 matches on the tour and, despite a lapse against Wales, was as sound on defence as attack.

A. S. BARTHOLOMEW,

419 & 420 HIGH ST., CHELTENHAM.

WINES.

SPIRITS.

Australian

WINES.

CHELTENHAM FOOTBALL CLUB.

OFFICIAL PROGRAMME

OF - THE

GRAND MATCH

CHELTENHAM v. NEW ZEALAND,

WEDNESDAY, DECEMBER 6th, 1905.

PRICE - ONE PENNY.

ALES.

STOUT.

TABLE

WATERS.

"INVICTA" Table Ale Pts. 2/6, ½ Pts. 1/6 per doz. LAGER Beer Pts. 4/-, ½ Pts. 2/3 per doz.

Printed and Published by the "Echo" Electric Press, Cheltenham.

PROGRAMME FOR THE Cheltenham match.

ATHLETIC NEWS

THE MAORI WAR SONG which the New Zealanders sing before victory is a rather weird chant. We persuaded W. Cunningham, the chief soloist to write out the words with an English translation, and further acquaintance does not tend to remove the impression of the dangerous character of the language.

When we gave the copy of the verse to the Master Printer he read the words over twice and then went and killed a compositor. There is something in the song when it gets into cold type that excites the blood, what effect it has when people sing it can be imagined by watching the New Zealanders shaking their frenzied fingers and stamping on the earth as if they were letting Dick Seddon in the land beneath know they were just about starting on a scalping excursion.

THE MORNING LEADER

To the Editor

Sir,

The review of the England versus New Zealand match in your columns by 'Rover' is so ungenerous to the English team, and so wide of the mark in its criticism of the Rugby Union, that it ought not to be passed over without protest.

After the handsome reservation that he does not blame the English team, your critic describes them as 'playing the fool' instead of the game and as 'a miserable rabble of resisters'.

To the impartial onlooker the game was a desperate struggle of determined men with a team their superior in combination and tactics. The English played hard and gallantly throughout, and were going stronger at the end than at the beginning. It should be remembered when indulging in virulent condemnation that they were only beaten by the same number of points as the Irish.

On another issue, that anyone considering football as a sport and not as an exhibition could congratulate the Football Association on the 'expansion in its natural way' which it has brought about passes comprehension.

If the Association had taken up a firm position and set its face against professionalism as the Union has done, the all-hired teams would have been relegated to the League and its imitators, and we should have been spared the grotesque competitions between Football Companies Ltd which annually interchange each

other's men.

That anyone should wish Rugby Football to come to this pass in order to beat New Zealand, or any other colony, shows a fundamental lack of appreciation of the spirit of true sport.

The explanation of the whole talk of decadence is probably in the present temporary dearth of great players. This occurs periodically in all games. Witness Australia at cricket after the retirement of Murdoch. The Universities happen to be below the average; Richmond and Blackheath not so strong as in recent seasons; and in the

BILLY WALLACE'S RECOLLECTIONS

When our tour was first mooted the Cheltenham Club were among the first to offer the guarantee of £75 for a match. As their usual takings for a club match were £20 many people thought they were taking a very grave risk. Now, of course they were congratulating themselves on their foresight! They found that the ground was not big enough to hold the crowd that wanted to see the game — officials were doing their best to rectify this want, for as we practised, carpenters were busy with hammer and saw erecting new temporary stands.

On the day of the match all business was suspended in Cheltenham and all the schools were closed. Excursion trains ran from the surrounding districts and the Welsh contingent was very strong, for the game against Wales was drawing very near and they came across to study our tactics whenever they could.

After the match there was a big dinner in the Town Hall where both teams were the guests of the local MP Mr J.T. Agg-Gardner, who proposed our health in the most complimentary terms and said he regretted that we could not come back to Cheltenham again, as he felt sure the local team would have profited by the match that afternoon.

There was no doubt that our style of play was a great attraction to the English public and it was not uncommon for a player who had distinguished himself in a match to get letters from girls extremely anxious to meet him. Some girls went further and made offers of marriage!

In one of our matches at this time one of our five-eighths distinguished himself by scoring a beautiful try and this captivated the heart of a love-sick girl. Unfortunately the papers made a mistake in reporting the match and credited the try to one of the threequarters.

The latter received a very nice, affectionate letter from the girl offering marriage. But next day she discovered her mistake. She therefore wrote once more to the threequarter: 'Dear Sir,' she said, 'since writing, I discovered it was really —— who scored, the insertion of your name being a printer's error. Under these circumstances I wish you to hand the letter on to him. I can be no more than a sister to you.

Yours faithfully, —— '

North and West there is the same tale.
If England's supremacy can only be
maintained at the cost of her amateurism,
New Zealand is welcome to all her victories.
'Rover' indulges in some ingenious
speculation as to the number of New
Zealanders who could beat England in a
game played without scrums. He omits to
give the number required to beat England
in a game without a ball.

Yours, W.H.G., Regent Sq.

BILLY STEAD ABOUT HIS TEAM-MATES

Cunningham always wanted plum duff, I craved for a pot of apple jelly after
a game, whilst Gallaher always kept a cigar in reserve and 'General' Booth
generally managed to save a banana for half-time.

George Tyler always had a special oration to the ball, whilst George Smith kept
tying and untying his boots. Three 'yawns' a minute was characteristic of Billy
Wallace and I can still see Bob Deans expanding his chest and stretching himself.

Two of the front row men always played with a quid of tobacco, which they
chewed as long as it would last. When chewing gum came in I always accepted my
piece, though I never used it, but kept it along with a damp handkerchief and piece
of resin in a hip pocket I always had in my football pants.

Playing centre outside Dick McGregor in 1903 at Brisbane, I was asked by him
for my spare chewing gum, which he promptly put into action. After the game I
discovered that I still had the gum and he had got the resin. Opai Asher always
blamed Dick for his selfish play that day. No wonder!

THE SPORTSMAN

WHEN THE NEW ZEALANDERS return to the land down under
Mr Dixon intends to write his impressions of the tour.

Athletic News

The match which the New Zealanders played against Munster at
Limerick might for several reasons very well have been left out
of their programme.

Daily Mail

The New Zealanders are a great side, and they have given a new
phase to rugby football — a phase which can only be likened to
England v Australian cricket.

Glasgow News

To New Zealand we now stand indebted for two of the finest
international matches in the history of rugby football.

Hamish Stuart in A.M.

The Rugby Football Union is well known to be a most open-
minded and docile body. It has carried the *fas est ab hoste doceri*

principle about as far as it will go. Having spent ten years in
trying to imitate the Welsh style of play, with the most disastrous
results, it has now suddenly resolved to take a lesson from the
all-conquering New Zealand experts.

Field

In view of the splendid reception accorded the Antipodeans,
the question naturally arises, 'What will they do with their
revenue?'

Manchester Evening News

'EN PASSANT' IN ATHLETIC NEWS

JIMMY HUNTER

When British backs
His Strong attacks
Try hard to circumvent 'em
He'll simply grin
Like ancient sin
And easily prevent 'em;
With bursts so great
And eel-like gait
Towards the line zig-zagging
And tacklers keen
Look on in spleen
While he the tries is bagging.
Oh, don't the days seem drear and dun
When he don't score with a corkscrew run?
And isn't his life a dreadful bore
When there ain't a goalline to tumble o'er?

The critics stare
With baleful glare –
Their wits gone all 'a-flunter' –
To see our teams
Like men in dreams,
A-hunting of this HUNTER.
He's like a ray
Of light in play –
A hurricane, a blizzard –
A streak of grease
No hand can seize
A veritable wizard
In short, this aggravating 'fern'
Is clipper-built from stem to stern
And it's sad to think 'ere he leaves our shore
The number of lines he'll tumble o'er.

GAME 26 — SATURDAY 9 DECEMBER 1905 — at Birkenhead Park, Birkenhead

NEW ZEALAND
CHESHIRE

34
0

FOR NEW ZEALAND
Tries by Hunter 3, Thomson 3, Abbott,
Deans, Nicholson, Roberts;
conversions by Cunningham, Tyler.

NEW ZEALAND
Gillett, Thomson, Deans, Hunter, Abbott,
Stead, Roberts, Gallaher (captain), Seeling,
Nicholson, Corbett, Cunningham, O'Sullivan,
Tyler, Casey.

CHESHIRE
G.F. Tomes (New Brighton), E.S. Ashcroft
(Birkenhead Park), C.J. Clarke (New
Brighton), A.S. Anderson (Birkenhead Park),
A. Hartley (Sale), P.D. Kendall (captain,
Birkenhead Park), F.C. Hulme (Birkenhead
Park), E. Herschell (Birkenhead Park),
J.S. Francomb (Sale), E.A. Weir (New
Brighton), A.M. Johnstone (Birkenhead Park),
H.J.M. Edgar (Birkenhead Park),
A. Taylor (Birkenhead Park), G.C. Sanderson
(Birkenhead Park), S.J. Richardson
(Birkenhead Park).

Weather: Fine, ground firm
Referee: F.W. Nicholls (Leicester)
Crowd: 8000

KICK OFF
Nicholson scored after the fullback's kick was charged down. Gillett missed: 3-0.
Hunter and Deans combined to put Thomson across. Gillett missed: 6-0.
Roberts and Stead worked together to put Hunter acrosss. Tyler converted: 11-0.
The backline attacked from a scrum and Thomson scored. Gillett missed: 14-0.
Stead, Hunter and Deans conspired to put Abbott across. Thomson missed.

HALFTIME
New Zealand 17, Cheshire 0

Deans gathered in a Roberts crosskick to score. Thomson missed: 20-0.
Stead, Hunter and Deans combined to put Thomson in again. Gillett missed: 23-0.
Stead broke clear in loose play and put Hunter across. Abbott missed: 26-0.
Roberts and Deans worked the blindside and Hunter scored. Gillett missed: 29-0.
Roberts pounced on a loose ball from a scrum near the line. Cunningham converted.

FULLTIME
New Zealand 34, Cheshire 0

FROM THE SIDELINES

DAILY EXPRESS

THE NEW ZEALANDERS' TRIUMPH at Cheshire was another tribute to the all-round strength of the tourists. The absence of some of the 'stars' of the team seems to make little difference to its scoring powers. Some of the biggest scores of the tour have been registered when the New Zealand fifteen has included a number of lesser lights in this galaxy of football talent.

At Birkenhead on Saturday the Colonials, despite the absence of Smith, Wallace, McGregor, McDonald and Glasgow, were fully equal to every demand made upon them and defeated Cheshire with apparently the greatest ease to the tune of 34 points to nothing.

Had the place-kicking been up to the high standard set by Harper at Cheltenham, the score would have been huge indeed for no fewer than ten tries were scored.

As a social affair the game was a great attraction, over 8000 people gaining admission, though about 1000 managed this by the aid of bogus tickets, which had been freely sold in neighbouring towns when it was understood that it was to be a case of admission by ticket only.

THE TIMES

BOTH IN THE SCRUM and out of it the fifteen separate 'All Black' pieces fitted together in all their varying combinations with the harmonious precision of a kaleidoscope. Not one change, nor three, nor six changes affects the smoothness of the New Zealand machinery. It is a complex, highly-polished mechanism, composed of a number of interchangeable units. And if one gets a littly rusty or worn there is always its exact counterpart in the selection committee's locker.

NEW ZEALAND TIMES' UK CORRESPONDENT

THE NEW ZEALANDERS WERE ENTERTAINED at the Adelphi Hotel, Liverpool, on Saturday night by the Cheshire Committee. Cheshire's hospitality took the form of 'high tea' with some speechmaking afterwards. Mr Thorpe, who has been president of Cheshire for 21 years, toasted the New Zealanders and Mr Gallaher in return toasted Cheshire.

The Cheshire men sang 'For he's a jolly good fellow' in English, and the New Zealanders in turn sang something in Maori to the same tune.

LIVERPOOL COURIER

THE PLAIN TRUTH OF THE MATTER is that the Cheshire team was no match for the New Zealanders. Individually, the All Blacks were incomparably superior. Collectively, they were ridiculously superior.

Their forwards invariably won the scrums and their backs showed a combination, judgement, cleverness, pluck and pace which left their opponents miles behind. Nothing prettier or more inspiriting could be imagined than the breakneck bursts of straight sprinting, safe and sure passing, and brilliant dodging by which time and again they carried the ball over the line.

BILLY WALLACE'S RECOLLECTIONS

Our headquarters were not at Birkenhead (where the game was played) but at New Brighton, and there we had an invitation to go to a theatre and see a performance of 'Merry England'. As soon as we entered the place the whole audience rose and cheered us and called upon us for the haka, which we had to give.

When we got back to the hotel we were pretty hungry, so we went down to the bar to see if we could get anything to eat. The proprietress of the hotel was a great sport and had taken us to her heart. There was no food lying about but she pointed out the safe to us and told us to help ourselves. We needed no second invitation. We made a great job of the eatables and cleaned up everything in the safe.

Then George Dixon appeared and all the boys playing in the match the next day were ordered to bed. I was among the 'breathers' again and so was able to stay on and see the fun.

In the bar were two Scotchmen and when they saw our merry little party they said to the good lady, 'Who are these boys?'

'That is the New Zealand team,' she replied proudly.

'What,' said the Scotchman, 'the All Blacks! Here boys, come and have a drink with us. By Jingo! We'll have champagne.'

Again we needed no further persuasion and the champagne battle went on. We filled our glasses and sang 'Tenei te tangata' to the chap who had shouted, and gave the haka.

They were immensely pleased and the other chap said, 'Now, boys you must have some with me.' So again we filled our glasses and toasted him in similar fashion.

Not to be outdone, the proprietress, to keep the ball rolling, was next to 'turn it on' and she also got 'Tenei te tangata pai rawa atu' and the haka.

We had a whispered conversation amongst ourselves for we thought we were bound to return the hospitality. We collected our stray threepences and sixpences and mustered enough cash to send the champagne around again. By this time we were a most enthusiastic party.

We were having a great time when one of the Scotchmen said to 'Dougie' Corbett, 'How are you boys going to play tomorrow after all this?' Dougie did not quite see what he was driving at and said, 'Oh, we're only the breathers. The team for tomorrow are all upstairs in bed.' That put the lid on things and finished the champagne and poor old Corbett came in for a bad time. So we faded away quietly to bed.

One player was collared round the waist two yards from the Cheshire goalline. He turned a complete somersault, his tackler still clinging to him, and planted the ball over the line.

Several times a galloping back, hemmed in by grasping, panting enemies close to the coveted line, dived literally headforemost across with the ball. When they tackled a man, you heard the arms lock and saw that man bounce. A pluckier or more determined set of players never trod the turf, but it is their deadly machine-like combination and tactful skill which make them so absolutely pre-eminent.

By contrast with them, the weak, nervous fumbling, the futile straight-into-touch kicking and the hopeless want of cohesion displayed by some of the home team appeared weak indeed. Some of the backs really seemed to dread being found in possession of the ball.

◆ DAILY MAIL

YOU HAVE TO WATCH very closely to see how the deed is done. The formation of the pack has something to do with the smartness of the operation.

There is a channel running from the first row to the last, and when Cunningham, the lock — the centre man of the second row — gets his tiny foot near the ball the next second it belongs to Roberts, or Gallaher, generally Roberts.

Then those movements start which invariably end in disaster — to the other side. It is not, as one Cheshire official said, that the New Zealand passing is good, it is the men who take part

GEORGE SMITH

Auckland — wing
31, 5ft 7in, 11st 12lb

Practising on the Stamford Bridge ground in London before the Middlesex match brought back happy memories for 'Smithy', for it was on that ground three years earlier he had broken the world 120-yard hurdles record, having been sent to England by the New Zealand Athletic Association to compete in the British AAA championships. A true speedster, Smith's try against Scotland was considered one of the finest individual efforts of the tour. In 14 matches, he scored 19 tries, but a broken collarbone against Ireland put him out of further test contention. Smith was reputed to have ridden a horse called Impulse to victory in the 1894 New Zealand Cup and was something of a mystery man, disappearing from the rugby scene for seasons at a time. He appeared for Auckland in 1896 and 1897 but not again till 1901. This was followed by another lengthy absence until the chance of a tour of Britain lured him back to the rugby field.

BRANSCOMBE'S ORIGINAL CRICKET AND FOOTBALL PROGRAMME 9 DECEMBER 1905. PRICE, 2d.

Almost every footballer of renown in New Zealand has a pet name generally depictive of some marked characteristic on the field of play. The 'All Blacks' now touring this country are no exceptions to the rule. One is sometimes puzzled when in their company to understand who is being addressed or spoken of. These are some of the names they are familiarly known by:

ABBOTT:	'Bunny' (because he darts about like a rabbit).
BOOTH:	'General' (probably on account of his possible relationship to the Salvation Army Chief).
WALLACE:	'Carbine' (after the New Zealand racehorse, the winner of the Melbourne Cup and famous for its speed).
HUNTER AND MYNOTT:	'The Taranaki Twins', (both hailing from that province and always playing together. The latter 'Maori' through his dark complexion and having some knowledge of Maori).
THOMSON:	'Mona' (from his fondness for the song 'Mona').
McGREGOR:	'Dunk', short for Duncan, his first name. The last British team in New Zealand called him 'the Flying Scotchman' as he scored two brilliant tries against them in the New Zealand v. Britain match by sheer speed).
GILLETT:	'Akiriki' (Maori for Auckland, where he was born).
SMITH:	'Smithy'.
HARPER:	'Dean Eric' (through his relationship to the famous bishop of that name in Canterbury, New Zealand).
STEAD:	'Billy'.
ROBERTS:	'Freddy'.
DEANS:	'The Farmer Boy' (he is a well-to-do 'squatter').
CASEY:	'Ginger' or 'Hot Stuff' (though his activity in the scrums and close work).
TYLER:	'Bubs' (short for 'Bubbles' for he is a fast amateur swimmer).
GLASGOW:	'Glassy'.
O'SULLIVAN:	'Sully'.
GLENN:	'Opunake' (the name of his home).
McDONALD:	'Fighting Mac' or 'Madrid', generally the latter. He sings the song of that name very nicely.
SEELING:	'Bronco Bill' (after an American rider in New Zealand of that name).
JOHNSTON:	'Massa' (owing to his proclivity for singing Negro melodies).
NEWTON:	'Babby' (he has a sweet, open face).
CORBETT:	'Hokitika' (the place he hails from).
NICHOLSON:	'Nick'.
GALLAHER:	'Davy' or 'Skipper'.
MR DIXON, (Manager):	No one dares address him with familiarity.
DUNCAN:	'The old horse' (being an old player, with a wonderfully good record — practically the 'grand old man' of football in New Zealand).

When a team is selected to play a match the players who are not selected are called 'breathers'.

A CHESHIRE PLAYER rests up following another New Zealand try at Birkenhead.

in it that are so darn quick. And they believe in going straight for the posts and transferring when the opponent is right on them, and when they are so unfortunate as to be collared with the ball they have a mysterious way of throwing the leather to a spot where, at the moment, there is no one, but, as if by magic, something black in human shape rises up and scoops that ball.

It is the never-tiring, always-exerting system which prevails through every operation that makes for victory. As (Billy) Wallace told me after the match — he was on the touchline and saw the game in all its glory — the first try ought never to have been scored.

But every man in the team knows the value of following up. He said you might follow up twelve times and not gain anything for your troubles, but on the thirteenth such a chance as came to Nicholson and O'Sullivan might happen, and that would repay for all the other efforts.

Besides, following up has a very disconcerting effect on opponents. That was particularly noticed on Saturday.

The kicking of the Colonials in any and every position is so good, and so true in its direction, that opponents who have managed to gain yards of ground by dribbling or running find all the advantage taken from them by a judicious and powerful punt into touch. And even when the touchline is not aimed at, the ball is sent so lofty that when it descends there is a black crowd waiting for it like flies round a honey pot.

It was remarkable to notice the influence which the New Zealanders exerted over their rivals before the game finished. The final five minutes previously referred to saw the Cheshire backs doing something in passing and re-passing the ball and in dashing ahead that was a very colourable imitation of the dexterous and daring methods of the Colonials.

It was a pity they started so late, but probably they had not been allowed to put their ideas into operation for obvious reasons. But there is no doubt the lesson learned on Saturday will bear fruit.

At all events, the hon secretary, Mr C.C. Harvey, told the players after the match to go home — and think, and not to stir out of the house until they had thought, which no doubt they will do.

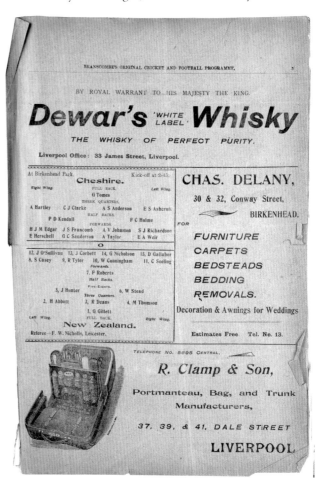

THE PROGRAMME for the game at Birkenhead.

GAME 27 — WEDNESDAY 13 DECEMBER 1905 — at Northern Union Ground, Headingley

NEW ZEALAND
YORKSHIRE

40
0

FOR NEW ZEALAND
Tries by Booth 2, Deans 2, Hunter 2,
McGregor 2, Mynott 2;
conversions by Wallace 4, Tyler.

NEW ZEALAND
Wallace, Booth, Deans, Stead, McGregor,
Mynott, Hunter, Gallaher (captain), Mackrell,
McDonald, Nicholson, Newton, Corbett,
Cunningham, Tyler.

YORKSHIRE
J.S. Auty (Headingley), A.S. Pickering
(Harrogate), W. Lynch (Castleford),
R.C. Dobson (Headingley), T. Orton
(Harrogate), B. Oughtred (captain, Barrow-
in-Furness), B. Moss-Blundell (Harrogate),
B. Dalton (Castleford), J. Green (Skipton),
R. Duckett (Skipton), W. Knox (Skipton),
T. Chapman (Harrogate), W. Smith
(Harrogate), W.H. Hutchinson (Hull),
J. Dobson (Wakefield).

Weather: Cold, ground firm
Referee: Percy Coles (England)
Crowd: 24,000

KICK OFF
Hunter, Stead and McGregor combined to put Booth across. Wallace missed: 3-0.
Gallaher linked with the backs to put Mynott over. Wallace missed: 6-0.
Hunter probed the blindside to score. Wallace converted: 11-0.
Stead and Mynott confused the defence and Deans scored. Wallace converted: 16-0.
Stead broke clear from loose play, putting Deans across. Tyler converted: 21-0.
Mynott handled twice from a scrum before scoring. Wallace missed.

HALFTIME
New Zealand 24, Yorkshire 0

A forward rush produced a try for Booth. Wallace converted: 29-0.
Mynott, Deans and McGregor combined to put Hunter over. Wallace converted: 34-0.
Deans made a great run and kicked for McGregor who scored. Wallace missed: 37-0.
Stead, Mynott and Hunter conjured up another try for McGregor. Wallace missed.

FULLTIME
New Zealand 40, Yorkshire 0

FROM THE SIDELINES

DAILY MAIL

THERE WAS A FINE SPORTING crowd, from which a great volume of cheering went up that greeted the constant flashes of 'All Black' brilliancy. The game was very fast, the Yorkshiremen being run off their feet, and the visitors carried scrum after scrum. The Tykes in their first half were fairly flabbergasted at the extraordinary speed of their opponents.

In twenty-seven matches the Colonials have now scored 801 points to twenty-two. Splendidly fine weather prevailed and the attendance was estimated at about 25,000. The gate receipts amounted to over £1,100.

NEW ZEALAND TIMES' UK CORRESPONDENT

IN SOME OF THE YORKSHIRE INDUSTRIAL and mining districts the nickname 'All Blacks' has led to a curious misapprehension. Many a miner and ironworker trudged his way Headingley-wards in the belief that he was going to see the triumph of the black race over the white, and their astonishment was great when there trooped out on to the green as stalwart and agile a set of Caucasians as ever were seen west of the Balkans.

'They're a very fine set of men,' said an old Yorkshire international player. 'They look a jolly sight more like Yorkshiremen than our team.'

◆ ❖ ◆

Mr George Dixon, manager of the New Zealand team, who is a native of Marsh, Huddersfield, was entertained on Tuesday night at the Huddersfield Liberal Club by some of his Marsh friends and members of the Huddersfield Juniors FC of which he was a member some 23 years ago.

He was presented with a case of pipes by Mr J.W. Crossley. In acknowledging the gift Mr Dixon attributed the success of the team largely to the forwards, who were, he said, picked for a certain position and played in it. Good back combinations was also a requisite.

J.H. SMITH, MANCHESTER EVENING NEWS

THE ALL-CONQUERING NEW ZEALANDERS continue to dominate the interest in Rugby football; indeed, attention is not confined to the devotees of the oval ball, but is, in a degree, shared by the leaders and followers of the Association code and by the 'man in the street' who has previously exhibited no concern regarding football matters at all.

Every match the Colonials play enhances their reputation, and their opponents appear to be quite content to act on the defensive. Certainly for any team to cross their lines, or even keep them from scoring for, say, twenty minutes, is regarded as an indication of exceptional merit.

A GROUP OF PLAYERS enjoys a relaxing day out in the country.

BILLY WALLACE'S RECOLLECTIONS

Soon after our arrival two strangers called on me and introduced themselves. It seemed they were in the wool trade and on opening a bale of wool that had come from New Zealand they found a note inside to the effect that Billy Wallace was coming Home and they should look him up. The note was from a friend of mine who was a wool classer in Marlborough. They were excellent fellows and they took me away for the rest of the day and we had a great time.

◆

There were many wild rumours floating around Leeds about us. Most of the people were league followers and could not conceive the idea that anyone should play for the love of the game. We were told on good authority that we were the highest paid footballers in the world and some of us were supposed to be getting £12 per week. Alas! It was only three bob a day!

The Tuesday morning was spent in practice and the afternoon in sightseeing. We retired early that night, for not only had we the match the next day but we had the great game of the tour on the following Saturday — against Wales. We gave Freddy Roberts a spell for this game and though we eventually won by a large margin, his presence at the back of the scrum was very much missed.

The game was a one-sided affair with ten tries and five conversions and at the dinner that evening the President of the Yorkshire County Committee, Mr Barron Kilmer, asked the company to rise and drink to the 'best team that has ever visited these shores'. George Dixon in his reply thanked our hosts for the wonderful hospitality accorded us.

We left Bradford the next morning for Cardiff. The great day was almost at hand when that great argument as to who would win — Wales or New Zealand — would be settled.

Ever since we had commenced our tour we had heard the same cry: 'Wait till you get to Wales' and now we were bound for Wales at last.

GAME 28 — SATURDAY 16 DECEMBER 1905 — at Cardiff Arms Park, Cardiff

WALES

NEW ZEALAND

3

0

FOR WALES
Try by Morgan.

WALES
H.B. Winfield (Cardiff), W.M. Llewellyn
(Penygraig), R.T. Gabe (Cardiff),
E.G. Nicholls (captain, Cardiff), E. Morgan
(London Welsh), C.C. Pritchard (Pontypool),
P.F. Bush (Cardiff), R.M. Owen (Swansea),
A.F. Harding (London Welsh), W. Joseph
(Swansea), J.J. Hodges (Newport), J.F. Williams
(London Welsh), C.M. Pritchard (Newport),
G. Travers (Pill Harriers), D. Jones (Aberdare).

NEW ZEALAND
Gillett, Wallace, Deans, Hunter, McGregor,
Mynott, Roberts, Gallaher (captain), Seeling,
McDonald, O'Sullivan, Newton, Glasgow,
Casey, Tyler.

Weather: Cloudy and calm, ground firm
Referee: John Dallas (Scotland)
Crowd: 47,000

KICK OFF
Owen dummied to Bush, passed to Pritchard and Morgan scored. Winfield missed.

HALFTIME
Wales 3, New Zealand 0

FULLTIME
Wales 3, New Zealand 0

FROM THE SIDELINES

WANTED—A GIANT-KILLER.

HOW THE ALL BLACKS were perceived prior to their arrival in Wales.

WELSH CAPTAIN GWYN NICHOLLS' TEAM TALK

Gather round, men

The eyes of the rugby world are on Wales today. It is up to us to prove that the Old country is not quite barren of a team that is capable of giving New Zealand at least a hard fight. It has been suggested by some of the English papers that they come to Wales more or less stale; but as they played two English Counties last week and won each match by forty to fifty points with half their best players resting for today's game, the staleness is not very apparent.

We have already discussed tactics. So it only remains to me to appeal to you to be resolute in your tackling. You all know what New Zealand are like if they are given latitude. They throw the ball about, and their system of intensive backing-up makes them very dangerous.

So there must be no hair-combing. Every man in possession must be put down, ball and all. As for the forwards, you already know what to do to get the loose head.

Come on. Let's get out!

◆ WESTERN MAIL

WALES HAD AN OMINOUS DUTY to perform on Saturday and, to the intense delight of Welshmen all the world over, she proved equal to the task of inflicting the first defeat upon the world-famed New Zealanders.

Other victories have been won in other years, and while they served to establish the supremacy of Welsh football in these islands, they pale into dimness in comparison with the great triumph of Saturday.

Such a game had never been played before, and such a victory had never been won. It was virtually a contest for the rugby championship of the world, and now that one can look back upon a result that was gratifying to Wales it requires no small amount of self restraint to review the game in a spirit of calmness, and thus take the proper perspective of the event.

That Wales fully and thoroughly deserved to win is a point upon which there is universal agreement, and it is satisfactory to know that the Colonials, keenly as they must have felt their defeat, were good sportsmen enough to acknowledge that they had at least met a team superior to their own.

It is doubtful whether there has ever been an occasion which so thrilled the whole country with intense emotion, and whatever may be said for or against the part played by football in the national life of Wales, there is no blinking the fact that it exercises a remarkable fascination upon all classes of people. Not

BILLY WALLACE'S RECOLLECTIONS

In the train the selection committee had a prolonged meeting to look over our resources and see what was available. When we looked around us we were dismayed to see just how limited our resources were and it seemed impossible that we could field a sound team against our most redoubtable opponents. We had done a vast amount of travelling in the past four weeks and this was to be our fourth International in four weeks.

We had several injuries, but our greatest drawback was the evident staleness of the team. It is very difficult to describe what this staleness is. But in the main it is caused by players being cooped up in trains without exercise, causing them to put on superfluous

weight and making them sluggish. To give an example with our two locks, Cunningham, when he was in the pink of condition, was about 14 stone and Newton 15 stone. Both were now carrying about 17 stone.

All of us had put on weight in the same way and lost that sparkle and vivacity that was so characteristic of us. No longer were we eagerly looking forward to the next game.

We arrived in Cardiff at 11 p.m. but nobody was in bed. Those who weren't in the station were out on the streets and there was tremendous excitement when our train pulled into the station. As soon as we stepped out of the carriage we were greeted by the Lord Mayor and the officials of the Welsh Rugby Union.

There was hardly room to breathe, let alone move. The police with great difficulty forced a lane for us through the dense throng and we emerged from the station into a big square which was similarly packed.

As soon as we appeared we were cheered to the echo and we had a great struggle to reach our drag which was to take us to the Queen's Hotel. The streets and footpaths were filled with a cheering throng while from the tops of every verandah and from practically every window on the route people waved to us as we passed. It was the finest reception we had received anywhere and it showed the tremendous interest the Welsh people were taking in the coming match.

only in the homeland, but in all the remote parts of the world where a few Welshmen are gathered together, the news of Wales' victory has been, or will be, received with unbounded joy.

One can imagine every Cymro in New Zealand holding his head higher than ever, and declaring with greater gladness his pride of his race.

These are days in which responsible men who have the future welfare of Britain at heart proclaim from the housetops that stay-at-home Britons are gradually losing that virility and grit upon which the greatness of the Empire has been founded, and the time had come when it was necessary to furnish some tangible proof to the country.

We looked in vain for that evidence to England, Scotland and Ireland and it seemed somewhat incongruous and lacking in the element of due proportion that the onus of that proof should have been cast upon the little Principality of Wales.

It was a great responsibility and all the world wondered whether Wales would prove equal to the duty of vindicating the trust. Well, she has done it. The prestige of Wales has been enhanced tremendously as a nation possessed of those splendid qualities — pluck and determination.

These were exemplified almost in an unparalleled degree in Saturday's historic battle. It was the hardest, keenest and most vigorous contest ever waged between two representative teams on the football field, and the triumph of Wales was due not only to those qualities named but also to masterly strategy, intelligence and skill of the highest order.

The Colonials, by their own confession, were beaten at their own game, and this entitles the governing authorities of rugby in Wales to a tribute of the sincerest praise for their wisdom and foresight and courage in abandoning the old formation in favour of the new system of seven forwards and eight backs.

The deciding score came 10 minutes before halftime when the Welsh backs put into effect a move that had been practised at a special training session. Scrumhalf Dicky Owen had continually plied the ball out to Percy Bush, ignoring Cliff Pritchard, the rover back.

Then from a scrum in midfield, Wales heeled, and Bush, Gwyn Nicholls and Willie Llewellyn raced right. Owen made as if to pass to Bush as usual but instead sent one of his famous reverse passes towards Pritchard. Although the ball bounced, Pritchard picked it up, swerved and passed to Rhys Gabe who unloaded to Morgan. The winger rounded Duncan McGregor and darted past George Gillett to score.

THE WELSH SUPPORTERS erupt with delight following Teddy Morgan's epic try.

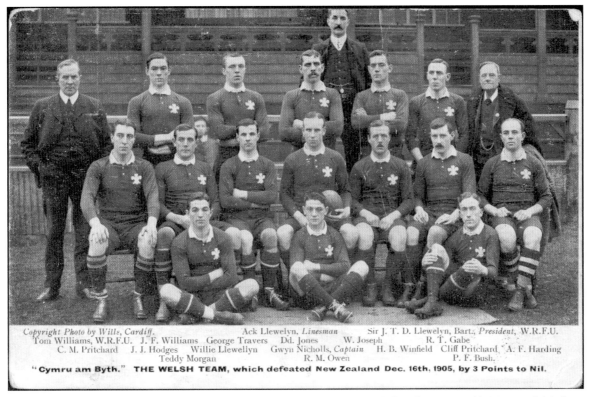

Copyright *Photo by Wills, Cardiff.* Ack Llewelyn, *Linesman* Sir J. T. D. Llewelyn, Bart., *President*, W.R.F.U.
Tom Williams, W.R.F.U. J. F. Williams George Travers Dd. Jones W. Joseph R. T. Gabe
C. M. Pritchard J. J. Hodges Willie Llewellyn Gwyn Nicholls, *Captain* H. B. Winfield Cliff Pritchard A. F. Harding
Teddy Morgan R. M. Owen P. F. Bush.
"Cymru am Byth." THE WELSH TEAM, which defeated New Zealand Dec. 16th, 1905, by 3 Points to Nil.

THE WELSH TEAM that defeated the All Blacks 3-0. Holding the ball is captain Gwyn Nicholls with tryscorer Teddy Morgan at left in front.

SOUTH WALES ECHO

IT SOON BECAME CLEAR that this was not a day when the New Zealand machine would function smoothly. Spanners were thrown into its works from the opening minutes — more than once by Gwyn Nicholls, who was leading by example.

His first big tackle drew a grunt of anguish from the Taranaki first five eight James Hunter, who groaned, 'You're too old for this game — why don't you give up?'

Nicholls also stopped Wallace in the Welsh 25, lifting him bodily, bearing him back yards and dumping him down hard.

SOUTH WALES DAILY NEWS

IT WOULD BE IDLE TO DENY that the New Zealanders were not formidable opponents, for there are points about their play which demand recognition. Their following up and speed all round as a side has probably never been excelled, but in opportunism and in tactics, as in strategy, they were a long way behind not only their Welsh opponents, but many of the English, Scottish and Irish sides that could be named, while given a referee of the impartial strictness of Mr Dallas the three Welsh invincible sides would have defeated them at every time of meeting.

There have been occasions when individual Welshmen have shown greater powers of defence than individual members of the present team did, but never has there been a Welsh side which, from forward to fullback, showed such uniform excellence as the 15 men whose names will live as having defeated the hitherto all-conquering New Zealanders, every man of whom played

with a grim determination that deserved the honour of victory.

As a spectacle, the game was a great one. Seldom was the ball hidden from sight for more than a moment.

Wales proved that their forwards could stand the strain of play at ding dong pace for 80 minutes as well as any, and the writers of the nonsense about the victories of the New Zealanders having proved the decadence of the men of the Mother Country would feel silly could they have witnessed this match.

Every man did more than he was expected to do and the samples of collectivism in skilled attack were such as to give every warrant for the belief that but for the fouls artfully committed out of sight of the referee, the New Zealand defence would have been penetrated on other occasions.

GEORGE DIXON'S DIARIES

That [Deans'] was an absolutely fair try there is overwhelming evidence . . . including Gabe who tackled Deans as he was falling and pulled him back into play, and Llewellyn the Welsh line umpire.

The referee was not what could be called first-class according to my standard — no referee who is commonly 30 or so yards behind the play when a fast bit of work occurs, can be classed A1 — what would be thought in New Zealand of a referee who runs out to control a first class game, on a greasy ground, in ordinary walking boots, no buttons or bars, and clad in heavy clothing, including the orthodox stiff high collar?

In the evening were dined by the Welsh Union. Mr Philips in the chair — a number of good speeches.

THE REFEREE

IT WAS ONE OF THE HARDEST matches ever played. Wales deserved to win on the day, and they owed their success mostly to the superb fullback work of Winfield and the pace and robustness of the forwards.

Cliff Pritchard did his 'spoiling' work like a master. But the New Zealanders played a poor game outside the scrimmage.

Mynott at five-eighths made a terrible number of mistakes, and his inability to field the ball let his side down.

The team lacked the 'sting' in attack that had been common to them, and Wallace and McGregor, the wing threequarters, were forgotten.

As a spectacle, it was not a great game to watch. The teams were too terribly keen and, although quick and hard, never found an easily precise game.

When the New Zealand Premier saw the side off, his final words were, 'Be sure and beat Wales.' The New Zealanders have failed. It was something of a mistake leaving such an important match to the fag end of the tour.

The Welsh forwards were terrific and if it was a case of a side playing as well as its opponents let it, then New Zealand quite merited defeat, for our Colonial friends were not in anything like the form they showed at Inverleith. The wear and tear of the exacting tour had told on the side, and they had to meet the Welshmen at the time when the footballers of the Mother Country are perhaps at their best.

THE 1905 WELSH test programme.

LONDON DAILY CHRONICLE

THE CHIEF EXPLANATION OF THE New Zealanders' defeat is to be found in a staleness which must have evidenced itself before had they encountered a foe almost as strong as themselves.

Think of what the New Zealanders have done — playing three national fifteens, in Scotland, Ireland and England, on consecutive Saturdays, with exhibition games and exhaustive train travelling in between — and then it is easy to understand how they came to be beaten by a side which in respect of physical, and one may say mental, fitness must be considered superior to any combination of players the tourists have hitherto encountered.

Wales at least merits the credit of being sufficiently strong to benefit from the hardships which beset the Colonials' perpetual programme in a game which breeds casualties, but the fact that Wales did nothing more than just win, and that one is left dubious of the moral legitimacy of the victory, are circumstances that protect this great New Zealand team and their greater record from any argument of belittlement.

WALES AND NEW ZEALAND do battle at scrum time.

'MAJOR', THE SPORTSMAN

I WAS WITHIN SIX YARDS of the spot where the New Zealanders scored the disallowed try. It was the unanimous verdict of a goodly number of Welsh supporters next to me, and also my own, that no fairer try has been scored on the football field. The one question uppermost in my mind is, should not the separate Rugby Unions in the future insist on independent linesmen?

I readily concede that on the day's form the better team won, but the legitimate result should unquestionably have been a draw. The experience of the Colonials in having a try disallowed is, of course, merely the luck of the game — like an umpire's decision in cricket, or a rub of the green in golf, it has to be borne cheerfully.

But when men are charged with trickery and unfairness something forcible may be said, and this is just where the Colonials have cause for complaint.

Mr Dixon, the New Zealand manager, who I know to be one of the most reserved of men, has found it necessary to officially state that, 'A great many untrue, unfair and unsportsmanlike statements have been made in various papers, alleging, amongst other things, that the New Zealanders put the ball unfairly into the scrum. I have suggested to the Welsh Football Union that in any of our future matches in Wales the referee be asked to put the ball into the scrimmage on every occasion. If this is done, the public will be able to judge by results which side has been the greater offender in this respect.' Unfair, untrue and unsportsmanlike are strong words and they are especially strong when coming from the pen of Mr Dixon, who is not in the habit of using them. The reader may be assured the words would not have been used save under a great sense of injustice.

TELEGRAM SENT BY BOB DEANS TO *DAILY MAIL*

Grounded ball six inches over line. Some of Welsh players admit try. Hunter and Glasgow can confirm. Was pulled back by Welshmen before referee arrived. *Deans.*

DAILY MAIL

EXTRAORDINARY THINGS ARE REPORTED to have happened in the Rhondda Valley after the game. It appears that scores of Welsh colliers had staked their full fortnight's wages on the Welsh team. Never in the history of rugby football has such unbounded confidence in Welsh sport been shown by the mining inhabitants of South Wales.

One enterprising collier at Porth, having bought a house and furnished it nearly, staked the whole of his property on Wales. Though betting has not got a very firm hold on the more respectable Welsh colliers, the most extraordinary bets have taken place over the match. Two Rhondda tradesmen staked £100 of merchandise each that Wales would win.

As soon as the news of victory arrived at Teddy Morgan's home at Abernant, near Aberdare, the town crier was sent around the village with the glorious tidings.

Cliff Pritchard, who played five-eighth for Wales and had a hand in 'the' try, met with a great reception on his return to Pontypool on Saturday night.

A large crowd met the train, and Pritchard was carried shoulder high through the principal streets of the town, the crowd singing 'Land of My Fathers', 'Sospan Fach' and other national songs.

The Devonport and Torquay excursion train for the great match arrived at Cardiff after the gates were closed. Three to five shillings was paid to stand on the roofs of hansom cabs in Westgate Street, so as to obtain a glimpse of the game.

THE ALL BLACKS secure lineout possession.

THE GALLAHER CONTROVERSY

The better team won and ought to have scored at least two more tries. My opinion is that the New Zealand team played an unscientific and brutal game, and especially the man Gallaher. Every time he put the ball into the scrum he twisted it under his own men's legs, and he ought to have been penalised. There is no doubt they are a dirty team.

Ex-Welsh Vice-President James Livingstone

I think Gallaher is occasionally guilty of obstructing the opposing halfback, but my experience is that he puts the ball into the scrum properly. In fact, when I officiated he offered to let me put the ball into the scrum myself. Yes, the New Zealanders are a good lot of sportsmen.

A.L. Soper, who refereed the Oxford game

I consider Gallaher an obstructionist, but the referee is the best judge of whether or not he puts the ball in the scrum fairly.

Former Welsh international Wallace Watts

He has always given me the impression that he plays fairly.

F.J. Sellick, London RUSR

While the Welsh players have raised the art of 'heeling' to a high standard of excellence, the New Zealanders have worked it out to an even greater nicety, and have consequently suffered their share of adverse criticism.

That their superiority is brought about by any unfairness on the part of the Colonial captain in the way he throws the ball into the scrum is a suspicion that should at once be dispelled. The rapidity with which the ball emerges is, in my opinion, entirely due to their better formation in the pack. Their arrangement of a 2-3-2, properly formed, allows for a clearer exit.

Gallaher as a wing forward has certainly been unduly abused. The only thing I have against him is that he was a thorn in our side. He, like every other player, is not infallible and occasionally got around the scrummage too quickly, and was penalised in consequence. The reason for this, I believe, was due to the fact that, in heeling, the Welsh forwards sometimes allowed the ball to hang in the back row, and Gallaher, more used to the 'lightning heels' of a New Zealand pack, darted round, fully expecting to find our halves already in possession. Gallaher rightly plays 'bang right up to the whistle'.

Too much in praise cannot be said of Gallaher and his men, and we in Wales, being progressive in football matters, are thankful for the lessons which are to be gathered from their visit. Their record is one of which they should be justly proud.

May this Colonial invasion not be the last!

Welsh captain Gwyn Nicholls

DUNCAN McGREGOR, IN A LETTER HOME

On the day's play at Cardiff the Welshmen were the better side. Hunter, our great five-eighth, let us down. He couldn't do anything right. The referee was not too good. One of our fellows got over the line, but the referee would not give a try. We have had postcards from Welsh people who saw it, and when they say so it must be very nearly right.

EVERY CONCEIVABLE VANTAGE spot at Cardiff Arms Park was taken up.

NEW ZEALAND TIMES' UK CORRESPONDENT

BEAT WALES — never mind the rest — beat Wales,' we are told were the last words of Mr Seddon, the New Zealand Premier, when he cheered the Colonial rugby footballers on their quest in the old country.

For a minute the crowd stood still, not realising the fact that Wales had won, was still champion of the world at rugby football and that the New Zealanders had failed to carry out Mr Seddon's behest.

Then pandemonium broke loose. Hats, umbrellas, coats were flung to the heavens. Men hugged one another, rushed across the pitch and mobbed the players; gibbered with delight, and then slowly, still in a dream, filed out of the famous arena on which Wales have not lost a match since 1899.

'Man,' said one leek-decorated enthusiast to a friend who asked him what he thought of it all, 'I couldn't speak for five minutes after it was all over, I was that excited.' Said another: 'Of course, I'm glad we won, but now it's all over I wish it had been a draw. The New Zealanders deserved to score, and I believe Deans did in the far corner.' But the majority of the crowd continued to cheer and sing.

THE TIMES

FOR ROBUSTNESS AND KEENNESS the game could not be surpassed. Mr Dallas, the referee, had a very difficult task. He administered the law of the game unflinchingly and the New Zealanders had to pay dearly for sailing so near to the wind on the question of offside.

Many penalties were given against them in the first 15 minutes which obviously affected their organisation, and the pace and vigour of the Welsh forwards gave them no repose in which to steady themselves.

DAILY EXPRESS' WEST OF ENGLAND CORRESPONDENT

IT IS MUCH TO BE REGRETTED that towards the end of a phenomenally successful tour the New Zealand football teams should be called upon to repudiate charges of unfair play, and I am convinced that the attitude of the Welsh critics, who are entirely to blame in this matter, will be resented by every Britisher to whom the term 'sportsmanship' is something more than an idle phrase.

In the course of 20 years' experience of representative rugby football, I do not remember an occasion on which one side was so heavily handicapped by a hostile crowd as was the case with the Colonials last Saturday. The unwarranted aspersions cast upon Gallaher's play by contributors to Welsh football journalism, had produced a general distrust in the Colonial captain's fairness.

More than seventy-five per cent of the huge assembly took it for granted that Gallaher's main object was to obtain an advantage by means that were opposed to the spirit as well as the letter of the law.

The result was a continuous flow of barracking that completely unnerved the Colonial players and enabled Wales to achieve a success which I, for one, believe would not be repeated if the sides met one hundred times on a neutral field.

◆ ❖ ◆

In the highest circles there was animated debate on the New Zealand methods and discussion centred on Gallaher's wing forward play and his method of putting the ball in the scrummage. Mr Dixon, the manager of the New Zealand team, was emphatic

THE NEW ZEALANDERS' war cry that prompted 47,000 Welshmen to burst into 'Land of Our Fathers'.

BOB DEANS, IN A LETTER HOME

There was a huge crowd of about 45,000 people, who in response to our war cry, all sang 'Land of Our Fathers', the national song. The game was very even but not of the highest order. Morgan scored from a passing run for Wales, and after this they played a defensive game, finding touch instead of passing.

We attacked a good deal in the second spell, but our men were too eager, for time and again the passing was spoiled or else the ground we had gained would be lost by a fine kick from a Welsh threequarter.

After several attempts at last got over for New Zealand, but while lying over the line was pulled back by the Welsh forwards, and the referee, who was about 30 yards behind, gave it no score. After this Wales had somewhat the better of the play, and time was called with them three points to the good.

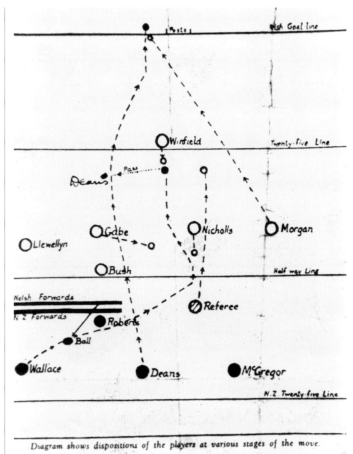

Diagram shows dispositions of the players at various stages of the move.

TEDDY MORGAN'S DEPICTION of Bob Dean's famous non-try.

in his opinion that Gallaher's methods were perfectly fair and did not infringe the letter or spirit of the rules.

That the penalties given against him are mostly due to a failure to appreciate the finest point of the game; Welsh opinion was wholly antagonistic to this and the fact of the matter is that the New Zealanders' conception of some of the rules is greatly at variance with the conception by the Motherland.

◆ ❖ ◆

As for the New Zealand players, Casey and Tyler were prominent all day, tackling and hooking the ball most successfully. Newton probably never played a better game in his career. All round his style was first class, his 16st 7lb and strength were invaluable. All the New Zealand pack played a 'game of games' and deserve every credit. Gallaher experienced a trying ordeal. His keenness made him most conspicuous and his play was a novelty to the Welsh. Mr Dallas evidently blamed him for twisting the ball into the scrums . . .

The Welsh team had a triumphal return to the Queen's Hotel. The 'All Blacks' returned in a leisurely manner, feeling more hurt about the decision on the try than about the game. During the evening a dinner was held, and the utmost enthusiasm and good feeling prevailed. This convivial meeting ended early, and the teams mingled and strolled through the admiring throngs outside. The streets had the appearance presented after a huge British victory in South Africa (Boer War).

◆

ATHLETIC NEWS

DAVE GALLAHER, THE CAPTAIN of the New Zealanders, was one of the first to congratulate Gwyn Nicholls on the triumph of his team. Nicholls heartily reciprocated the compliments, and then the rival captains exchanged jerseys.

Gallaher was wearing the red dragon raiment of the victors when he gave his opinion of the match. 'It was a rattling good game, played out to the bitter end, with the result that the best team won,' he said.

'Is there any point about the defeat which you regard as unsatisfactory?'

'No,' was the reply: 'the better team won, and I am content.'

'What of the refereeing? Have you any opinion favourable or otherwise to express?'

Gallaher smiled as he replied, 'I have always made it a point never to express a view regarding the referee in any match in which I have played, so you must excuse me now.'

The Welsh captain, Gwyn Nicholls, looking radiantly happy, wore the black jersey of the New Zealand captain and was drinking a cup of tea with evident satisfaction when asked for his views.

'There really was practically nothing between the teams,' he said. 'The real difference was that we took advantage of our only opportunity to score and the New Zealanders didn't.'

'Any other point?'

'Well, I think the fielding of our men was certainly superior on the day's form.'

'Would you single out any for special mention?'

'No, it isn't needful,' replied Gwyn, 'for all did so well.'

I think it was a grand game, but a draw would have more fairly represented the play. Of course I am delighted with the result, but the New Zealanders are to be condoled with on losing.

Welsh player Percy Bush

GAME 29 — THURSDAY 21 December 1905 — at St Helen's Ground, Swansea

NEW ZEALAND
GLAMORGAN COUNTY

9
0

FOR NEW ZEALAND
Tries by McDonald, Smith, Wallace.

FOR NEW ZEALAND
Booth, Abbott, Smith, Stead, Wallace,
Mynott, Roberts, Gallaher (captain), Seeling,
McDonald, O'Sullivan, Cunningham,
Newton, Glasgow, Casey.

GLAMORGAN GOUNTY
J.C.M. Dyke (Penarth), W. Arnold (Swansea),
J.L. Williams (Cardiff), H. Jones (Neath),
W. Pullen (Cardiff), R.A. Gibbs (Cardiff),
J. Jones (Aberavon), P. Hopkins (Swansea),
W. Joseph (captain, Swansea), D. Jones
(Aberdare), J.F. Williams (London Welsh),
R. Thomas (Mountain Ash), D. Westacott
(Cardiff), J. Powell (Cardiff), H. Hunt
(Swansea).

Weather: Fine and windy, ground soft
Referee: James Games (Glamorgan)
Crowd: 20,000

KICK OFF
Smith and Abbott attacked from a scrum and Smith scored. Wallace missed.

HALFTIME
New Zealand 3, Glamorgan County 0

McDonald snapped up a loose ball and ran away to score. Wallace missed: 6-0.
Wallace latched on to a well-judged crosskick from Smith to score. Wallace missed.

FULLTIME
New Zealand 9, Glamorgan County 0

FROM THE SIDELINES

ATHLETIC NEWS

THERE HAS BEEN SOME TROUBLE over the appointment of the referee for today's match and yesterday it was stated that New Zealand had intimated to the Welsh Rugby Union that unless some other person than Mr Games, of Newport, was appointed they would not only cancel the fixture with Glamorganshire, but also the remaining fixtures in Cardiff, Newport and Swansea. It is alleged that Colonials have discovered that Mr Games is on the 'black list' of the English union.

The ultimatum of the New Zealanders was considered at a meeting of the Welsh Rugby Union at Cardiff last evening, when it was decided to stand by Mr Games. The New Zealanders were given two hours in which to make their final decision. At the end of that time the Welsh Rugby Union received a message from the Colonials accepting the appointment of Mr Games as referee, and the match will therefore now be played.

◆

SOUTH WALES ARGUS

THOSE WHO EXPECTED TO FIND in the contest between Glamorgan and the New Zealanders at Swansea a sort of return 'test match' were sorely disappointed. The Glamorgan team as originally contemplated was practically the Welsh side, but abstentions — in some cases due to injuries received in the great match, and in others owing to the prior claims of business — so weakened the combination that it was practically a Welsh 'A' team that eventually took the field.

It would be ungenerous to say that the Welsh cracks, having achieved their object and defeated the hitherto invincible 'All Blacks' did not care to run the risks of a second trial of strength, but so it happened that, although about twelve were available, only three of last Saturday's victorious team took the field yesterday.

It was a game of missed chances. The New Zealanders won by 9 points to nil, but they were exceedingly lucky to do so and if one were an 'All Black' one would shudder to contemplate what would have happened if Nicholls and Gabe had been playing in the centre instead of the two substitutes who did duty for Glamorgan yesterday, considering that one of these centres has for years been best known as a forward and that the other is only a member of the Cardiff reserve team.

The only two men on the New Zealand side to do themselves justice were Roberts and Wallace. The others were good and bad by turns, and with most of them the bad periods far outnumbered the good. Gallaher set his men a good example by always throwing the ball swiftly hip high . . .

Towards the close the New Zealanders rallied, and first

THE GLAMORGAN TEAM that held the All Blacks to 9-nil at Swansea.

BILLY WALLACE'S RECOLLECTIONS

Trouble arose over the appointment of a referee for the Glamorgan match when we were notified that a Mr Games had been appointed referee by the Glamorgan County. We knew nothing for or against the gentleman in question, but we objected on principle to the appointment of anyone without reference to us.

We felt very strongly that the Welsh authorities were trying to put another one across us, as had been done in the appointment of the referee for the Welsh match. After discussing the matter very thoroughly we decided to communicate with the New Zealand Rugby Union to cancel the match if necessary. We got a reply leaving the matter in our hands.

So we notified Glamorgan that the match was off. There was, of course, great disappointment on the part of the public and several newspapers took our part.

Then a deputation of businessmen waited on Gallaher and pointed out that great preparations had been made for the match. Tickets had been sold, excursion trains had been organised, factories had arranged to close.

Dave called the team committee together and after another long discussion we eventually decided to play the game and accept the referee. As events turned out, the gentleman gave a really good display of refereeing and we had no cause for complaint whatever. No doubt after all the hullabaloo he was out to show just what he

could do and he was certainly absolutely fair and kept up with the game very well.

Our display in the game was not in keeping with the reputation we had gained and several Welsh papers deplored the fact that the original Glamorgan team had not taken the field so the prestige of Welsh football might have further been enhanced with another victory against the All Blacks.

We were a thoroughly jaded team and did not care how soon the tour finished. Had we met the Welsh team earlier in the tour I think there would have been a very different story to tell.

McDonald and then Wallace scored tries for them, after two exceptionally clever pieces of work. The brilliancy came too late, however, to satisfy the spectators, who went away frankly disappointed with the New Zealanders' display.

◆

NEW ZEALAND TIMES'
UK CORRESPONDENT

A MISTAKE WHICH IS NOT LIKELY to be repeated is the inclusion of so many comparatively unimportant matches. Had the Glasgow and Munster matches been omitted, the wear and tear upon the present team would have been considerably less, for these matches were sandwiched in between the internationals — a most awkward arrangement — and, in the case of the Munster fixture, involving a good deal of fatiguing travel.

ALEX McDONALD

Otago — loose forward
22, 5ft 10in, 12st 12lb

Educated at the George St School and a member of the Kaikorai club of Dunedin, McDonald first represented his province in 1904. He was subsequently selected for the 1905 tour to Australia and later that same year on the Originals tour . . . he played in the internationals against Scotland and Ireland on the side of the scrum and against England and Wales in the back row. Team-mate George Gillett, in an interview upon his return to New Zealand, labelled McDonald and Seeling the best forwards in the team.

The fixture at Limerick was a particularly unfortunate one for the New Zealanders, for it was there that G. W. Smith was rendered useless for the rest of the tour. He was very badly missed in the match against Wales.

It is easy, of course, to be wise after the event but there is no gainsaying the fact that the playing of Smith in the unimportant Limerick match was a blunder. His absence was hardly likely to mean a New Zealand defeat at Limerick, but it would have been better to lose that match than to lose his services against Wales.

◆

NEW ZEALAND TIMES'
UK CORRESPONDENT

S OME OF THE WELSH PAPERS came down very heavily and most unfairly on the New Zealanders over their play in the international match. They accused the All Blacks of being 'decidedly unfair and unduly rough', of unfairly putting the ball into the scrum, of 'improper tackling', of violation of rules that removed the breakers of them outside the pale of pure sportsmanship,' and so on.

Gallaher, in particular, came in for severe condemnation for his delinquencies in the matter of putting the ball into the scrum and for his 'obstructionist tactics'.

I showed a Welshman who was present at the match these allegations against the New Zealanders. His reply was, 'Bally rot.' Another has written to the 'Sportsman' protesting against the accusations levelled against the All Blacks, and actually says he was struck by the 'almost fatherly forbearance which the big men meted out to little Owen, when nothing would have been easier than to put him hors de combat'.

Owen, be it said, was the only member of the Welsh team to receive a knock hard enough to lay him out for a couple of minutes. So much for the 'roughness' of the New Zealanders.

As for Gallaher's unfair tactics, I think Owen, the Welsh half, should know a good deal about them. In an interview with a *Western Mail* scribe he said in reply to a question as to Gallaher's methods:

'Well, he is a most useful man to his inside half. At times I could not get round the scrummages to gather the ball in consequence of his cutting in between and preventing me getting to it, and that was why Roberts beat me occasionally.'

Anything unfair as to his other work?

'No,' responded the little man. 'He knew his work thoroughly well, and is a great player.'

It is thought that he was paying you unusual attention.

'Oh no. He was on me whenever he had the chance, and made no mistake in tackling, which was exceptionally keen throughout.'

What may be termed 'Gallaher tactics' have been objected to in England chiefly on the ground of his being an obstructionist and getting off-side. Few acknowledged judges of the game have ever raised the point that he puts the ball into the scrum with an unfair twist on it.

But a number of Welshmen firmly believe that he does so. Very early in the New Zealand tour this subject was broached to a well-known referee who, after closely watching the New Zealand 'winger' in several games, was quite satisfied that he does not put the ball in unfairly.

The attacks upon him prompted the team manager, Mr George Dixon, to write to the 'Sportsman' suggesting that for all matches in Wales the referee be asked to put the ball into the scrum.

Gallaher critics are not, being it said, having matters all their own way. He has plenty of defenders among the journalists who have followed the New Zealanders on tour, and among competent referees. Several of the latter say that he is occasionally 'an obstructionist' but scout the idea that he either puts the ball into the scrum unfairly or wilfully trespasses against the rules of the game in any other direction.

The journalists who have taken up the cudgels on his behalf belabour the New Zealanders' Welsh detractors particularly severely, intimating that their 'partisan spirit has dominated all other feelings.'

It was clear at Cardiff that the Welshmen had made up their minds to 'barrack' against Gallaher, whatever he did. Their local scribes had insisted that his methods were unfair, and the result was that the 'winger' could do nothing that was correct in the eyes of the Welsh spectators.

◆ ❖ ◆

At one time it appeared to be an odds-on chance of the match against Glamorgan being scratched, but happily the contretemps was avoided.

The trouble originated over the selection of a referee. Mr Games, of the Welsh Rugby Union, had been appointed as referee in the match, but the New Zealanders, who had evidently been informed that Mr Games was referee in the Leicester-Swansea match, when the Welsh Union altered his decision, objected strongly to his appointment.

Manager Mr Dixon, who had cabled to the New Zealand Rugby Union early on Wednesday morning, informed the Welsh union later in the day to the effect that he had received a message from the ruling body in the colonies stating that they were prepared to abide by the decision arrived at by the team.

In the meantime, Mr Dixon had issued a letter to the local press, explaining that all the New Zealanders asked and insisted upon was that they should have a voice in the appointment; in other words, that the referee should be mutually agreed upon, as provided in the laws of the game.

The New Zealanders intimated that they were willing to accept Mr Bowen (Llanelly) or Mr Gil Evans (London) as referee. The Welsh Union, however, considered that they could not for a moment consider that question. A meeting of the committee of the union was held at Cardiff and it was decided that Mr Games must be referee or the game could not be played.

At six o'clock on Wednesday night, New Zealand was communicated with, and during the evening frequent messages passed between the two parties. At eight o'clock relations were such that the printer of the official card, on asking for the names and numbers, was told that New Zealand hardly thought it necessary to give them, as they were not likely to be required.

It was nine o'clock before the tension was relieved, and then the Welsh Union officials again got into communication with the New Zealanders and, after a long discussion on the telephone, Mr Walter Rees announced officially that the match would be played, and that Mr Games had been accepted by New Zealand as referee.

Teddy Triumphant or Morgan and Maori

Every Druid with his sickle,
Every milkman with his cry,
Chants the name of Teddy Morgan
And his ever-glorious try:
And the 'Milk-oos' of the morning
Are a paean on the gales,
Chanting Cymric Teddy's prowess,
Worthy son of worthy Wales.
Oh, his name shall live in story,
He of Cardiff, county Glam.,
Who has proved that good Welsh mutton
Beats your Canterbury lamb.

[Chorus —
Maori had a little lamb
'Twas a wonder without question
But when it ate a raw Welsh leek
Little Maori had indigestion.
— Help! Murder!]

Then erect on highest Snowdon
Mid the clouds of Cymric fame,
A grand statue, all enduring,
On it carve our Teddy's name.
Poise the Morgan of true manhood
On a pedestal of rock,
Emblematic of the country
Which withstood Maori shock,
And around his classic forehead
Carve a crown in stone, to speak
Unto future generations
Of the Fern beneath the Leek.

A popular Welsh Song celebrating Morgan's try

GAME 30 — SATURDAY 23 DECEMBER 1905 — at Athletic Ground, Newport

NEW ZEALAND
NEWPORT

6
3

FOR NEW ZEALAND
Try by Harper; penalty goal by Wallace.

NEW ZEALAND
Wallace, Thomson, Deans, Stead (captain), Harper, Mynott, Roberts, Gillett, Seeling, Glenn, McDonald, Cunningham, O'Sullivan, Tyler, Casey.

FOR NEWPORT
Penalty goal by Griffiths.

NEWPORT
R.B. Griffiths, W. Thomas, C.C. Pritchard, S. Adams, A. Davies, G, Jones, G.H. Vile, W.J. Martin; C.M. Pritchard, J.J. Hodges, G. Boots, E. Thomas, W.H. Williams, W.H. Dowell, J.E. Jenkins.

Weather: Fine, ground good
Referee: Gil Evans (Birmingham)
Crowd: 12,000

KICK OFF
Stead and Mynott attacked from a scrum, Harper scoring. Wallace missed: 3-0.
Wallace drop-kicked a penalty goal from 30 metres.

HALFTIME
New Zealand 6, Newport 0

Griffiths landed a magnificent penalty goal from halfway.

FULLTIME
New Zealand 6, Newport 3

FROM THE SIDELINES

WESTERN MAIL

IT IS STRIKING TESTIMONY to the high standard of Welsh football efficiency that in the three matches already played on Welsh soil the Colonials have only crossed the line four times, and those who witnessed the Glamorgan match, at Swansea, will readily agree that two of the three tries were wholly undeserved on the run of play. Still, they were scored.

But those people who imagine that the Colonials were possessed of supernatural powers must be convinced by this time that they have feet of clay, after all.

Their play against Newport was not above the standard of ordinary club football among the leading Welsh clubs, and, indeed, fell considerably below the level of excellence attained by Swansea last season, and the preceding six or seven seasons, without mentioning the great Newport team led by Graham a dozen years ago.

It was surprising to find the Colonial backs on Saturday, when opportunities presented of showing their skill in passing and running, doing nothing but kick into touch whenever the ball came their way. This style of play was reminiscent of English club football rather than of the deftness and attractiveness which have been such marked features of Welsh football in the last couple of decades.

They have by this time lost all the terror which previously attached to the glamour of their name by reason of the great reputation they had gained by their victorious march through the three countries.

They have found that Welsh soil is not so congenial to their methods as that of the sister countries, and they have found, what is more to the point, that Welsh football is a very different quantity, and also a very different quality, to what they experienced elsewhere.

There is very little to be said in praise of the New Zealand back

THE PROGRAMME FOR the Newport game.

BILLY WALLACE'S RECOLLECTIONS

The Newport game was very evenly contested even though the Welsh papers reckoned that Newport had much the better of the game. The London papers were able to take a more impartial view of the game. 'The All Blacks are either meeting foemen in South Wales far more worthy of their steel than they have met elsewhere or else the strain of their tremendous tour is beginning to take its inevitable toll,' said one leading London paper.

After the game we went straight back to Cardiff, but this time there was not much rest for us. This was Saturday, 23 December, and was to all intents and purposes Christmas Eve.

Consequently the town had a holiday atmosphere about it and we took part in the fun, looking at the displays of Christmas goods in the windows and wishing we hadn't spent our cash reserve quite so early in the tour!

On Sunday, Freddy Roberts and I went for a drive in the afternoon with Llewellyn, Harding, Teddy Morgan and J.L. Williams, who entertained us to afternoon tea.

On Christmas Day we had the dining room to ourselves and we had a great Christmas dinner. We were able to have all the fun we wanted and the proprietor of the hotel looked after us in a wonderful manner. In addition to the fare provided by the hotel we had quite a number of puddings sent us from friends in different parts of the country and these were very popular, not only for their flavour but because of the uncertainty as to how many sovereigns they contained!

Needless to say we had scores of telegrams wishing us the best of luck from friends in the Old Country and New Zealand and we filled our glasses and drank heartily to 'Absent Friends'. The dining room was all decorated with streamers and we all sat around one big table.

And so as we sat there with paper hats on our heads and pulling bon-bons with each other, we forgot all about the fog outside and thought of those far away across the sea, who were enjoying Christmas under summer skies.

play; in fact, there is nothing to be said, because there was nothing new and nothing to be compared with the back play of the Welsh teams that have held a leading place in rugby football for many years past.

DAILY MAIL

THE GAME AT NEWPORT produced a remarkable effect on the hundreds of ladies who watched its varying fortunes from the stands. The average woman in Newport, judging from the expert feminine criticisms punctuating Saturday's play, apparently knows nearly as much of the science of rugby as any man.

They enter heart and soul into every contest, urging on their players with impassioned cries of approval and encouragement, visiting their failures and shortcomings with mournful wails of disappointment that very often drown their brothers' and fathers' gusts of despair.

There is scarcely a trick of the game with which the Newport girl is not familiar. She is not a bit like the Blackheath or Richmond girl, who goes to a football match more because it is 'the thing' socially than for any real pleasure she derives from watching the game. The Newport girl, on the other hand, enters into the spirit of the contest with all the ardour and abandon of her brother. And not only the Newport girl, but the Newport matron too, and in not a few cases even the Newport grandmother.

On Saturday the most vehement cries of denunciation and encouragement on the principal stand came from several smartly attired elderly ladies, who unquestionably possessed footballing sons, if not footballing grandsons.

'TOUCH JUDGE', DAILY MIRROR

I WAS MUCH INTERESTED in an article appearing one day last week in the *Daily Mail* and written by Mr R.G.T. Coventry, an old Oxford Blue on the subject of the theory of rugby. Briefly summarised, Mr Coventry holds the view that no good is to be gained from lectures on football, and that footballers are born not made. Taking the New Zealanders as a case in point, he remarks: 'Their football is an evolution, not of the lecture room, but of the football field itself.'

Is he quite right in his general contention that football can only be learned on the field itself? I take leave to doubt it and venture to assert that much of our mediocrity, principally in back play, has been brought about by our men not taking the trouble to quietly talk over and think out some of the nice points with the assistance of a first-class exponent.

I do not know the lines on which New Zealand football is conducted or inculcated into the youthful mind, but I should imagine that they attach much value to thoughtful and serious study of the game away from the field itself. The Welshmen most certainly do, and they represent nearly all that is best and most skilful in rugby in this country.

Wales have not disdained the use of a blackboard and lectures by experienced players. They have proved very valuable in educating the minor clubs in the outlying villages and hamlets in the possibilities of their own style.

E.H. SEWELL, LONDON STANDARD

ALL IN ALL THE NEW ZEALANDERS could place the finest fifteen in the field that has ever been seen. I think after due reflection, the majority of good judges of the game will agree with this verdict.

Many, of course, will not agree, and that does not show their opinion wrong, for the majority are not always right. I do not pretend to have seen all the great teams since 'the year one' of the rugby game, as some of my more fortunate confreres have, but to nearly every case where I have made inquiry of past internationals and men of great rugby knowledge, there has been but one answer.

I have never attempted to make out the New Zealanders as possessing a monopoly of how to play football, but I have all along

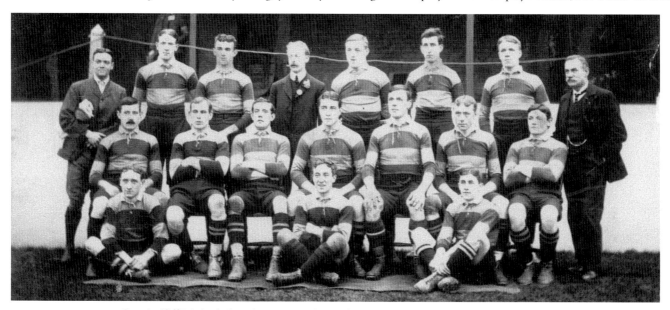

THE NEWPORT TEAM. Captain Cliff Pritchard, the only international, is in the middle of the seven seated.

DAVE GALLAHER,
INTERVIEWED AFTER NEWPORT GAME

'What do you think of our club football?'

'I can only say that we are meeting in your clubs players of our own calibre. I never wish to see a finer game than that at Newport today.'

'What about the referee question?'

'Surely we are within our rights in desiring a voice in the selection? It is such a simple matter after all.'

'Do you think your team is getting stale?'

'I will not say that, but we should have preferred to have met you earlier in the tour.'

'The same may be said of Sivright's team — the 1904 Great Britain team led by 'Darkie' Bedell-Sivright — in New Zealand then?'

'Yes, that is so.'

'What is your opinion of the two remaining Welsh matches?'

'I think the Cardiff match will be a hard one.'

'Are you playing?'

'Oh yes, I shall turn out.'

ACTION FROM THE ALL BLACKS' GAME against Newport. A try and a penalty goal gave them a hard-fought victory.

for them, in several instances — their fielding, especially — the referee penalised Gallaher out of usefulness, in more than one instance quite wrongly, and was not 'up' with the ball when Deans scored. On the run of the game Wales deserved the victory, but it was wretched luck for the New Zealanders to be deprived of as genuine a try as was ever scored, and on such an occasion.

The try meant a drawn game. The ball was touched down over the Welsh line about twenty yards from the left-hand post. There was practically no wind and the ball was dry. From such a position a goal was at any rate an even money chance.

Then came a deal of unnecessary trouble over the referee for the Glamorgan match at Swansea, the New Zealanders not being given any say whatever in the appointment of Mr Games.

It is not generally known that right up to the last moment, when the visitors gave way, it was touch and go whether the New Zealanders did not, on a question of principle, scratch the remaining three matches in Wales and, returning to England, finish the tour with two or three of the numerous games they might have had without asking. The decision to give in to the Welsh authorities was done solely not to cause ill-feeling.

thought, and think still, despite the paper result of December 16, they are better players as a team than any other team in the British Isles.

When I saw them play their second match, at Camborne, I was certain they stood a great chance of returning unbeaten, and as it is now certain that they scored a try on December 16 at Cardiff — as some of the Welsh players know, and some of the body of journalists who formed themselves into anti-New Zealanders of the most pronounced type, for some reason best known to themselves, admit — the team does actually return unbeaten.

But on the records, they have lost one match. It is neither here nor there whether any other combination of players could have endured the strain of thirty-plus matches in fifteen weeks, together with its incessant travelling and the amount of hanging about hotels inseparable from a football tour.

The tour was not a success owing to physical degeneracy on our part but to superiority in playing ability on theirs. In the seventh match, against Durham, the Colonial line was crossed for the first time, by a wing threequarter Phil Clarkson. Three more successful weeks passed before it was crossed again, at Leicester. J.G. Cooper kicked the first of only two goals from tries scored against them. Only two goals from tries in thirty matches. What a team!

Does anyone suggest that the best team that ever played for Wales, Scotland, England or Ireland could play thirty matches in more than three months and have only two goals from tries scored against it? It was evident as the Welsh international approached that some of the players were beginning to feel the strain, and it is a positive fact, despite scoffers and unbelievers, that the team went into Wales nothing so fit as it had been during the period from October 21 to November 28.

Then came the match of the tour. The Colonials played badly,

JIM O'SULLIVAN

Taranaki — loose forward
22, 5ft 10in, 13st 7lb

Born at Okaiawa in Taranaki, O'Sullivan first played for Taranaki as an 18-year-old in 1901. Three years later he had his first taste of an international, for a combined Taranaki-Wanganui-Manawatu team against Great Britain. The following season he was chosen to play for North Island, then featured on the New Zealand tour of Australia and, from that, the Originals tour. He was in great form on tour as a hard-working forward, useful in lineouts. He played in four tests but broke his collarbone against Cardiff, effectively ending his tour.

GAME 31 — TUESDAY 26 DECEMBER 1905 — at Cardiff Arms Park, Cardiff

NEW ZEALAND
CARDIFF

10
8

FOR NEW ZEALAND
Tries by Nicholson, Thomson;
conversions by Wallace 2.

NEW ZEALAND
Wallace, Thomson, Deans, Hunter,
Booth, Stead, Roberts, Gallaher (captain),
Seeling, McDonald, Nicholson, Newton,
O'Sullivan, Glasgow, Casey.

FOR CARDIFF
Tries by Nicholls, Thomas;
conversion by Winfield.

CARDIFF
H.B. Winfield, R.C. Thomas,
E.G. Nicholls, R.T. Gabe, J.L. Williams,
R. David, P.F. Bush (captain), R.A. Gibbs,
G. Northmore, W. Neil, J. Brown, J. Powell,
Sgt Smith, L. George, E. Rumbelow.

Weather: Fine, ground firm
Referee: Gil Evans (Birmingham)
Crowd: 50,000

KICK OFF
Gabe worked the ball acrossfield to Nicholls who scored. Winfield converted: 5-0.
Thomson swerved past Nicholls and Winfield to score a great try. Wallace converted.

HALFTIME
New Zealand 5, Cardiff 5

Bush carelessly failed to force, giving Nicholson a try. Wallace converted: 10-5.
With time up Thomson scored in the corner but Winfield could not convert.

FULLTIME
New Zealand 10, Cardiff 8

FROM THE SIDELINES

SOUTH WALES DAILY NEWS

CARDIFF LOST THE GAME solely and simply through a temporary lapse on the part of one of the most resourceful players in the rugby game. Captain Percy Bush's breakdown baffles adequate explanation.

It is true that he had been confined to bed since the London Welsh match, in which he performed brilliantly, but his play in other stages of the game was marked by his best skill.

It seemed an instance of sudden mental paralysis, and his 'toying' with the ball was as though there was not a New Zealander within 100 yards of him. He had only to touch down to save the position, instead of making a present of a try to New Zealand after the ball had gone over the line as a result of poor and aimless workmanship, not skilful attack. Seeling's kick over the line was a wild one, and his disgust at his hard kick was palpably shown by him.

Still, it was a flash of inspiration that sent Nicholson and Thomson over the line on to the ball, when they saw that Bush had not immediately fallen on it, so that what started with accident wound up with a smart example of opportunism.

The New Zealanders deserve highest credit for making a courageous fight. To have lost one of their men before the first half was over in a game in which up to then they had had the worst of play was a great handicap, and as it meant that the side lost the incalculable assistance of Gallaher as wing forward and left Roberts alone to feed the backs, it entirely disorganised the style of play which the New Zealanders have adopted in every one of their matches on the present tour. But while they are entitled to this mead of praise for indomitable persistence, they can regard themselves as once more having triumphed when, on actual play, territorially and otherwise, they were a beaten side.

The game is one that will be long remembered. Even before O'Sullivan was off the field the Colonial forwards were unable to command the ball in the scrummage and the Cardiff forwards quite held their own up to that time.

Frequent shouts of delight were raised at the wonderful saving work of Wallace, and though his kicking was not as lengthy or so well directed all through as that of Winfield, yet the intelligence with which he perceived where danger was threatening, and broke in to stem it, were features which commended themselves to the crowd who often cheered him to the echo.

'Kill-danger' Wallace never more merited his happy cognomen than he did in this game and he is justly entitled to be classed as great a fullback as he is a wing threequarter.

HAMISH STUART, ATHLETIC NEWS

THE NEW ZEALANDERS OWED their narrow victory to Bush's error and to the two chief characteristics of their play, speed and strength. No other side would have been 'up' to avail themselves

of Bush's mistake, or have disconcerted that player into making his mistake.

To call the New Zealanders a scientific side in the sense that Cardiff are scientific is a misnomer. Many people mistake effective football for scientific football.

Speed, strength and stamina will win as many if not more games than sheer science, combined with less of the said three qualities than the New Zealanders possess.

EVENING STANDARD

THERE IS NO SHADOW of a doubt that the New Zealanders have had too much football. They only just managed to beat Newport and although with only fourteen men for about two-thirds of the game, they beat the best Welsh club yesterday.

Still, they played in both matches before most of the form I know them to possess. As I have seen them play nineteen of their thirty-one matches, I may be perhaps permitted to know something about their real form.

Their huge scores were run up in this country mainly owing to their seizing the many opportunities which came their way.

In Wales, in the international and Cardiff matches particularly, they handled, for them, very badly indeed.

'PENDRAGON', WESTERN MAIL

THE NEW ZEALANDERS OUGHT to consider themselves the luckiest team that ever played football. They have played four games in Wales, lost one and won the other three by pure unadulterated luck.

It would be hard to imagine what Percy Bush felt like after

A PRIZED TICKET to the Cardiff match at the Arms Park.

making that wretched slip that gave the All Blacks the victory. In fact, it seems incredible that a player of Percy Bush's reputation could make such a blunder.

But there it is, and the Colonists ought to feel mightily thankful for their good fortune.

Percy was spoken to soon after the match and his acute mental distress at his acknowledged blunder was obviously great. Tears welled into his eyes as he said, 'I don't know why I did it, but it will be a life-long memory for me.'

BILLY WALLACE'S RECOLLECTIONS

The day after Christmas would not seem a very good day for playing football, but we were due to meet Cardiff on that day. It was good business for Cardiff for, as the morning broke fine, crowds began to pour into the city from an early hour and by the time the match started there was an even larger crowd than had witnessed the international match against Wales.

The day was ideal for football and in the interval the crowd amused themselves by singing all sorts of songs including the latest 'hit' that had been specially composed since the Welsh test — 'Teddy Morgan, The One Who Scored The Try'.

The Cardiff team was an exceptionally strong one especially in the backs, for Winfield, Gabe, Nicholls and Bush were all playing. The club was the premier team of Wales and had put up a wonderful record for the past few seasons, and so everybody was anticipating that our colours would be lowered once more. Our position as regards fit players was almost desperate.

We continued to attack and before long we equalised the scores thanks to a splendid try by Mona Thomson. The ball was brought out for me to place for the kick at goal and so dense were the spectators that they had to move their chairs and open up a lane to allow me to take my run. The kick was a beauty and sailed fair between the posts, thus making the hundredth goal I had kicked on the tour.

DAILY MAIL

The boxing day match at Cardiff against the Cardiff Club was a most exciting one, and it was a better game than the international which took place on the same ground, the Arms Park. It attracted, beyond a doubt, the biggest gate ever known at Cardiff.

The crowd were mute with disappointment after Bush's dreadful mistake. Poor Bush, who has done such great things for Cardiff and had played such a sterling game all through, ousted Gallaher from his position of 'the best hated man in Wales'.

Urged on by the incensed crowd, who had seen what at first seemed an assured victory for Cardiff slipping out of their grasp, the Cardiffians made heroic efforts to pierce the desperate 'All Black' defence. Gwyn Nicholls particularly summoned all the speed and strength of his halcyon days and with the coolness and skill the veteran made opening after opening in the seemingly impenetrable wall of grim defenders.

The breach, however, was never quite wide enough, and time after time Wallace and Booth and Deans repelled the attack. At

A RARE PHOTO in tour blazers of Fred Roberts, Mona Thomson and Billy Wallace.

last, after a short visit to the Cardiff half, the Welshmen returned to the attack with a fiery onslaught that pierced the defence, Thomas getting over in the corner after another fine display of typical Welsh threequarter passing.

The crowd were frantic with delight and the sky suddenly grew dark with hats, many of which doubtless never found their owners again. They had given up the game as lost, yet here, at the very last moment, there was the chance of averting defeat.

All that was needed was for Winfield to place the goal. He had won many games both for Wales and his club in the hour of gloom, by his marvellous kicking. Surely he would not fail now, even though the angle was an extremely difficult one, and the odds against him.

The crowd and the players, too, held their breath as Winfield went about the usual preliminaries to his fateful effort. A whisper could have been heard as he poised the ball and the tension was almost unsupportable as he drew back the few steps for his short run. The ball soared high to the air straight towards the posts, and to all save the referee and the linesmen standing beneath it seemed as though it had reached the goal.

The crowd evidently thought it had, as they broke into another deafening roar that must have echoed down the ghostly lists of Camelot, leagues away, enough to startle the spectral heroes of the Arthurian legend.

But the wish of the crowd had been father to the thought. The ball had been deflected — perhaps by a little wind — and passed on the wrong side of the post. It was a very near thing indeed, but the referee could have had no difficulty about making his decision.

This was Cardiff's last chance as the end came a minute or two after. But a very large section of the crowd left the field under

THE CARDIFF TEAM. Captain Percy Bush, holding the ball, cost his team victory with a calamitous mistake.

the impression that Cardiff had made a draw of it, and many telegrams to that effect were sent away ere the final score of 'ten points to eight' in cold print convinced the doubting.

Although Cardiff had hard times, it must not be forgotten that the 'All Blacks' played only fourteen men for the greater part of the game, and they are to be congratulated, at the fag end of an exhausting tour, which by this time must have become physically nauseous, on having beaten the strongest club team in Wales.

The total gate receipts were £1861, of which the Colonials take seventy per cent.

◆

EVENING STANDARD

I CAN ONLY HOPE THOSE CRITICS who so unfairly and falsely accused Gallaher of dirty tactics in the Welsh match noticed one thing of the Cardiff match. After O'Sullivan retired hurt, Gallaher went into the scrum. The ball was put in the scrum from that moment to the end of the game by the Cardiff halfbacks.

Despite the absence of Gallaher's alleged unfair tactics and his alleged insistent offside and rough play as wing forward, the New Zealanders — playing all the time one short — won the match against the leading and unbeaten Welsh club.

This in itself gives the lie direct to all the baseless charges made against the New Zealand captain who, by the result of the Cardiff match, stands completely vindicated.

FRED ROBERTS

Wellington — halfback
23, 5ft 7in, 12st 4lb

A tough, nuggety player, Roberts enjoyed a phenomenally successful tour. At its conclusion one correspondent wrote: 'Roberts was the hardest-working man in the team. He played in 29 of the 32 matches in the UK, including all four internationals. How admirably he fulfilled his arduous task is well known to everyone who has followed the fortunes of the All Blacks. In all the galaxy of talent Roberts was the man whom the team could least have spared. It is a question whether a finer scrumhalf has ever been seen in the UK.' He succumbed to an attack of tonsillitis in San Francisco and could not return home with the team. His great friend Billy Wallace remained behind to take care of him, the pair being fortunate to miss the massive San Francisco earthquake of 1906 that demolished their hotel just days after they sailed for New Zealand.

GAME 32 — SATURDAY 30 DECEMBER 1905 — at St Helen's Ground, Swansea

NEW ZEALAND
SWANSEA

4

3

FOR NEW ZEALAND
Dropped goal by Wallace.

NEW ZEALAND
Wallace, Thomson, Deans, Stead, McGregor,
Mynott, Roberts, Gillett, Seeling, Glenn,
Glasgow, Cunningham, Corbett, Gallaher
(captain), Casey.

FOR SWANSEA
Try by Scrine.

SWANSEA
G. Davies, W. Trew, W.W. Arnold, F. Gordon
(captain), R. Scale, F. Scrine, R.M. Owen,
P. Hopkins, I. Morgan, D.J. Thomas, W. Cole,
H. Hunt, W. Parker, A. Smith, W. Joseph.

Weather: Fine and windy, ground firm
Referee: Gil Evans (Birmingham)
Crowd: 20,000

KICK OFF
Good passing by Swansea's backs and forward gave Scrine a try. Davies missed.

HALFTIME
Swansea 3, New Zealand 0

With 10 minutes play remaining Wallace drop-kicked a goal from wide out.

FULLTIME
New Zealand 4, Swansea 3

FROM THE SIDELINES

DAILY EXPRESS

THE GAME HAD FLASHES of real brilliancy, but it ended unfortunately, because the best team lost when it should have won. Swansea's luck has been thoroughly bad throughout this season; drops and penalty goals having contributed to nearly every defeat suffered.

On this occasion, after giving the Colonials one of the hardest games of their tour, and crossing their line, they were eventually beaten by a lucky kick with the wind. This was cruelly hard for the homesters.

In the result, we have this singular feature in the New Zealanders' scoring against the Welsh teams — against Newport they won by three points, against Cardiff by two points and against Swansea by one point.

Of the seven tries conceded in 32 matches, four were against Welsh opponents.

DAILY POST

IT WAS A GAME in which the All Whites displayed their greatest effort of the season. They rose to the occasion brilliantly, and had the satisfaction of crossing their opponents' line, whereas the Colonials were unable to pierce the Swansea defence.

That they had equal opportunities to score will not be disputed for one moment. It was only by the keenest of hard luck that the Swansea players were not awarded further scores. Their efforts were not concentrated on dropping goals, but on making for the line.

They thoroughly merited at least two additional scores, the critical transfer alone failing when the course seemed clear. I cannot get away from the fact that the All Whites had the game in hand.

They, for three parts of the game, had the All Blacks well held, and succeeded once in crossing the line.

For the other part, the Colonials pressed, but could only notch a dropped goal, through Wallace's grand effort.

As a pack the All Whites were superior to the All Blacks, and have

to be sympathised with at the unsatisfactory result of the match. They deserved to win without the shadow of a doubt.

WESTERN MAIL

THE ONE TOPIC OF CONVERSATION in Swansea on Saturday night was the relative values of a dropped goal and a score from a try, and the opinion was generally expressed that the rule which decrees that a dropped goal shall count one more point than a try should be altered without delay.

This sudden outbreak of zeal for reformation seems to have set in with great virulence and extraordinary unanimity.

SOUTH WALES DAILY NEWS

AT 2.30 THERE WERE 20,000 PEOPLE present . . . the irrepressible crowd on the bank now came out at their best to greet the New Zealanders. They chanted a refrain, accompanied by appropriate actions, which sounded something like —

Ter rer! Ra, ra, ra!

Um, um! Ra, ra, ra!

This was repeated four times and created much amusement for the New Zealanders.

The loyal home crowd saw the Colonials beaten at their own game, Swansea being unlucky to lose the match on the general run of play.

After the match all the Swansea players and officials interviewed were unanimous in the opinion that the New Zealanders were fortunate to pull the match off. Mr Walter Rees, secretary of the Welsh Rugby Union: 'Swansea didn't deserve to lose. It was very hard to be beaten under such circumstances.'

Mr Gallaher: 'It was a very fine, fair game.'

Mr Seeling: 'Very hot.'

Mr Gillett: 'Rattling good, but we won!'

Mr R.M. Owen: 'A hard game and we had the worst of the luck.'

BILLY WALLACE'S RECOLLECTIONS

This was the 32nd match of the tour and our hearts rejoiced at the thought that this was to be our last. The day was fine but a really strong wind was blowing which spoilt all chance of really good football. Another unsatisfactory thing was that the ground was covered in straw to protect it against frost and this was then swept to the side lines and piled in heaps.

With the players retrieving the ball from touch and the spectators moving about a good deal the straw was brought back again and at times it was impossible to see the touch line. During the second spell Duncan

McGregor grounded the ball over the goalline but the line umpire raised his flag for stepping into touch. Our chaps protested and when the straw was cleared away we found Duncan had missed stepping into touch by at least a couple of yards!

A couple of minutes later I got my chance and the lost try was avenged. The ball came to me right on the halfway line and right near the touchline. Turning round I ran infield and up towards the twenty-five-yard line. Then I let fly with my left foot and the ball flew fair and square between the posts. The kick was described

by all the Welsh scribes as the greatest fluke, but it was one of the best goals I ever kicked. Had I kicked direct for the goal posts it would have missed by yards. We were, of course, delighted but the Welsh people were greatly disappointed.

After the match we had to return to the hotel and pack, then catch the train to London. We had a great send off from Swansea, all our faults were apparently forgotten and forgiven and the train pulled out amid rousing cheers.

STRAW ON THE GROUND at Swansea caused the All Blacks considerable frustration. A stunning dropped goal by Billy Wallace rescued the day.

GEORGE NICHOLSON

Auckland — lock

27, 6ft 3in, 13st 10lb

Exceptionally tall for his era, Nicholson earned the nickname 'Long Nick' and was a member of New Zealand's first test team in 1903. He was then selected for the test against Great Britain in 1904 and was a natural choice for the Originals tour. He played 20 matches on tour but was surprisingly overlooked for the tests. A high point of his tour was scoring the winning try against Cardiff when he took advantage of a fateful miskick by Cardiff's Percy Bush. Nicholson and teammate Billy Stead, both bootmakers, kept their hand in trade-wise by looking after their teammates' boots.

NEW ZEALAND TIMES' UK CORRESPONDENT

THE NEW ZEALANDERS left Swansea by the 8.55 p.m. mail train for Paddington on Saturday night. Their journey to London was one of triumphal progress.

At nearly all the stations at which the train stopped crowds of people assembled to give the All Blacks a parting cheer, and at Cardiff the throng was so dense that it was some time before a way could be cleared for the mails to be put into the train.

'Sospan Fach' and 'Auld Lang Syne' were sung. At Gloucester some members of the local team turned up to wish their old opponents 'God speed' and there was another demonstration at Swindon.

It was reserved for Paddington, however, to provide the most spontaneous welcome of the night. All the porters and others on duty were ranged up on the platform, and as the train arrived they greeted the All Blacks with enthusiastic cheers.

'They are Jolly Good Fellows' was sung with fervour, and the New Zealanders' luggage was transferred from train to car with a rapidity which was the best proof of enthusiasm.

Johnston, who has been laid up in London with a bad leg since the northern tour, rejoined the team at Victoria Station on Sunday and accompanied them to Paris. O'Sullivan also made the trip, despite his broken collar-bone. The only absentee was Gillett, who is staying on with friends.

◆ ❖ ◆

The New Zealand authorities did not have the least idea before their team came over to England how successful they would be. A writer in an Otago paper remarked: 'But New Zealand takes its football very seriously, and what will happen if that crowd of footballers gets dished is just too horrible to think of. Chaka, the Zulu Napoleon, used to butcher troops that returned after a defeat. New Zealand will probably drop its team into a geyser.'

FOR THE RECORD

Only seven men have crossed the New Zealand lines. They are Phil Clarkson for Durham, R.F. Russell for the Midland Counties, Teddy Morgan for Wales, Frank Scrine for Swansea, John McCallum for Scotland, Ralph Thomas and Gwyn Nicholls for Cardiff.

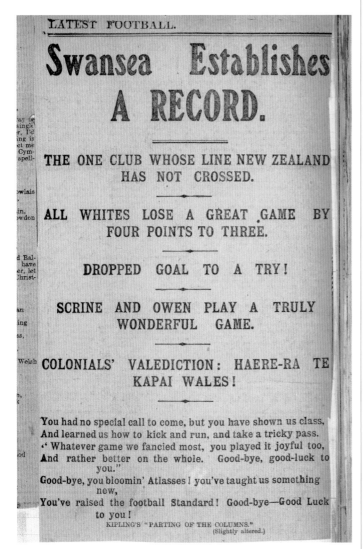

LATEST FOOTBALL.

Swansea Establishes A RECORD.

THE ONE CLUB WHOSE LINE NEW ZEALAND HAS NOT CROSSED.

ALL WHITES LOSE A GREAT GAME BY FOUR POINTS TO THREE.

DROPPED GOAL TO A TRY!

SCRINE AND OWEN PLAY A TRULY WONDERFUL GAME.

COLONIALS' VALEDICTION: HAERE-RA TE KAPAI WALES!

You had no special call to come, but you have shown us class,
And learned us how to kick and run, and take a tricky pass.
" Whatever game we fancied most, you played it joyful too,
And rather better on the whole. Good-bye, good-luck to you."
Good-bye, you bloomin' Atlasses ! you've taught us something new,
You've raised the football Standard ! Good-bye—Good Luck to you !
KIPLING'S "PARTING OF THE COLUMNS."
(Slightly altered.)

THE WESTERN MAIL describing Swansea's agonising one-point loss.

GEORGE DIXON'S DIARIES

154th day, SATURDAY 30 DECEMBER.

Up at 5.30 and writing continuously until lunch time — getting ready to get away to London, en route Paris, after match today. Left at 9 p.m. for London, great send off at station also at Neath, Swansea, Newport also at other stations Gloster [sic] and Swindon and at Paddington, big concourse of porters.

155th day, SUNDAY 31 DECEMBER.

A few hours sleep at Paddington Hotel and en route again for Paris at 9 a.m. Crossed via Folkestone and Boulogne and arrived at Paris 6 p.m. Stayed at St Petersburgh Hotel. House greatly patronised by Englishman.

DAVE GALLAHER, WRITING IN THE *DAILY MAIL*

WHY THE ALL BLACKS TRIUMPHED

I must confess that the unfair criticism to which I have been subjected, while in Wales especially, has annoyed me. For instance, what is one to say about the remarks of Mr Livingstone, an ex-president of the Welsh Union, who is reported to have said that I played an 'absolutely dirty and unfair game'?

The demonstrations against me at the Cardiff international and Swansea were altogether uncalled for and were directly attributable to the utterances of presumably responsible officials. However, I shall try to forget them. I shall doubtless have a complete revenge if ever I visit England again in seeing that the Welsh Union has adopted the wing forward game in all its nakedness, as they have already modified their back and scrum formation in keeping with ours – perhaps the greatest compliment the New Zealanders have received during their tour.

In my opinion, the majority of cases of injury in these countries are attributable to the player deliberately lying upon the ball.

THE DAILY MAIL TOUR BOOK was rushed out at the conclusion of the tour and became an instant best seller.

GAME 33 — MONDAY 1 JANUARY 1906 — at Parc des Princes, Paris

NEW ZEALAND
FRANCE

38
8

FOR NEW ZEALAND
Tries by Wallace 3, Abbott 2,
Harper 2, Hunter 2, Glasgow;
conversions by Wallace 2, Abbott, Tyler.

NEW ZEALAND
Booth, Abbott, Wallace, Hunter, Harper,
Mynott, Stead, Gallaher (captain), Seeling,
Glenn, Glasgow, Newton, Cunningham, Tyler,
Mackrell.

FOR FRANCE
Tries by Cessieux, Jerome;
conversion by Pujol.

FRANCE
W.H. Crichton, G. Lane, H. Levee, P. Sagot,
J. Pujol, H. Amand (captain), A. Lacassagne,
P. Dedeyn, A. Verges, A. Branlat, A.H. Muhr,
G. Jerome, M. Communeau, N. Cessieux,
F. Dufourcq.

Weather: Raining, ground firm
Referee: L.O. Dedet (France)
Crowd: 10,000

KICK OFF
Mynott and Hunter combined to put Wallace in for a try. Wallace converted: 5-0.
Wallace turned defence into attack and Abbott scored. Wallace missed: 8-0.
Jerome launched a counterattack, Cessieux scoring. Pujol missed: 8-3.
Hunter handled twice from a lineout before scoring. Wallace converted: 13-3.
Wallace joined the backline and put Harper across wide out. Tyler converted.

HALFTIME
New Zealand 18, France 3

A rush by the French forwards produced a try for Jerome. Pujol converted: 18-8.
Mynott put Wallace into a gap and he scored from a scrum. Harper missed: 21-8.
Glasgow crosskicked from a lineout and Wallace scored. Wallace missed: 24-8.
Mynott and Wallace worked together to put Hunter over. Harper missed: 27-8.
Mynott and Wallace combined again for Glasgow to score. Newton missed: 30-8.
Hunter's pace created a try for Harper. Glasgow missed: 33-8.
Abbott snapped up a loose ball and raced 75 metres for a try, adding the conversion.

FULLTIME
New Zealand 38, France 8

FROM THE SIDELINES

NEW ZEALAND TIMES' UK CORRESPONDENT

THE ALL BLACKS AFTER ONLY a couple of hours' rest in London yesterday morning, went on to Paris, where they arrived in the evening and met the cream of French rugby today. Quarters had been engaged at the Hotel St Petersbourg, which is conveniently situated in the centre of town. A wash and a good dinner had a wonderfully refreshing effect on the energies of the travellers and within an hour of their arrival the whole party were scattered about the town, taking their first glimpse of life in a Continental city.

In the course of the evening most of the New Zealanders found their way to the Folies Bergères and the Olympia Theatre, where Paris in its gayest dress was busily engaged in seeing in the New Year. At the Olympia café under the theatre, a party of the Colonials were given a most vociferous reception by an excited crowd of young French and Dutch sportsmen; the latter were a soccer team from Rotterdam.

They could all speak English of sorts, and proclaimed themselves frantic admirers of the 'All Blacks'. Much to the embarrassment of the New Zealand manager, they joined hands and danced around that modest fellow singing 'For he's a jolly goot fellow'. And not content with that they lifted Mr Dixon shoulder high and cheered until the very glasses rattled.

Whenever they sighted a silver fern leaf the cheering broke out again, and the 'Jolly Goot Fellow' chorus was in constant demand.

◆ ❖ ◆

None of the New Zealand team seemed to be speakers of French, although one or two remembered snatches of the language — relics of their schooldays. They derived much amusement, if little profit, from firing these off upon the Parisians, whose faces during the ordeal were generally a study. It was certainly amusing at dinner on the first evening at the St Petersbourg Hotel, when one member of the team proudly aired the following slice of French: '*Garçon, donnez-moi les pommes-de-terres.*' To which the deferential Swiss replied: 'Potatoes, sir? Yes, sir.'

◆ ❖ ◆

Duncan, the team's coach, had an experience on the first night in Paris. He went out alone for a stroll through the streets, and, very naturally in a strange city on a dark night, he lost his way.

He could not remember the name of the street he wanted to return to, nor could he speak the language of the gendarmes and the cabmen. His efforts to make them understand where he wanted to be directed to were futile, and after walking about for a couple of hours it began to look as though he might be kept walking the streets all night, when by a sudden piece of luck he ran across Mr Dixon and 'Captain' Gallaher on their way back to the hotel from the Olympia Theatre. When Duncan got his bearings from them, he found to his disgust that he had been within three minutes' walk of the hotel without knowing it.

GEORGE DIXON'S DIARIES

156th day, Monday 1 January. Unfortunately weather was unfavourable this morning. We were driven out to the ground in motor cars. The attendance was affected by the weather but still there was some 8000 spectators present. The ground was level but hard with frost, notwithstanding the drizzling rain which fell throughout the afternoon.

If this game was not distinguished by first-class football, it was at any rate a fine sporting game, played in the best possible spirit and witnessed by an impartial and enthusiastic crowd of spectators, the best a man could desire. The Frenchmen have a lot to learn yet regarding the finer phases of the game — in the matter of passing particularly their ideas are very rudimentary. But there can be no mistake regarding the vigour which they impart to their play. They are moreover keenly enthusiastic and it can only be a question of time for them to develop into very respectable exponents of rugby. Possibly their best feature at present is tackling which was in many cases very solid indeed.

The referee, an old French player, proved himself very capable and gave a capital interpretation of the rules — moreover he was invariably with the game. In the evening were dined by the French Union and in spite of the difficulty in understanding each other, a most enjoyable time was spent.

EVER ROMANTIC, the French composed a song to commemorate the All Blacks' visit . . . *Amour et Football* — Love and Football.

BILLY WALLACE'S RECOLLECTIONS

About an hour before the match was due to start, eight motor cars lined up outside the doors of the hotel. These were to take us to the Parc des Princes. We saw more cars in France than we saw during the whole of our stay in England. They were private cars and the drivers had evidently decided to have a race to the grounds. There were no speed limits in Paris and off they went like the wind. People were ducking and diving out of the way and the horns were tooting like mad and we wondered if we would get to the ground alive. General Booth was sitting in the front seat of one car and the speed was so great his hat blew off his head and through a hole in the celluloid window behind!

Somehow or other we got the impression that the French players would be small and effeminate chaps, but that was quite wrong and we got the surprise of our lives to find that the French players were of splendid physique — quite equal to our own.

The French captain would not hear of tossing. We were the honoured visitors and therefore it was their pleasure to allow us to choose which way we would play and also to have the right to kick off. It was a very nice and unique compliment.

I might say that the French captain Armand and Dave Gallaher took an instant liking to each other, as one would expect from two such fine sportsmen. Of course we returned the compliment by choosing to play against the wind and rain.

When Cessieux dived over for a try the French players were in ecstasies of delight and turned somersaults and Catherine wheels and handsprings and back flips. The spectators all had their umbrellas up to keep off the rain and it was a great sight to see thousands of umbrellas waving excitedly up and down.

DAILY TELEGRAPH

NEW YEAR'S DAY WAS A GREAT DAY for football in France — perhaps the greatest day ever known, for France scored 8 points against New Zealand. The French people were delighted with their achievement against the wonderful New Zealanders; it was a red-letter day for French football and the New Zealanders' cries of 'Bravo France!' 'Well played, France!' with which they encouraged the Frenchmen at the close of the game will long ring in the ears and hearts of the home team.

British teams have from time to time visited Paris, but never anything approaching the stir which prevailed on this occasion has been caused. The match, which was expected to prove a record one in the matter of attendance, was a failure, for only about 10,000 spectators were present. The ground was in a terribly bad state, frost having made it hard, while the surface was rendered slippery by the sleet and chilling rain which fell throughout the game. Had the weather been fine it is estimated that fully 20,000 people would have attended.

The Frenchmen looked slenderly built beside the tremendous physique of most of the colonials. Considerable difficulty was experienced by Mr Dixon in the making up of his team, owing to the number of his men on the 'crocked' list and it was not until after breakfast on the morning of the match that he, with the other members of the New Zealand selection committee, decided on their team as they wished to pick their most fit players. Fortunately a very strong side was placed in the field.

◆ ❖ ◆

The 'Blacks' were eight points up and near the French line but Jerome made a fine catch, and the Frenchmen for once backing each other up, the ball reached Cessieux, who by this time was right across the field, and he grounded it in the coveted ground beneath the New Zealand line. There was cheering then, with war-whoops and war-dances among the French spectators and the Englishmen, who were present in thousands, cheered enthusiastically too. The goal was missed, but that was nothing. France had scored a try against New Zealand; it was more than any Frenchman had hoped.

'Up went a great shout,' observed another spectator. '"Le Brave! Cessieux, Cessieux! Un essai, un essai!" Beautifully dressed Parisiennes waved their umbrellas and added their pretty voices to the tumult.'

When play was resumed (second half) the Frenchmen started finely and in a good rush secured a second try by Jerome. This was far more than any Frenchman had ever dreamed of and the cheers were good to hear. When the try was converted (by Pujol) there was a burst of enthusiasm in which we all joined, for the Frenchmen deserved it.

◆ ❖ ◆

I came back from the game in a delirious crowd of young Frenchmen. They dreamed of the day when football shall become a national game in this country. They were intoxicated with triumph, measuring the distance between what France showed this afternoon she can do in the field, and the miserable achievements of but half-a-dozen years ago.

One had only to see and hear the delight of all young boys, and elderly boys as well, when France scored a try, then actually a second try, and converted it, to understand what strides athletics have made in France within the last few years.

France actually equalled the top score recorded against New Zealand during the entire tour. Eight points against the All Blacks, the same score as Cardiff — it was wonderful.

It was indeed a great day for football in France and all the greater because the French crowd appreciated thoroughly how great it was. Of course, the Frenchmen do not delude themselves that the New Zealanders played up to their best form.

DAILY MAIL

THE TAKINGS AT THE GATE were £480, which is a record in the history of French football.

After the match the opponents met at a banquet in the winter garden of the famous Champeaux Restaurant. The teams fraternised from the start, and as most of the Frenchmen could speak a little English — one or two spoke it very fluently — they soon became the best of friends.

Autographs were exchanged, and menu-cards circulated round

the table to receive the signatures of the respective teams.

After the coffee and liqueurs and a few words spoken on both sides, a move was made to the Boulevards and the heights of Montmartre. The party adjourned to a New Year ball, where another enthusiastic welcome awaited the Colonials.

By special request they mustered in the centre of the ballroom and gave their famous war-cry, with which the Parisians seem hugely delighted. It went particularly well on this occasion and evoked a storm of applause. Dancing was kept up to a late hour and the wearers of the silver fern-leaf had no difficulty in finding partners for the waltz among the pretty Parisians.

The stay in Paris has been, perhaps, more enjoyable than any other portion of the tour, and the Colonials will carry home with them pleasant memories of a generous, hospitable and 'sporting' people.

ATHLETIC NEWS

IT WAS ONE OF THE brightest and most interesting games of the tour. The Frenchmen lost the game, but they quite won the hearts of the New Zealanders by their sportsmanlike conduct on the field, and their abounding hospitality and good fellowship after the match. It was very sporting of the French Union of Athletic Sports Societies to arrange the match at all when they knew how much superior to their best fifteen the renowned 'All Blacks' must be.

The French team, too, showed no lack of courage and determination on the field, and although hopelessly outclassed, kept pegging gamely away to the end. Everyone was delighted (the New Zealand party too) to see the Frenchmen score two tries. As for scoring against the 'Les terribles Touts Noirs' they had hardly dared to hope for such a possibility. No wonder, then, that the French team, overwhelmingly defeated, were proud and happy men that night.

A TICKET FOR the All Blacks test in Paris.

As for the French spectators, they too showed a very sporting spirit, and applauded the 'All Blacks' in a way that would have put some of our British assemblages to shame. The New Zealand team enjoyed their novel experience immensely. The Frenchmen gave them a better game than they had anticipated and proved themselves 'good sports' as well. 'It was a pleasure to play against such a team,' said the New Zealand captain after the match. 'One of the most sportsmanlike games of the tour,' was Mr Dixon's verdict.

'We are charmed with the sporting spirit of the Frenchman,' said another New Zealander and on this point the team were unanimous.

The New Zealanders could teach the French a good deal about football, perhaps, but the latter have little to learn in the matter of sportsmanship and camaraderie.

LA PRESSE

NATURALLY, THE NEW ZEALANDERS WON, how, indeed could it have been otherwise? These New Zealanders are all athletes of the first order, thick-set, adroit, full of dash and we have literally marvelled.

'MAJOR TREVOR', IN THE SPORTSMAN

I HAVE RECEIVED A LETTER from a French Rugby Unionist asking me whether I think the New Zealanders 'allowed' the French to score those eight points in Paris.

Personally, I do not believe for a moment that they did. The New Zealanders are fine sportsmen, and they would be the first to recognise that to do such a thing would be to pay their hosts a doubtful compliment indeed, and would also be a poor way of requiting the generous French hospitality which they received.

Moreover, if they meant to flatter France intentionally, they would hardly have piled up a score of thirty-eight points. Certainly, it seems to me that the Frenchmen are entitled to the full and fair credit of what they have achieved.

Perhaps one may be allowed to say this much on the question at issue. The New Zealanders did not 'allow' the Frenchmen to score those eight points if the word is used in the sense that the 'All Blacks' deliberately paved the way for their opponents to score.

At the same time, it would be nonsensical to allege that the New Zealanders took the French game as seriously as they did their engagement at Cardiff.

In Wales, the 'All Blacks' were, so to speak, 'out for blood' all the time and went on to the field at Cardiff, Swansea and Newport with the intention of piling up as many points against their adversaries as they could.

In France all that they really cared about was to give the Frenchmen a good game and to win.

Had they set themselves to achieve such a feat I am confident that they could have equalled or beaten their record score against Hartlepool. But the Frenchmen's tries were, nevertheless, genuinely earned as the play went.

GEORGE DIXON'S DIARIES

157th day, TUESDAY 2 JANUARY.

Started off after breakfast to Versailles and had lunch at a village. Lots of state carriages at V. The latter baffles description, the paintings are wonderful — one would require days, nay weeks to assimilate.

3 JANUARY.

Spent the day driving about in a motor car — a 40hp Mercedes. There is no speed limit in Paris and the way one moved along was a caution. Saw a great many of the public buildings in this way and the outskirts of the city.

159th day, 4 JANUARY.

After a walk around the streets and a visit to the tomb of Napoleon — left after lunch and arrived in London at the Manchester Hotel, just before midnight.

160th day, 5 JANUARY.

Waited upon Palliser and with him visited Canadian office, re trip through America. This trip is a confounded nuisance. Would much rather have gone aboard the steamer to enjoy a six-week rest and immunity from letters, callers, newspapers and worries generally. After lunch at Rugby Union office, also the Bank, and in the evening visited Jack and spent the evening with him.

10 JANUARY.

Good deal of worry about Johnston. Arranged with Dr for consultation.

167th day, 12 JANUARY.

Visited Johnston this morning and after early lunch started for Penmaenmaw. Found mater and Aunt Jenny at shop and accompanied them home for tea. Found Jenny very jolly, sat up late yarning and slept really well.

Saturday, 14 JANUARY.

In the afternoon visited an old farmhouse where grandmother and of them once lived and which they state is haunted. Jenny tells stories of noises of a door fastened by a chair fall against it, inside a room which has no other means of ingress or egress. Mother states she once saw a figure which tallies with the descriptions given by other people.

Tuesday 16 JANUARY.

Stayed in with Mother all morning and after dinner started for station. The poor old mater didn't like me leaving at all nor did I like leaving her — in all human probability never to see her again. Arrived Paddington at Manchester Hotel about 11.30 p.m. — found a big budget of correspondence awaiting me.

172nd day, WEDNESDAY 17 JANUARY.

Called upon Johnston and afterwards Palliser to get information re American arrangement — lunched with Reeves at his club and Palliser and afterwards called up Coles and Rowland Hill. Arranged with latter to lunch with him on Thursday and talk over N.Y. Union matters — afterwards saw NY Shipping Co re rebate of passengers and got money.

173rd day.

After breakfast went to see Johnston again.

174th day.

Saw Johnston and paid his allowance to Dr. Also Palliser and after lunch Coles with view of picking up tab of England match a/c — found Crystal Palace people had not settled lawyers and arranged that it should be paid to Palliser — I took out Letter of Credit for £900 and arranged for remittance of balance. Dinner with Gallaher, Roberts after which they attended social launched by London NY society. I spent remainder of evening with Jack — returning to hotel about I a.m.

175th day, SATURDAY 20 JANUARY.

Last day in England — all hustle from an early hour. Luggage had to get away by 8 a.m. and we left for Waterloo Station at 9. Found a big crowd waiting to see us off, including a lot of rugby people. And left amidst much cheering and heartily expressed good wishes.

On arrival at Southampton found a goodly crowd also. Donne (Somerset) of the English Union, who met us on arrival at Plymouth, had come down to see the last of us — a number of people also accompanied us down in the train. We were cinematographed going on board the SS *New York* — had a very enthusiastic send off and as we finally cast off, the crowd on the dock and our party in singing 'Auld Lang Syne'. Found our quarters very comfortable.

176th day, 21 JANUARY.

Spent a quiet day, which included a good deal of sleep — as did all the boys. Very few first-class passengers on board, and our party forms fully half of the second-class lot. Got an attack of lumbago.

Thursday, 25 JANUARY.

Up to now experienced fair weather and mild, but this morning struck fog and turned suddenly very cold. There is a good deal of vibration in these high-speed boats and whatever part of the ship you may be on, it is felt.

27 JANUARY.

Getting near end and passed a lot of vessels. Passed Savoy Hook and docked at New York about 7 p.m. All examined by doctor for some form of disease which is common among some Europeans. Met by Denbigh and driven to Astor House, a confidently old-fashioned hotel, right in centre part of city. You pay so much per night for a bedroom and pay for your meals as you take them. All menus being a la carte and the charge very high. A very ordinary meal costs a dollar. For instance a cup or tea or coffee (former very poor) costs 15 cents (7½d). Everything is priced, even the different kinds of vegetables.

183rd day, 28 JANUARY.

After breakfast took a walk over the Brooklyn Bridge. This is a very fine suspension bridge. What surprised us was the constant streams of elevated trains and trams passing and repassing the bridge. Surprising how the structure stands the strain. Two of the tallest skyscrapers in NY are situated opposite the Astor House.

184th day.

Found cost of living at Astor House so high that decided to allow each man $2 a day for meals which they took at restaurants, thus saving at least a dollar a head per day. Went into details of journey across continent with Denbigh — also met an official from Philadelphia who wished to arrange a match there.

THE MENU FOR the banquet at the Restaurant Champeaux following the international in Paris.

Tuesday, 30 JANUARY.

Finally decided play exhibition game on Thursday leaving same night for Niagara — left at 12 o'clock for Philadelphia and arrived about 2.15. Had no difficulty in finding Alfred Smethurst's house and found [relatives] waiting for me.

187th day, 1 FEBRUARY.

During morning cashed cheques and paid boys' allowance. After lunch to a park in Brooklyn to play in game. This is a baseball ground where spectators number only about 500. Match was nominally NZ v NY but NY team includes six of our players — Abbott, McGregor, Mynott, Duncan, Newton and Casey. Referee G.H. Dixon.

The game was too one-sided to be properly called a contest — but was nevertheless a pretty exhibition of passing and running and pleased the onlookers. New Zealand played with 14 members in first half and at times Roberts changed over to help them. Gallaher playing, came in at half time. Score final 46-13. (NY scorers Abbott, and Abbott goaled 5. McGregor 2, McGregor goaled one. 13 points.)

After dinner left by train for Niagara, several of the boys cutting it very fine and barely catching ferry to New Jersey connection with train. Pullman sleeper reserved for us and I was early to bed. Too hot in cars.

FRIDAY, 2 FEBRUARY.

On arrival at Niagara in early morning found ground covered in snow and temperatures below freezing. Went to Prospect Hotel over frozen snow. Very pleasant hotel but heated (as are all American hotels) to an oppressive degree. After breakfast went out to view the falls. Fine snow falling and it was too thick to see anything. Found cold very severe on ears and nearly everyone in a cap with deep ear flaps. After lunch went across Goat Island and see falls from many different points of view.

189th day, 3 FEBRUARY.

Arrived at Chicago about 4.20 p.m. — 2½ hours late, met at station by local rugby enthusiasts, who regretted very much that we were unable to play a match at Chicago. Had we been able to, however, the frozen state of the ground would have rendered it impossible. Boys went off with said enthusiasts who showed them the town. What I saw of Chicago was impressive though — noticed some very fine big buildings — no one would think that this big city of 200,000 people was only 70 years old.

190th and 191st day.

All of both days in train, broken by stoppage for meals.

192nd day, 5 FEBRUARY.

Country passed through very poor-looking. Arrived 'Williams' about 1 o'clock and after not very good lunch, proceeded by train to The Canyon. A most desolate region — not enough feed in sight for a rabbit. Arrived at Canyon and proceeded to Bright Angel Camp — a boarding house (one storey) constructed partly of weatherboards and partly of logs situated on edge of canyon. About a dozen of the boys visited the bottom of the canyon — access only by a narrow trail that zigzags across the more sloping part of the cliffs.

8 FEBRUARY.

On train again, today gradually ran into better country and warmer weather — at the stations found buildings surrounded by palms. Arrived at Railway terminus in the evening and across the Bay of San Francisco in a ferry boat. Met on landing by a number of New Zealand and Australian residents, also representatives of the Oceanic committee. After dinner at California hotel subjected to interviews, photographs, etc. Boys visited Olympic Club, a large splendidly appointed club for Amateur Athletics — it contains a very fine swimming bath. Had some talk about tomorrow's match arrangements.

GAME 34 — SATURDAY 10 FEBRUARY 1906 — at UCLA Ground, Berkeley

NEW ZEALAND
BRITISH COLUMBIA

43
6

FOR NEW ZEALAND
Tries by Thomson 6, Roberts 2,
Abbott, Cunningham, Deans;
conversions by Roberts 3, Booth, Glasgow.

NEW ZEALAND
Booth, Thomson, Deans, Stead, Abbott, Mynott,
Roberts, Gallaher (captain), Macrell, McDonald,
Glasgow, Cunningham, Nicholson, Tyler, Casey.

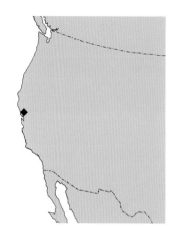

FOR BRITISH COLUMBIA
Tries by Schofield and M. Sawers

BRITISH COLUMBIA
Bell-Irving, Schofield, Marshall, Marpole,
Jenkins, Johnston, O. Sawers, Bispham,
Ritchie, Templeton, Barclay, Worsnop,
Barnacle, M. Sawers, Thomson.

Weather: raining, ground muddy
Referee: Jimmy Duncan (New Zealand)
Crowd: 1200

Run of play not available for this game

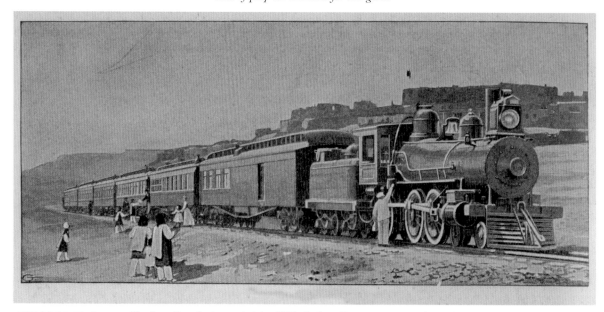

THE SANTE FE JOURNEY The Sante Fe train that carried the All Blacks from Chicago to Los Angeles made 21 stops along the way, at the
following stations: Kansas City, Newton, Dodge City, La Junta, Trinidad, Raton Tunnel, Raton, Las Vegas, Glorieta, Albuquerque, Continental
Divide, Gallop, Adamana, Winslow, Flagstaff, Williams, Grand Canyon (Rim), Needles, Barstow, Summit, Cajon Pass and San Bernardino.

FROM THE SIDELINES

SAN FRANCISCO CHRONICLE

RUGBY FOOTBALL HAS TAKEN a long step forward as the probable inter-collegiate sport on the Pacific Coast.

The exhibition game played on the University of California campus, between the famous New Zealand team and a sturdy aggregation from Vancouver created enthusiasts, won over lukewarm spectators and silenced many critics.

On the left side of the field there were a couple of clergymen standing on benches and yelling away like 10-year-old urchins. 'Go to it, New Zealand!' 'Give it to 'em, Vancouver!'

Of course, the result of the game was a foregone conclusion. The lusty lads from the Antipodes are practically invincible and so it proved, to the score of forty-three points to six. The disagreeable weather kept the crowds down. The Vancouver team wore funny-looking woollen mits to hold the ball while the 'kangaroos' had their hands covered with linen bandages.

During the game, which was comparatively fierce, not a single man was obliged to leave the field, and only two had the wind temporarily knocked out of them.

Both teams were entertained at a banquet given in the Olympic Club. The tenor of the speeches was an expression of hope that rugby would be adopted throughout America so that the whole Anglo-Saxon race might be playing the same game of football.

THE COMMEMORATIVE BOOKLET produced to mark the All Blacks' grand train journey across America.

GEORGE DIXON'S DIARIES

Left for Berkeley by ferry, found that the usual ground had been rendered a perfect quagmire by the rain — they don't play the American game on turf, but on earth which is harrowed before a match to make it soft — very greasy and muddy. Found on arrival that playing area had been marked out only 50 yards wide and had to have it widened another 15–16 yards, leaving goal posts where originally fixed!

Considering the state of the ground the game was fast and the passing and tackling on the greasy ground wonderfully accurate. BC put up a hard game. They were no match, however, for the skills of the All Blacks who won 43–6. Spectators 1000–1200. In evening both teams entertained at Olympic Club. President Harrison (an ex-New Zealand resident who went to Colony in 1856 and left in 1872). Enthusiastic gathering and a great desire to see New Zealand play again.

197th day, 11 February.
Stroll through streets. Looked at Majestic Theatre, all shops lit up in evening, and numerous others open. Also photographers, parlours, theatres in full swing — understand no limit to hours pubs kept open — but have seen no cases of drunkenness.

Monday, 12 February.
For tomorrow's match. Freddy Roberts not so well this morning. Temperature up and Dr seems afraid of diptheria — suggested to him that nurse be got. Stayed with Freddy all afternoon and nearly missed the game.

BILLY WALLACE'S RECOLLECTIONS

The match against British Columbia which we won by 43 points to 6 was really an exhibition game for the benefit of the colleges of San Francisco, who were considering the possibilities of substituting rugby for their local game. From the accounts given in the papers the critics were greatly impressed with the dazzling speed and sensational passing of the All Blacks, and most of them considered rugby the better game.

At any rate, they were satisfied that some of the phases of rugby — particularly the passing rushes — could, with advantage, be introduced into their game. The day was not suited to a good exhibition of the passing game, for it rained solidly and the ground that had been prepared was simply a sea of mud, for in America they did not play on turf but on the bare soil. At the last minute the ground had to be changed and it was very narrow.

Mona Thomson had a field day for he scored no fewer than six tries; Freddy Roberts got two, and Bob Deans, Bunny Abbott and Bill Cunningham one each. Freddy kicked three goals and Booth and Frank Glasgow one each. Our opponents were lacking in knowledge of the finer points of the game, especially in the art of backing up.

GAME 35 — TUESDAY 13 FEBRUARY 1906 — at Recreation Park, San Francisco

NEW ZEALAND
BRITISH COLUMBIA

65
6

FOR NEW ZEALAND
Tries by Wallace 4, Mynott 4, Deans 3, Hunter 2, Stead 2, Glasgow, Mackrell; conversions by Wallace 2, Mynott 2, Gallaher, McGregor, Thomson.

NEW ZEALAND
Thomson, Wallace, Deans, Hunter, McGregor, Mynott, Stead, Gallaher (captain), Gillett, Booth, Glasgow, Cunningham, Nicholson, Mackrell, Casey.

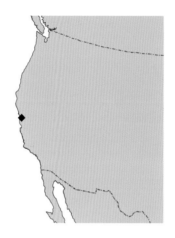

FOR BRITISH COLUMBIA
Tries by Abbott and Barnacle

BRITISH COLUMBIA
Bell-Irving, Schofield, Abbott (New Zealand), Marpole, Jenkins, Johnston, O. Sawers, Bispham, Ritchie, Templeton, Barclay, Worsnop, Barnacle, M. Sawers, Thomas.

Weather: Fine, ground firm
Referee: Jimmy Duncan (New Zealand)
Crowd: 2000

Run of play not available for this game

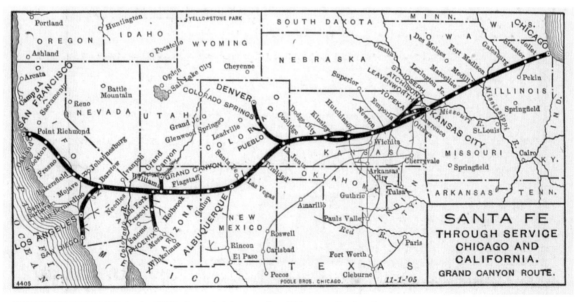

THE ROUTE TRAVERSED by the All Blacks on their journey from Chicago to Los Angeles.

FROM THE SIDELINES

PRESS ASSOCIATION

WHEN THE NEW ZEALAND Premier Richard John Seddon, who had amazed British officials with his stream of 'Keep it up boys' cables — and his government — paid for the All Blacks' return via North America the team were elated about the new return route. The only man with his head in his hands was George Dixon — he had been only days away from getting all his high-spirited individualistic group on to the boat in one piece and incident-free.

The New Zealand footballers, now in Los Angeles, were farewelled by a large and enthusiastic crowd at Southampton and sailed by the American liner *New York*. Arrangements were made for their transportation across the States in a private Pullman car. After spending a day or two in New York, the team visited Niagara Falls, Chicago and after staying there two days, travelled the Santa Fe route to San Francisco, stopping a day each at Kansas City and the Grand Canyon of Arizona, and two days at Los Angeles before preparing to sail home to New Zealand.

◆ ❖ ◆

THE NEW ZEALAND TEAM IN SAN FRANCISCO

GIVE THE CONTEST the adjuncts of an inter-collegiate game, packed benches, rival colours and singing and the cheers and you would have a rare spectacle as breathlessly thrilling as any of the 14 historic gridiron battles between Stanford and Berkeley. Big numbers displayed on the backs of the New Zealanders gave a racy touch to the proceedings.

The New Zealanders say that throughout their whole tour but one man was hurt and he only had his collarbone broken, yet the tackling is determined and no child's play. However it is evidently the desire of the contestants to avoid roughness, and again and again a tackler sacrificed a yard or so by supporting his man in order that no injury might result from the impact. Yards count too much in an inter-collegiate game to permit that sort of chivalry, and an advancing man is forced back if possible, if his face is scraped off in the process.

In every department of play New Zealand excelled her antagonists in passing, in running, in kicking and in what the British call 'combination' and what we term 'team work'.

GEORGE DIXON'S DIARIES

1500 people and game one-sided. Judging by what one hears, probability that our missionary work will bear fruit in near future. Boys at Olympic Club, they have been most hospitably treated during stay.

◆

NEW YORK GLOBE

THE NEW ZEALAND RUGBY TEAM's Maori war cry, the 'haka' sounded like a mixture of Yale's frog chorus, Princeton's locomotive yell and a Chinaman explaining his laundry bill!

BILLY WALLACE'S RECOLLECTIONS

Better appreciation for our game here than in New York where we played an exhibition match. There we had to lend the local side six of our men — Abbott, McGregor, Duncan, Casey, Newton and Mynott — and won 46 to 13. The Americans did not seem greatly impressed, apparently thinking it was not vigorous enough. They were accustomed to seeing men knocked out in nearly every match and they reckoned rugby was a 'sister's game'.

On our way over here we spent some time looking around Chicago and as Jimmy (Hunter) was a farmer he was naturally interested in the great meat works and in the cattle and sheep. In these great works they say they use every part but the squeal — the pig goes in one end of the machine and comes out the other end as hams, sausages, lard, margerine and binding for Bibles! And all in a quarter of an hour!

On 13 February, we played a return match against British Columbia and on this occasion we lent the services of Bunny Abbott, to replace one of the British Columbia team who had been injured on the Saturday. Jimmy Duncan refereed the game, which was played in better weather conditions than the game in Berkeley.

This game was played at Recreation Park before a crowd of about 1500, including a fair sprinkling of the ladies.

Here is an account of the game as it impressed an American reporter: 'The beauties of rugby football as it is played by champions were again shown to an applauding American crowd yesterday afternoon. The New Zealand team, champions of the world at the famous English game, met and vanquished for a second time by an overwhelming score the All-British Columbia team from Vancouver.

'The turf field made it possible for the New Zealanders to show their wonderful speed and skill and passing, with the result that the Vancouver team was beaten by a score of 65 to 6. Approximately 1500 people viewed the match and that these spectators, most of whom were Americans new to the game, liked the exhibition was evidenced throughout the game by the cheering and hand clapping at this or that brilliant play.

'And, as on Saturday, there were plenty of plays that could be styled brilliant. Long runs, with difficult passes at just the moment when the runner was tackled made the exhibition more than just a pretty sight to see. It was beautiful.'

Chapter 6

THE
RETURN
HOME

MORE THAN SIX MONTHS after leaving New Zealand the All Blacks were finally on their way home. Hawaii, their final stopover, had been farewelled and now it was full steam ahead for Auckland and the huge welcoming reception that awaited the colony's conquering heroes.

On board the S.S. *Sonoma*, the All Blacks' astute and hard-worked manager, George Dixon, must surely have permitted himself a quiet smile of satisfaction as he contemplated a tour that had exceeded all expectations. A tour embarked on with such shaky financial foundations that the team had left New Zealand with no surety that it could afford to pay for the return voyage . . . why, just a couple of weeks earlier he had cabled the New Zealand Rugby Football Union from San Francisco to inform them that total tour receipts amounted to a staggering £14,700! This was a sum beyond everyone's wildest dreams and, when all bills and outgoings were paid, would net the rugby union £9500 to put the national body on a sound financial footing ever after.

The team had been impatient to return home direct from England, but this was countered by the realisation that the union's coffers would be bolstered by an NZRFU decision to agree to a short tour in the United States, after the New Zealand government had expressed its keenness to capitalise on the success of the All Blacks by showcasing them before the powerful American market.

While the New Zealand team was in France, on 2 January 1906, the NZRFU had held an informal meeting accepting the Government's offer to pay for the All Blacks to come back via America. At the meeting a resolution was passed that NZRFU chairman George Campbell convey to the Premier 'That this Committee desires to express its high appreciation of the Government's generous offer.'

Of the 28 members of the team who left New Zealand on 30 July 1905, only 22 were returning on the *Sonoma*. (Harper and Glenn had opted to travel back via the Suez Canal on the *Orontes*, while Wallace had remained behind in San Francisco to care for Roberts, who had been laid low by an attack of tonsillitis and Seeling had acted similarly in England with his sick All Black teammate Johnston — Wallace and Roberts returning on the *Ventura* and *Seeling* and Johnston on the *Gothic*.)

BILLY WALLACE'S RECOLLECTIONS

Freddy Roberts had not been able to play in the last game and was sickening for something. This turned out to be tonsillitis and we were all very sorry when next morning after the match the doctor refused to allow him to travel. Freddy and I had been great chums throughout the tour and I felt I could not leave him, so I volunteered to stay and follow with him on the next boat.

I went down to the wharf to see the boys off and it brought a lump to my throat to see them off. We had been a very happy party and I knew we would be missing the fun of the homeward voyage. Three weeks later we left by the *Ventura* and the members of the Australian Club turned up to give us a good send-off and their 'coo-ees' could be heard long after the vessel had left the wharf.

◆

NEW ZEALAND HERALD

AUCKLAND, 6 MARCH 1906

IT BEING KNOWN that the mailboat was eight hours later leaving Honolulu she was calculated to reach Auckland somewhere about midnight of Monday, but it was thought that if a good passage was made the lost time might be made up and Auckland reached about four o'clock, so that those whose duty it was to meet the vessel held themselves in readiness then.

And from that time till dark the signal station on the North Shore was anxiously watched. Still there was no sign of the liner.

As the evening wore on crowds thronged the streets in anticipation of witnessing the landing of the footballers, but when ten o'clock came round, it was realised there was no hope of a landing that night, and the hosts of friends, relatives or enthusiasts wended their way homewards, determined to be up at dawn.

About half past six on Tuesday residents who could command a view of the harbour saw a dark hull and the two funnels of a vessel coming in, and quickly the word was passed round that the *Sonoma* was arriving, and thousands hurried to the wharf. The arrival proved to be one of the war vessels of the squadron and she stole silently to an anchorage close to where the *Powerful* and *Cambrian* lay, grey and sinister in the early morning light.

Still there was no sign of the long-expected mailboat. So many inquiries were received on Monday evening and Tuesday morning by the operators at the Telephone Exchange as to whether the vessel had been sighted that little wonder if those courteous officials should wish the New Zealand team in Timbuctoo or Peking and, instead of the familiar 'Number, please' yell into receiver upon getting a call, 'No, not sighted!'

Nine o'clock came, ten o'clock, but still the much-expected boat was not in sight, and then other vessels were sighted and the signals dangled out for them, while frantic telephone rings sounded all over the city, as inquirers asked, 'Is that mailboat sighted?'

How fervently everyone concerned wished that the mailboats were provided with wireless telegraph outfits to communicate with a station in Auckland. Boats were in readiness for the

A MULTITUDE FLOCKED to the wharf in Auckland to welcome the All Blacks.

meeting on the waters and reception officials perched on the wharf or wandered aimlessly about.

No one knew anything, and the long wait lengthened out to a longer and still a longer one. Flagpoles were decorated, tramcars bore 'Welcome' pennants on the trolley-pole ropes but still the ship came not, and a grey haze settled over the gulf.

At noon the *Sonoma* was seen coming steadily up from the grey horizon 15 miles north of Tiritiri, and instantly the news was flashed to the waiting thousands in the city. Dense crowds soon surged around the waterfront and at half past one the ferry steamer *Eagle*, with members of the Rugby Union committee, relatives of members of the team, representatives of various athletic bodies, and former footballers of note, left to meet the mailboat.

A course was steered straight towards Orakei until the *Sonoma*'s long trail of smoke could be seen over on the other side of Devonport and a few minutes later the vessel came out of the Rangitoto Channel.

The two vessels came closer together until the white Panama hats of the New Zealanders were distinguished on the hurricane deck and to the accompaniment of roars of cheering and

THE PLAYERS manage a steep descent from the S.S. *Rimutaka*.

PHILSON'S SQUARE, AUCKLAND, where the All Blacks were officially welcomed home.

of the strains of 'Home Sweet Home', played by the band, much waving of hats and handkerchiefs, the ferry boat raced alongside the great liner, to the anchorage near where the vessels of the squadron lay at rest.

Very soon vessels of all descriptions surrounded the mailboat. There were several ferry boats crowded with cheering men, women, boys and girls, white-winged yachts, motor boats and rowing boats and they all crowded around the *Sonoma*.

NEW ZEALAND HERALD

AUCKLAND, 6 MARCH 1906

AS SOON AS IT BECAME known that the steamer was sighted people poured in from all parts of the city. By a quarter past two, when the vessel dropped her anchor, thousands had assembled along the wharves and waterfront. Shops were closed, factories were idle and offices were empty so that admirers of the victorious athletes might join in greeting them as they came ashore. Upwards of thirty thousand people were crowded on the wharves, in the streets, and covering points of vantage on the roofs and at the windows of buildings, and on the high land around the city. From the time the steamer dropped anchor the scene was one of tumultuous excitement and stirring enthusiasm.

At half-past two the health officer went out to clear the boat, accompanied by the Premier, who had come up from the south to welcome the team and Mr A.E.G. Rhodes, president of the New Zealand Rugby Football Union.

Mackrell provided a rare piece of comedy while the footballers were lined along the rail of the mailsteamer — and the *Eagle*, with the welcome party on board, was approaching. Mr Seddon, in frock coat and top hat, had just stepped on board and shaking hands with the footballers, advanced to the rail to display himself to the cheering crowds on the excursion steamer.

Mackrell in frock coat and top hat also, and with 'eye-glass in his ocular' anticipated the smiling Premier, and interposing himself in front of the burly personality of King Dick, smilingly took off his topper and bowed affably top left, right, and all round. It was prettily done, and, to strain a metaphor, literally brought down the house. King Dick's look of disgust as he realised that he had been outmanoeuvred was worth going miles to see, and aroused shrieks of laughter.

The team then gave three hearty cheers for Mr Seddon, who replied with the native greeting, 'Kia Ora' and extended a welcome home to the team on behalf of the colony.

It was at once seen that the men were in fine health. Every man carried more weight than when he went away and all looked fit and well. The players all expressed themselves delighted with the trip and equally delighted at returning home.

A couple of ferry steamers, with large crowds aboard, circled round the steamer as she lay at anchor, the passengers sending up cheer after cheer as they caught sight of the returning players.

When the vessel was cleared, one of the steamers chartered by the rugby union ranged alongside and the men then filed down the gangway to the deck of the steamer, to the strains of 'See the Conquering Hero Comes'.

When they reached the landing the crowd had swollen further, and to the accompaniment of continuous and enthusiastic cheering, they regained New Zealand soil after an absence of seven months. Followed by cheering crowds they were driven to their hotel and then to the Municipal Chambers where an official welcome took place. A dense crowd of people had assembled and a renewed outburst of cheering greeted the arrival of the team. The mayor, Mr Alfred Myers, presided, the Premier was on the platform and cheers were given for individual members of the team as they filed on the platform, the heartiest being for Gallaher, the team's popular captain.

To cheers, the Mayor congratulated the team on its splendid achievements. 'I need not tell you with what interest and pride your career has been watched. Your success has brought great credit to the whole colony. The most sanguine could hardly have anticipated the phenomenally successful tour which will never be forgotten.' The team went to England unnoticed, but came away as England's honoured guests from his Majesty the King downward, concluded the Mayor.

The Premier was warmly cheered. He expressed appreciation of the hearty manner in which Auckland had welcomed the team, a welcome of which the whole colony would be proud. The team went with the intention of playing the national game. In the Welsh international match the men had gallantly fought an uphill game to the finish. To cheers, Seddon said they had not questioned the result, but in their hearts and in the opinion of most people, it was recognised that morally this was not a defeat, but try to try. 'One reads of the New Zealanders as being footballers and one also reads of them as being true gentlemen — the generous captain of the vessel on which they came out spoke of them in the highest terms. In the whole course of his experience, the captain said, he had never met a large body of young men who were so well conducted.'

The Premier then read a letter he had received from the High Commissioner, in which Mr Reeves, after mentioning the assistance given to the team, said that of their athletic achievements he would not speak, because these were well known wherever football was a pastime. He bore testimony to the admirable personal conduct of the members of the team off the field as well as on.

Something that was no doubt due to the tact and firmness of their manager, Mr Dixon, and to the sportsmanlike example of Mr Gallaher, the captain, but the main credit was owing to the men themselves.

With regard to the wing-forward the Premier did not hesitate to say that in future their

kindred in the Mother Country would, in all their important matches, have their wing-forward, whom they would remember as one of the many things taught by the All Blacks. 'The triumph of the team is not only a credit to the colony but to the Empire.

'Much as it is to be commended, there is more in these visits than the mere question of dexterity and superiority in athleticism. They are of great material advantage, as they keep distant parts of the Empire in touch with the centre, remove false impressions, promote commerce and encourage interdependency and goodwill — and these principles are especially furthered when the visitors are men and gentlemen . . .'

Led by Mr Seddon, cheers, such as perhaps had never been heard before in Auckland, were given for the 'All Blacks' and later for the Premier, Mr Dixon and the captain of the team. The Mayor then called upon Mr Dixon to reply, and the manager rose amid another wild outburst of cheering. 'The members of the New Zealand team,' he said, appreciated to the fullest possible extent the honour that had been conferred upon them. 'We naturally thought that footballers would welcome us on our return, but we did not dream that the whole population — men and women alike — would become for a moment footballers, but that is what it appears. We are grateful for the manner in which we have been received, we have travelled many miles and met many people but none like you, our own folk.

'To a man, we are delighted to get back to New Zealand.'

The New Zealand captain was then called on by the crowd and again hearty cheers rang out as he rose. When they started on their redoubtable career they had hopes of winning every match, but as the Premier had said, they were beaten by the Welsh leek. They did not go behind their backs to talk about the Welshmen, but candidly said they were beaten by the better team. 'I have only one recommendation to make to the New Zealand Union

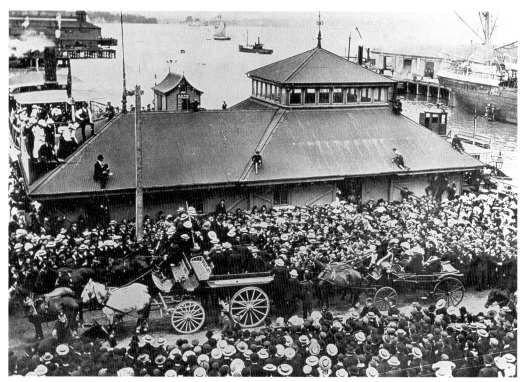

THE PLAYERS were taken from the wharf area in horse-drawn carriages.

if it ever undertakes such a similar tour and that is to play the Welsh matches first.'

He added that he would like to pay a tribute to the New Zealand Rugby Football Union for appointing Mr Dixon to control them. He called for three cheers for Mr Dixon, which were very heartily responded to. The reception concluded with more cheering for the team.

Minutes *of a* meeting *of* *the* NZRFU COUNCIL

JANUARY, 1906

Tuesday 6 March fixed on for official dinner and reception. It was decided to tender the team a complimentary dinner and to issue invitations. Cost not to exceed 12s 6d per head (excluding wines). Champagne to be provided if asked for.

Thirty medals to be ordered, each to contain 10 dwts New Zealand gold. Price not to exceed £5 each and to be ready for presentation at Auckland reception. Thirty Hardie-Shaw photographs price 16s 6d each with record complete and to present one to each member of the team and also to the Premier at the evening.

(Request from Auckland Union that invitations be extended to the Secretary and delegates of each club of that union, in common with clubs of other affiliated unions and to former New Zealand representative players.) Resolved that the ARU be advised that at present we are not prepared to issue invitations to club secretaries and delegates but the Secretary will confer on arrival.

The suggestion regarding ex-New Zealand reps was not entertained. The name of Mr Alf Warbrick of Rotorua, a member of the New Zealand Native Team who had been of service to the Union in Rotorua, was added to the list.

The Secretary was empowered to arrange, if necessary, that a limited number of tickets for the dinner be sold to the general public at £1 1s each.

NEW ZEALAND HERALD

An evening banquet followed in the Drill Hall in Wellesley Street, attended by two hundred guests including the Premier and leader of the Opposition. The proceedings were 'characterised by extraordinary enthusiasm' with close to twenty speeches, interspersed with songs including the popular 'On the Ball' and a piece especially composed for the occasion by a renowned musician, Alfred Hill, 'We Give You Welcome'. The menu matched the occasion:

COMPLIMENTARY DINNER

TENDERED BY
NEW ZEALAND RUGBY FOOTBALL UNION

TO THE
NEW ZEALAND FOOTBALL TEAM

ON ITS RETURN FROM THE UNITED KINGDOM
MARCH 6, 1906

ORCHESTRAL NUMBERS

March ...... 'Santiago'
Selection ...... 'Sea Songs'
Fantasia ...... 'Road to Moscow'
March ...... 'Rowsy Dowsy Girls'

MENU
❖
SOUPS
Clear Turtle
Ox Tail

FISH
Fried Flounder

ENTREES
Sweet Breads Jardinieres
Poulets a la Marengo

POULTRY
Roast Duckling, Boiled Fowl and Ox Tongue with Celery Sauce
Roast Turkey and York Ham

JOINTS
Roast Suckling Pig and Apple Sauce
Roast Sirloin Beef and Horse Radish Sauce
Roast Lamb and Mint Sauce

VEGETABLES
Roast and Boiled Potatoes
Kumaras
French Beans
Green Peas

SWEETS
Plum Pudding and Brandy Sauce
Apple Pie and Cream
Peach Pie and Cream
Trifle
Champagne, Maraschino and Macedoine Jellies
Forced Olives

DESSERT
❖

In a toast to the All Blacks, the Premier described the tour as the most wonderful in the history of football. The team had played two and sometimes three times a week against the muscle and football science of the United Kingdom. On many occasions they laboured under great disadvantages, but to win thirty-one of the thirty-two matches was a marvellous record. 'The names of the All Blacks will live on in the history of football.'

Each member of the team was then presented with a medal commemorative of the victories over Scotland, Ireland, England and France and framed photographs of the team were also presented, the Premier receiving a similar presentation.

Mr Dixon, manager of the team, was received with tumultuous cheering. He had been intensely proud of the conduct of the team during the tour. He took pride in the one defeat, since it was suffered under such disadvantageous circumstances. 'The team was sent Home primarily to help football in New Zealand and I am glad that in the endeavour to help ourselves, the team helped others. Many people in England are now speaking familiarly of New Zealand who were barely aware of its existence three months ago. I thank the team for its cordial, loyal support and Auckland for its splendid reception.'

Mr Gallaher was singled out for continuous loud applause. He said that it had been their one aim and object to play football as they thought it should be played and that was for the benefit of the colony. The team combined to do its task to its utmost and to do away with all provincialism, and in this it had been successful. It played the game right up to the hilt, it played it for all it was worth, and it played to win.

Captain Gallaher paid tribute to the NZRFU for appointing Mr Dixon to control the team. It had been due to Mr Dixon perhaps more than anyone else that the team had been so successful, for if the team had confidence in the management they would play well.

He had smoothed away the many little difficulties that had arisen. 'It was generally expected that we would win thirty per cent of the matches, but the team combined as a whole to do their utmost, and to do away with all provincialism, with the result that it was more like a club team than a representative international combination.'

THE OFFICIAL WELCOME was over, now it was time for the All Blacks to disband and for the southerners to embark on a triumphal train journey down country to their homes where they would face similar celebratory functions in their own centres.

The press clamoured for the stories every New Zealander craved to read. '. . . some people seemed to think there was too much of the Right Hon. The Premier and too little of the footballers, but the presence of Mr Seddon was a tribute to the achievements of the team, and if he did overspread the function a trifle it was surely his opportunity also . . .' George Tyler's 'hand that shook the King's' was an object of awed admiration in football circles . . . and as to the story that was telegraphed round the colony from Christchurch or Dunedin, three months previously, to the effect that there were serious dissensions in the New Zealand Football Team, and that an Aucklander had been thrashed by a Southerner over the issue of coach Jimmy Duncan, it was gratifying to learn that the story was an absolute fabrication. There were no serious dissensions at any period of the tour, the team throughout having been a happy family, while the story of the stand-up fight and the thrashing was a gross falsehood.

Canterbury representative George Gillett, formerly of Auckland, was happy to talk to the *Auckland Star*:

THE OFFICIAL BANQUET following the team's return.

During the tour Mr Gillett stated that he had played in every position from wing-forward to fullback, with the exception of halfback. He played in twenty-five matches of the thirty-two and said they had a most successful trip and thoroughly enjoyed themselves. The English crowds were the most impartial, Scotland and Ireland were good in the loose rushes and almost equalled New Zealand in that capacity, but New Zealand hooked the ball more often.

'Rumours were circulated here that there was a good deal of friction amongst the players?'

'That is absolutely rot. During the matches there was absolutely no friction.'

In answer to further questions Mr Gillett said that he considered the Devonport Albions a better team than that which represented England.

'There was a disputed try in the Welsh match?'

'Yes. Deans went over the line nine inches and grounded the ball. A man from behind pulled him back, and another who was on to him pushed him. I was close up to Deans at the time.'

Mr Gillett said that the New Zealanders were undoubtedly stale at the time of the Wales match, and besides that they did not have their full strength, for they were without the services of some of their most useful players in Nicholson, Johnston, Smith, Stead and Cunningham. The New Zealanders were fortunate in getting away from Wales without another defeat, for they were hardly able to place a team in the field.

'Can you single out any players for special mention?'

'Yes; I consider Wallace the best fullback that ever donned a jersey. Roberts was, perhaps, the most useful man in the team. McDonald and Seeling I consider the best forwards in the team, and Stead was the best of five-eighths. The treatment the team received in England was best of the tour from a social point of view.'

Interviewed shortly afterwards, George Tyler said the trip back was all right; 'none of the boys were seasick and we are all in really good form'.

'And will play again?'

'Rather! I believe practically every man in the team will be in the field next season.'

'How did you find the referees?'

'Very fair indeed on the whole. Of course you are bound to find some poor ones in every bunch. At first they did not understand the inside foot hooking in the scrum and penalised us; but when they dropped to our style and saw it was fair they were all right. We really enjoyed the trip but found the continuous travelling monotonous. It meant packing and unpacking all the time.'

'And the team appreciated the Government's offer of a return trip via America?'

'Yes; very much. We were, however, disappointed with the country. It was not up to what we expected after the booming we had heard.'

The elaborate ornamental boxes of chocolates with a picture of the 'All Blacks' lavished upon all of the New Zealand footballers on the eve of their departure — the gift of a well-known cocoa firm — would make lasting and handsome souvenirs of British hospitality, although the chocolates had soon disappeared.

NEW ZEALAND HERALD INTERVIEW OF GEORGE SMITH

REPORTER: I DON'T SUPPOSE FRANCE will ever become a great rugby centre?

Smith: It should make good progress there. Although they cannot pass or take a pass they form their scrum well.

Reporter: The team were treated well in France?

Smith: Yes; if a Frenchman grassed one of our players at all roughly they would turn around and say 'Pardon, monsieur.'

NEW ZEALAND HERALD

PONSONBY FOOTBALL CLUB told the press that it planned to give a welcome home social to their captain, Mr D. Gallaher, who returned with the New Zealand footballers on Tuesday. This club has a big reputation for its 'smokers' and is laying itself out for something special on this occasion.

But not everyone was happy . . .

AUCKLAND STAR

To the Editor
Sir,

Through the columns of your paper I beg to comment on the reception accorded the New Zealand football team. We have a team of men, a credit to New Zealand in football, who have had expenses paid and an allowance per day for a good holiday trip. I should like to know why such a fuss should be made of them.

When our gallant Contingent, the Seventh, arrived from South Africa no reception of any sort was prepared for them and no person of any importance welcomed the men home, although they had more casualties and did more gallant work than any other previous Contingent for our colony. And the authorities had not even the common courtesy to present their medals, but simply advertised that the medals were available at the Defence Office.

It seems to me that the pleasure seekers are thought considerably more of than a body of men like the Seventh Contingent, who spent twelve months of hardships fighting for their country.

And I consider that our Premier and others should have shown more common sense had they allowed our grand footballers to return to their respective homes quietly.

I am, etc.
SPORT.

CHRISTCHURCH PRESS

The southern section of the New Zealand football team, accompanied by Mr A.E.G. Rhodes, president of the New Zealand Rugby Union, and Mr E. Wylie, secretary, left for their homes by the *Rotoiti*. A large number of enthusiasts gathered on the railway platform to bid them farewell.

NEW ZEALAND TIMES

The southern members of the New Zealand football team passed through Aramoho yesterday and a very large crowd of football enthusiasts assembled at the station to greet the famous All Blacks.

When the express drew up at the station there was a great rush to greet the All Blacks, and naturally H.D. ('Mona') Thomson, Wanganui's representative, especially came in for a most enthusiastic reception. During the short time allowed the members of the team were simply besieged with eager questions and anything in the nature of an interview in the ordinary sense was out of the question.

The Wanganui man is looking first class, but apparently had no luck on the tour at all, as he ruptured a sinew in his right leg early in the tour, and played under difficulties all through the later matches.

EVENING POST

The new zealand footballers have returned to their breezy isles and the wild hurrahs of the blatant barracker still deafen the ears of the saner portion of the population. The Premier, who is the wildest barracker of them all, rushed to Auckland to welcome them and at the banquet held in their honour tried to crown them as the victors of Wales willy-nilly. But to the credit of Captain Gallaher, who returns unspoiled after all his triumphs, speaking for the team, modestly declined to be invested with any such undeserved honour in addition to those which already lay thick upon them, and frankly declared that on the day New Zealand met Wales the better team won.

All along the overland route travelled by the Wellington and Southern contingent of the team the same wild desire to shout hosannas and fall at their feet in worship was manifested and, on their arrival at Manawatu Station, all Bedlam seemed to have been let loose to welcome them. The small-brained, vast-lunged section of the inhabitants of this city of blow had gathered to yell themselves hoarse and act the Angora generally. Silly females who had gone along to do their little part in the acclamation had a very bad time in the stampede along the platform. The All Blacks themselves, who are looking particularly well after their travels, have so far given no startling evidence of swelled head . . .

EVENING POST

'Rather,' was the reply when [Deans and Duncan] were asked if they were glad to get back. 'It did get rather tiresome towards the end,' Deans added, 'and the fellows were pretty sick of it before we finished up in England. It was the travelling, the want of rest, and then the hard matches were left to the last.' But they enjoyed the games in America very much, having had a spell. 'We were very fortunate in the weather,' said Deans, 'for it was one of the mildest winters England has had for years. No rain to speak of, and no snow, with frost only in Scotland.'

It appears that if the tour had not opened so sensationally it might not have attracted much notice, but the first big wins focused attention on the team. Even then interest seemed to wane a little until the sixty-three points victory over Hartlepool stirred things up again. The New Zealanders at Home turned up to every match. 'Sometimes,' said Duncan, 'it was like walking along a Wellington street.'

'And now about that Welsh match?' said the reporter. 'You mean my try?' said Deans thoughtfully. 'Well,' with a convincing deliberation that spoke eloquently of the number of times he has had to talk about it, 'it was as fair a try as ever was scored.'

'I can't see how the referee could not see it,' put in Duncan, 'as we could see it from the far end.' 'No,' said Deans, 'I don't think he did see it.' Duncan added that the referee ought to have asked the line-umpire at all events, as that official was heard to say that the try was a fair one.

'And what about Gallaher?' was the next question. 'The referee,' was Deans' reply, 'went out to penalise Gallaher. There is no doubt about that.' 'But Dave never turned a hair,' added Duncan, 'and as to his unfairness in putting the ball in the scrum, look at the Cardiff match. Gallaher had to go in the scrum and yet we got the ball pretty well all the time.'

It is interesting to learn that the members of the team have thickened and broadened, and have all gained in weight. It was, Deans, explained, due to the hard work and the resultant ability to eat well. Newton is now 16st 6lb and many of the other men have gained a stone in weight. Asked whether he would play again this season, Deans replied that it was doubtful. He did not think he would play except in country matches. 'Rats!' was Duncan's comment.

CHRISTCHURCH PRESS

The homecoming of the southern members of the team which so worthily upheld the honour of New Zealand in the Old World excited considerable interest among the crowd which awaited the arrival of the *Mararoa* at Lyttelton wharf this morning. In view of the public welcome to be held in Christchurch, the greetings at the Lyttelton wharf were informal, though hearty. The representatives of the Rugby Union — Messrs G.H. Mason, W.G. Garrard, W. Walton, F.T. Evans, G. Scott and E.R. Guthrie — then escorted their guests to a carriage in the waiting train, which left at eleven o'clock for the city . . .

Those who waited to receive the homecomers at the Christchurch railway station were doomed to pace the platform until 11.30, when the small boy lookout sent forth the welcome news that the train was in sight, and in a few seconds the seven internationals were among their friends. The two Canterbury men, Messrs R.G. Deans and F. Newton, were quickly surrounded by their eager admirers, and many friends were waiting to shake hands with the Southerners Messrs Duncan,

McDonald, Casey and Booth (Otago) and Stead (Southland). The New Zealand football team and each of the players in turn were cheered vociferously.

At the reception at the City Council chambers, the players were toasted and Mr Deans, who was received with cheers, said that they were very glad to have reached home. The players felt that they had done what they could, and if others had had the luck to be picked in their places, they would have done the same. He believed that they had done well also in bringing back a little foreign capital, and so far as football was concerned, he thought that the tour would benefit both England and New Zealand. He thanked the Mayor and the people for their warm welcome.

Mr Newton rose, amid cheers, to say he was too hoarse to make a speech. The players had always tried to do their best, and they had had a great time, especially in Paris. They found that the Frenchmen were not great footballers but they knew a good bit about the game, and were great sports. They were not privileged to see an American football game played in America, but they understood as the Americans played it, football was a battle. 'I think I'm getting blown,' concluded the speaker. 'Thank you very much.' Cheers were given and the gathering dispersed.

At the invitation of the headmaster, Mr Bevan-Brown, Messrs Deans and Harper, two Christchurch High School old boys who were members of the 'All Blacks' football team, visited the school yesterday to meet the present pupils as well as a number of old boys who were present by invitation. Mr Deans gave a very interesting speech to the boys; Mr Harper also spoke and greatly amused his audience with a number of 'All Blacks' anecdotes. The boys were very enthusiastic and the speakers were accorded lusty rounds of cheers. Further cheers were given when Mr Deans was presented with the Canterbury Union's presentation gold medal. Mr Deans had been out of town when a similar presentation was made to Mr Harper.

◆

OTAGO DAILY TIMES

THE OTAGO AND SOUTHLAND members of the famous 'All Blacks' team were accorded an enthusiastic reception as they passed through Palmerston by the second express on Saturday evening. Long before the train was due to arrive people began to congregate at the railway station and when members stepped from the train there must have been three or four hundred persons present, including the Mayor, Mr E.H. Clark. On Mr Clark's invitation three hearty cheers were then given for the team and an additional cheer for 'Jimmy' Duncan.

By special request the team then gave the now-famous 'war-cry' and a minute later the train left amid renewed cheering and the singing of 'For they are jolly good fellows'.

◆

OTAGO DAILY TIMES

THE KNOWLEDGE THAT Messrs Duncan, Casey, Booth, McDonald and Stead of the now historically famous 'All Blacks' team would arrive in Dunedin again by the second express on Saturday night was the cause of a steady set of the tide of population in the direction of the Railway Station about the hour appointed, and thousands accorded the returned footballers the heartiest of welcomes home.

The expressions of gratification with which football enthusiasts hailed a sight of the features of the much-travelled Mr Duncan and his associates were characteristically fervent if limited. 'Good old Jimmy' seemed to exhaust the vocabulary of the beaming barracker.

Mr Stead, on rising to reply to the Mayor's words on behalf of the team, was received with enthusiastic applause. He said they could hardly express how much they had all been overwhelmed by the homecoming. On behalf of present and absent members of the team he thanked them all for their kindly welcome and interest and felt it his duty to express an emphatic denial to a report that had appeared in the press of the colony while the team was away.

The report as to the friction in the team in the Old Land was absolutely without truth or foundation. They had been a happy family from start to finish and all parochial feeling had been sunk. His own name and that of Mr Duncan had been drawn into that report and on Mr Duncan's behalf he would like to say that he had been a most useful man to the team. His advice had been freely given and freely asked for, though on so successful a tour it could be understood that it was not generally necessary to go into much detail about their play. But Mr Duncan was a second manager; he was particularly handy, and was the nurse of the team. (Applause and laughter.)

Stead said he gave the whole credit of the team's success to the forward division and he said this advisedly, because he had frequently heard it remarked that the forwards held their own, but the success of the team was due to the brilliant back division.

He had played behind a few forward teams, but never behind so brilliant a set and a set so versatile in all departments of the game as the combination that sailed from these shores last year.

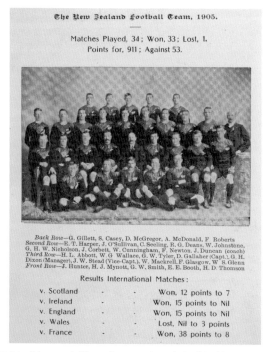

The New Zealand Football Team, 1905.

Matches Played, 34; Won, 33; Lost, 1.
Points for, 911; Against 53.

Back Row—G. Gillett, S. Casey, D. McGregor, A. McDonald, F. Roberts
Second Row—E. T. Harper, J. O'Sullivan, C. Seeling, R. G. Deans, W. Johnstone, G. H. W. Nicholson, J. Corbett, W. Cunningham, F. Newton, J. Duncan (coach)
Third Row—H. L. Abbott, W. G. Wallace, G. W. Tyler, D. Gallaher (Capt.), G. H. Dixon (Manager), J. W. Stead (Vice-Capt.), W. Mackrell, F. Glasgow, W. S. Glenn
Front Row—J. Hunter, H. J. Mynott, G. W. Smith, E. E. Booth, H. D. Thomson

Results International Matches:

v. Scotland	-	-	Won, 12 points to 7
v. Ireland	-	-	Won, 15 points to Nil
v. England	-	-	Won, 15 points to Nil
v. Wales	-	-	Lost, Nil to 3 points
v. France	-	-	Won, 38 points to 8

ONLY 34 of the team's 35 matches are acknowledged in this souvenir poster.

SOUTHLAND TIMES

Mr W.J. STEAD, DEPUTY captain of the famous 'All Blacks' team, returned to Invercargill by yesterday afternoon's express and was accorded a warm reception. The welcome though in a large degree official was nevertheless spontaneous and enthusiastic reflecting not only admiration of the splendid New Zealand team but an appreciation of the not inconsiderable contribution of Southland's representative to the success attained.

Though heavy rain was falling the station platform was crowded with waiting friends and at the entrance a large number of enthusiasts congregated to see the popular and familiar 'Billy Stead'. At a reception at the rotunda the Mayor said that when the All Blacks team left New Zealand there was a glow of satisfaction in this province in the knowledge that Southland had sent a representative who was so distinguished for his ability on the football field.

He said it was highly desirable as a matter of business that a colony such as New Zealand, where raw material was produced and sent out to the world, should be well known. New Zealand had suffered in the past by not being so well known as it might have been but the visit of the All Blacks to the Home Countries had made it known through the length and breadth of the Empire and other parts of the world. The success the team had achieved had given New Zealand a world-wide reputation. Mr Stead came of good stock and had worthily upheld the colony, his province and district. Mr Stead, who was received with renewed cheering, asked to be excused from making a long oration, as the team had been greeted with receptions all down the line, and coming to Invercargill had rather unnerved him. He felt as if he would like the rest of the team to be with him on this occasion.

They went Home with the intense purpose of doing their best for the colony on and off the field; the colony had been advertised in a way which no other medium of advertisement could have accomplished or had been able to accomplish in the past. It was most pleasing to him to look back upon the tour, and remember what an intensely happy family they were. One man's misfortune was every man's anxiety and it could be easily understood that when a spirit like that prevailed the manager and the heads of the team were saved a good deal of worry.

He had come back with a much broader conception of what the Empire really was — in their quiet life in the colonies they had no idea of the burden of empire at Home.

1906 ANNUAL GENERAL MEETING *of the* NZRFU

HELD AT THE CHAMBER OF COMMERCE, WELLINGTON ON THURSDAY, 3 MAY 1906

The Chairman Mr G.F.C. Campbell, in moving the adoption of the report and balance-sheet, remarked on the very favourable statement submitted. He thought the Union could be congratulated upon the success of the team during its tour of Great Britain.

Mr Hutchison (Otago) considered the action of the committee in allowing the Government to pay the return fare of the New Zealand team was open to criticism.

The committee had plenty of money, and further, some of the district unions had contributed to the fund for sending the team Home on the condition that no assistance was received by the Government.

In his opinion the first duty of the New Zealand Union would be to establish its finance on a sound basis, and to this end a portion of the money should be absolutely as a permanent fund. Other portions might be lent to affiliated unions on ample security for such purposes as securing grounds. The money might be advanced to unions at something under market rate of interest.

Much discussion on the tour's success and the excess of assets over liabilities (£12,027 16s 10d) as shown on the balance sheet.

Suggestion by mover Mr Isaacs 'that the surplus on the tour of the New Zealand team, be divided as follows: £5000 to be invested at fixed deposit for twelve months at 4 per cent, applications for £7000 to be invited from local unions for loans, either for the improvement or purchase of recreation grounds, only one loan to be granted to any one local union. Interest to be at the rate of 2 1/2 per cent. The mover pointed out that the £5000 invested at 4 per cent would bring in £200 per year.

In seconding the motion, Mr Weir said that if unions did not get some assistance they would soon be without grounds. He cited Wellington as an example.

Mr Goldie advised delegates to be cautious before this 'grab' was allowed. The surplus must be given where it was most needed and would do most good. Mr Pownall supported the motion. The Wanganui Union was overdrawn. When unions applied for loans they should send in their last balance-sheet and the fullest particulars. Mr Mason said the money belonged to the footballers of New Zealand and was held in trust for them. If the money was to be invested in good security, why not let the unions that had security to offer, have the opportunity of obtaining loans.

Mr Humphries spoke of the difficulties the Taranaki Union laboured under every time their team travelled. Private people had to finance them. Providing the unions could guarantee the money would be well used, why should not the New Zealand Union do as much for them as private individuals?

Mr Sheahan said that though Auckland was about to be turned out of its present ground, he did not appeal for that supposedly opulent body. He did, however, appeal for Taranaki.

Mr Walton said that Canterbury was prepared in every way to oppose a 'scramble' for the money. He thought it inadvisable to carry any motion. If his union wanted assistance it would ask for it in a proper manner.

An amended motion was put forward by G.H. Dixon: 'That £6000 be invested on fixed deposit and the balance be loaned to affiliated unions offering good security, at 2 ½ per cent.' He said there was a probability of an English team visiting the colony in 1908 and the New Zealand Union would probably have to guarantee the whole of the expenses. Assistance should be made to unions out of revenue and not out of capital. The amendment was carried.

The following motion was carried unanimously: 'This meeting desires to express its high appreciation of the services rendered by Mr Dixon as manager of the New Zealand team, and also of the spirit displayed by the team.'

The meeting closed at 1.30 a.m.

NEW ZEALAND HERALD

WELCOME HOME TO NEW ZEALAND

L IKE LAMBS THEY ENTERED, but like lions they departed from the Motherland, and yesterday, with something of the pomp and ceremony and triumph of a victorious army, the 'All Blacks' once more set foot in the streets of the city of Auckland.

So concluded the most remarkable tour of a body of athletes that has ever been known.

The New Zealand footballers arrived in England unostentatiously and unknown to the great bulk of the people of the Old Country, but left it in a blaze of glory. Yesterday they returned to their home, to a colony that is proud of their success, proud of the fact that whether on or off the field they 'played the game' — although in that they only acted as colonials do in amateur sport and as the colony expected them to do — and, moreover, their tour has taught the people in the Homeland more about the country and people of the Antipodes in a few months than would have been learned in years under ordinary circumstances.

There may still be some people at Home who imagine New Zealand people live in stockaded settlements, in fear and dread of savage Maoris who make the night hideous with wild, blood-curdling war cries, or who think New Zealand is a small group of islands off Australia, with barren, inhospitable coasts, but they have no excuse for remaining in ignorance after the great searchlights thrown upon this colony and the life here by the medium of the 'All Blacks' tour . . .

THE TEAM'S ACHIEVEMENTS are acknowledged — thousands turn out to welcome them.

Chapter 7

STATISTICS

1905 ALL BLACK TOUR STATISTICS

TOUR SUMMARY

beat DEVON COUNTY at Exeter **55-4**

beat CORNWALL at Camborne **41-0**

beat BRISTOL at Bristol **41-0**

beat NORTHAMPTON at Northampton **32-0**

beat LEICESTER at Leicester **28-0**

beat MIDDLESEX at London **34-0**

beat DURHAM COUNTY at Durham **16-3**

beat HARTLEPOOL CLUBS at Hartlepool **63-0**

beat NORTHUMBERLAND at North Shields **31-0**

beat GLOUCESTER at Gloucester **44-0**

beat SOMERSET COUNTY at Taunton **23-0**

beat DEVONPORT ALBION at Devonport **21-3**

beat MIDLAND COUNTIES at Leicester **21-5**

beat SURREY at London **11-0**

beat BLACKHEATH at London **32-0**

beat OXFORD UNIVERSITY at Oxford **47-0**

beat CAMBRIDGE UNIVERSITY at Cambridge **14-0**

beat RICHMOND at London **17-0**

beat BEDFORD at Bedford **41-0**

beat SCOTLAND at Edinburgh **12-7**

beat WEST OF SCOTLAND at Glasgow **22-0**

beat IRELAND at Dublin **15-0**

beat MUNSTER at Limerick **33-0**

beat ENGLAND at London **15-0**

beat CHELTENHAM at Cheltenham **18-0**

beat CHESHIRE at Birkenhead **34-0**

beat YORKSHIRE at Headingley **40-0**

lost to WALES at Cardiff **0-3**

beat GLAMORGAN COUNTY at Swansea **9-0**

beat NEWPORT at Newport **6-3**

beat CARDIFF at Cardiff **10-8**

beat SWANSEA at Swansea **4-3**

beat FRANCE at Paris **38-8**

beat BRITISH COLUMBIA at Berkeley **43-6**

beat BRITISH COLUMBIA at San Francisco **65-6**

Played 35, won 34, lost 1; points for 976, against 59.

Before leaving New Zealand the team played OTAGO-SOUTHLAND at Dunedin, drawing 10-all, CANTERBURY at Christchurch, winning 21-3, and WELLINGTON at Wellington, losing 0-3.

INDIVIDUAL RECORD

	GAMES	TRIES	CONS	PENS	POTS	MARKS	TOTAL
Billy Wallace	30	27	74	3	2	–	246
Jimmy Hunter	24	44	–	–	–	–	132
Bob Deans	21	20	–	–	–	–	60
George Smith	19	19	–	–	–	–	57
Duncan McGregor	14	16	1	–	–	–	50
Fred Roberts	30	14	3	–	–	–	48
Harold Abbott	10	15	1	–	–	–	47
Simon Mynott	22	14	2	–	–	–	46
Hector Thomson	11	14	1	–	–	–	44
Frank Glasgow	27	8	5	1	–	–	37
Billy Stead	29	11	–	–	–	–	33
Eric Harper	10	6	3	–	–	–	24
Charlie Seeling	25	8	–	–	–	–	24
Bill Cunningham	25	2	8	–	–	–	22
George Gillett	25	1	6	–	–	1	18
George Nicholson	20	6	–	–	–	–	18
George Tyler	23	2	6	–	–	–	18
Ernest Booth	16	5	1	–	–	–	17
Alex McDonald	17	4	–	–	–	–	12
William Johnston	13	3	–	–	–	–	9
Dave Gallaher	26	1	1	–	–	–	5
Jim O'Sullivan	20	1	–	–	–	–	3
Fred Newton	16	1	–	–	–	–	3
Bill Mackrell	6	1	–	–	–	–	3
Steve Casey	24	–	–	–	–	–	–
Bill Glenn	13	–	–	–	–	–	–
John Corbett	13	–	–	–	–	–	–
TOTAL		243	112	4	2	1	976

Opposition teams scored 13 tries, 3 conversions, 2 penalty goals and 2 dropped goals. Tries counted 3 points, conversions 2, penalty goals 3, dropped goals 4 and goals from a mark 3. Statistics do not include the exhibition match played in New York.